CHICAGO PUBLIC LIBRARY

W9-BRQ-238

VENEERING

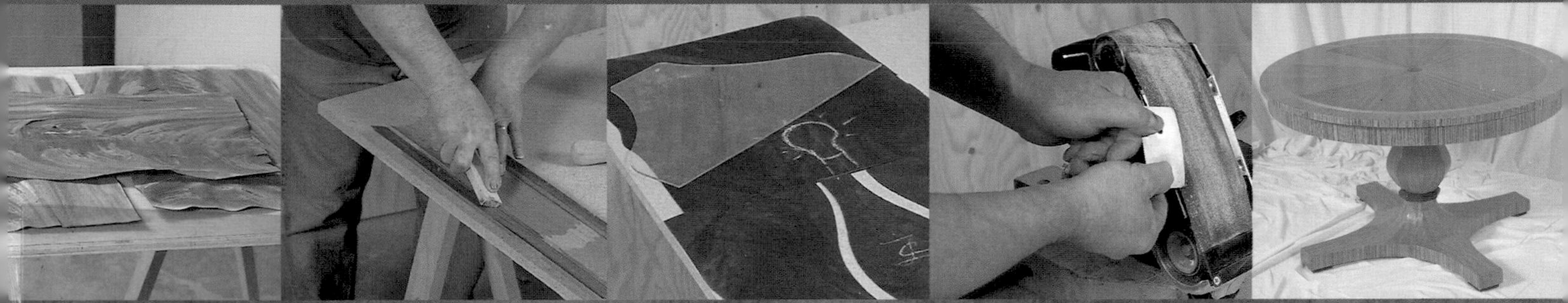

A FOUNDATION COURSE

Mike Burton

STERLING PUBLISHING CO., INC. ■ NEW YORK

To Carole and the Kids

Library of Congress Cataloging-in-Publication Data

Burton, Michael, 1944-
    Veneering: a foundation course / Michael Burton
       p. cm.
    Includes index.
    ISBN 0-8069-2855-7
    1. Veneers and veneering. I. Title.
    TS870.B87 2000
    674'.833—dc21   99-049675

Editor: Michael Cea
Designer: Chris Swirnoff

1 3 5 7 9 10 8 6 4 2
Published by Sterling Publishing Company, Inc.
387 Park Avenue South, New York, New York 10016
© 2000 by Mike Burton
Distributed in Canada by Sterling Publishing
c/o Canadian Manda Group, One Atlantic Avenue, Suite 105
Toronto, Ontario, Canada M6K 3E7
Distributed in Great Britain and Europe by Cassell PLC
Wellington House, 125 Strand, London WC2R 0BB, England
Distributed in Australia by Capricorn Link (Australia) Pty Ltd.
P.O. Box 6651, Baulkham Hills, Business Centre, NSW 2153, Australia
Printed in China
All rights reserved

Sterling ISBN 0-8069-2855-7

CHICAGO PUBLIC LIBRARY
SOUTH CHICAGO BRANCH
9055 S. HOUSTON

SOC

R01924 97561

CONTENTS

Introduction 7

19.95

PART ONE: **ALL ABOUT VENEER**

CHICAGO PUBLIC LIBRARY
SOUTH CHICAGO BRANCH
9055 S. HOUSTON 60617

CHAPTER 6
SHOP-MADE VENEERING EQUIPMENT AND MISCELLANEOUS TECHNIQUES 79

CHAPTER 7
ADDING A FINISH 94

INTRODUCTION

Many times I have been asked, "Where did you learn about veneering?" My usual reply has been, "Well, there's this big building on the corner of 25th and Jefferson . . ." I then look into the blank face of the questioner for a few seconds until he realizes or I inform him that that is the address of a public library. That's where my knowledge of veneering began and continues to this day, but through the years I have also had the opportunity and honor to watch and to work alongside some excellent craftsmen. Professionals all, these people built the project they were assigned with calm, step-by-step determination, filled with the pragmatism of the day.

I am not a hobbyist, and far too little of my work has ever found its way into my own home. I am a professional craftsman in several woodworking fields—which means I get paid for providing services in these fields. I have worked professionally in several crafts, and in this book I'll try to show some of the interrelated techniques I've learned through the years.

I received my first paid woodworking commission in 1962. After trying my hand in several other industries, I hung a shingle over the door of a woodworking shop in 1972; that shingle remains to this day. Through the years, that shop has engaged in a wide variety of woodworking-related enterprises, from general millwork to the cutting of dimensioned lumber to the manufacture of airplane propellers and guitar bodies to the production of custom furniture. In the following pages, I describe and show how some of the techniques I've learned through the years in these crafts can be applied to veneering.

Though the production of custom furniture has always been my goal, restoration and refinishing work have taken a great deal of time. I'm thankful for that work, as it has given me the opportunity to study many pieces from different periods, evaluating what ensures a piece's longevity and what contributes to its demise. I have always been a tinker and experimenter—often to the dismay of my sons, who have worked with me. But my tinkering and experimenting have proven to be a great way to obtain an education in veneering.

If you are a student of general woodworking, some of the tools and techniques that are presented here may seem a bit strange—certainly unconventional. Try them; they may work well for you. You don't have to tell your purest woodworking acquaintances about these unorthodox methods; I certainly won't.

One thing I've discovered is that there's no "right" way to do anything; nor is the "wrong" way always wrong. If the same project were assigned to five competent, professional woodworkers, they would probably take five different approaches to the task, but each finished product would be totally acceptable.

All of us have different backgrounds, tools, equipment, education, desires, ambitions . . . and the list goes on. Even our muscles have developed differently, and the ability to control those muscles varies from person to person. I myself am somewhat ambidextrous. This comes from my wood-carving work and is the result of sheer laziness. Rather than turn a project around and reclamp it, I learned to switch hands.

As you browse through the book and look at the photos, you'll see me working without eye protection or a dust mask while using a tool that generates a great deal of dust. With regard to dust, there are two large squirrel-cage fans in my workshop that circulate filtered air gently throughout it. The airflow clears fine dust in a matter of seconds, and for those seconds, I've learned to hold my breath. However, it is advisable that you use some sort of dust-collection system. And as for eye protection, I often feel that it's as important to clearly see what I'm doing as it is to protect my eyes.

In recent years, woodworking tools have been supplied with so many safety gadgets and guards that I sometimes wonder if these devices are not dangerous in themselves. Were I to pontificate upon table-saw guards, I'd eat up ten pages. Still, that said, in the following pages I indicate the safety precautions to take when appropriate. Also, it should be noted that the decision not to use the safety equipment is one I've made as a professional woodworker with years of experience, and the reader is advised to make his own decision based on his level of expertise and comfort level.

In the following pages, I take the reader step-by-step through the veneering process and describe and show how to build a variety of projects. I originally thought of buying a piece of inexpensive ready-to-finish pine furniture and changing it to mahogany before your very eyes, but rejected the idea. Rather, I incorporated the veneering of flat surfaces along

Author Mike Burton.

with curved surfaces in some rather unique pieces to present ideas on how to veneer even the simplest of projects. I've also used a number of different types of veneer for these projects that exhibit different properties.

I have dealt heavily with the veneering of curved surfaces, because many think that these surfaces are the most difficult. It goes without saying that if you can veneer a curved surface, you can veneer a flat one.

I have always believed that curved surfaces lend themselves to veneer in a very special way. Economy is one reason, to be sure, but there are effects that can be arrived at on a curved veneered surface that could never be created with solid wood. A bombé chest—one with outward curving lines—or a kidney-shaped desk always draws more compliments than its counterparts with square components. And, as I work for profit rather than fun, I've found the financial rewards are also far greater, while the effort is about the same—honest.

When reading the project section, don't look at the finished product photo and say, "I could never do that." Look carefully at the in-progress shots and read the accompanying text. Think about the tools and materials you have at hand. Adapt my ideas to that special project that you've always wanted to try. Then roll up your sleeves and get to work.

While reading, you may get the impression that I take a casual or even cavalier approach to my work. Nothing could be further from the truth, but I do accept the fact that I'm not perfect. If there is a slight defect in my work, I conceal it as best as possible, try to analyze what went wrong, and vow to try harder next time.

Read on. Try some different techniques—even those that may be considered "far out." Don't practice these techniques on your project, but rather on scrap wood. Most of all, enjoy the experience.

Mike Burton

PART ONE

All About Veneering

CHAPTER 1

From Log to Workshop: Cutting Characteristics of Veneer

During the Second World War there was a scarcity of good hardwood timber, glue—and craftsmen. But during that period, there was a fair amount of furniture produced. Not all, but a good deal of this furniture was built of vertical-grain fir and covered with veneer to disguise the not-so-appropriate lumber. Often the lumber was hastily cured and joints were poorly fit. As a result, far too many of these pieces fell apart of their own weight, finishes disintegrated, and veneers began to come loose. Consequently, the word "veneer" became synonymous with "cheap" and "inferior."

Unfortunately, this stigma from the war years has continued through several generations to the present day. It has been reinforced by stories and experiences with water damage, veneer's chief enemy. It's true that a veneered tabletop will not survive under a soggy potted plant. Even if the veneer survives, substrate materials such as particleboard and MDF (medium-density fiberboard) will swell to a point where the piece becomes irreparable. Too often people will not acknowledge their abuse of a product; it's far easier to blame the product. Few, if any, ever contemplate the damage that would result to solid wood under that same soggy plant.

So often I have mentioned using veneer to a client, only to hear, "Oh . . . well, I guess that would be okay, but do you think it will hold up?" At times like these, my eyes would begin to scan the shop for any veneered antique that might be there for restoration. For several years I had a clock case from the late 1700s in the showroom. I would lead the doubting client to the case and point out the beautiful "walnut" piece. Then I would open the door and let him or her see the pine on the interior. As they examined the case, I would say, "This piece has been around for a couple hundred years. What do you think?"

1–1. The information in this chapter describes the advantages of using veneer and its cutting characteristics.

Veneering—the technique of overlaying material over wood for protective or decorative purposes—is not a new craft. Artifacts covered with veneer have been found in the tombs of the pharaohs. The term "veneer" does not solely refer to wood—although wood is the focus of this book. Stone, shells, and metals can also be used as veneers.

Until modern times, veneered objects could be found only in the possession of the wealthy. The materials and talent to produce veneered pieces were beyond the means of the common man. Usually of exotic wood, often of unique design, and always elegant, veneered pieces were more appreciated by the well-to-do, for the common man was far more taken up with the practicalities of daily life.

In the area of furniture-making, veneer has been used a little differently during various time periods. It's interesting to observe the species of veneer used in a particular period and relate their availability to exploration, transportation, industrial development, and any wars being fought.

Not being a great student of history, I'll not pass along any specific observations in the following pages, instead concentrating on the technique itself.

Each time I'm commissioned to build a period veneered piece, I visit the library to research the species and designs of the period. Quite often my research is for naught. After the client thumbs through my veneer samples, a species is selected that was almost unheard of during that time, and the design is then changed to suit the client's own tastes. As a result, the only part of the furniture that reflects the time period may be its legs.

My own thinking is that, today, furniture-makers have a vast selection of materials at their disposal, so designs are limited only by the imagination—or, in my case, the imagination of my clients.

WHY USE VENEER RATHER THAN SOLID WOOD?

The reasons for using veneer rather than solid wood are many and varied. Economy immediately comes to mind. If you have ever used oak, walnut, or mahogany plywood in a project, the savings become obvious. The cost of the plywood might be almost the same per square foot as solid lumber, but there is no edge gluing and sanding involved, so you save time, and therefore money, on the project. This savings becomes even more obvious when we're dealing with exotic species, wherein the scarcity of solid wood and the cost of handling and transportation become major factors. And, of late we have become very conservation conscious. A rare tree sliced into veneer can adorn many more projects than it could if cut into lumber. It's unfortunate that so many exotic and beautiful trees cut in the rain forests are merely burned to make way for short-lived agriculture.

Economy is not the only reason for using veneer. Some designs are impractical in solid wood. An acquaintance of mine described a coffee table he had build out of diamond-shaped sections of solid oak. "None of that cheap veneer for me," he said. He went to great lengths to describe his trials in getting the pieces to fit perfectly and the number of biscuits (pieces of wood used when biscuit-joining) and amount of glue he used in each joint. I dryly commented, "Don't run your swamp cooler this summer." He did run his air conditioner, with dire consequences for the coffee table. As a matter of fact, you could drop a nickel through the openings that appeared at the center where the points of the diamonds met.

Effects can be achieved with veneer that are virtually impossible with solid wood. A piece of veneer wrapped in spiral fashion about a column lends a dramatic and unique effect to cabinetry or interior finish. (This is described in Chapter 6.) Veneer placed cross-grain in one character of a molding produces an effect that the eye doesn't expect. (This is described in Chapter 0.) Veneer is often used in Mission-style furniture to display the quartered figure of oak on all four sides of large components—an effect impossible in solid wood without four-piece construction.

Curved surfaces take on a far different and, to me, more pleasing look when veneered. The grain of veneer is smooth, flowing, and of even color and texture, while the grain of the wood beneath the veneer changes from end grain to flat grain, often varying in texture. Here, too, cost raises its ugly head, for the waste encountered in building anything curved is easier to tolerate in an economical species covered with exotic veneer than it would be in the exotic species of solid wood.

Some wood is not suitable for lumber. Satinwood

comes immediately to mind. Though satinwood makes a most beautiful veneer, lumber cut from this species checks—both across and through the grain. Zebrawood has similar characteristics. And can you imagine the complications involved in making a raised door panel out of a board cut from a crotch or a burl? I can, and the thought is not pleasant. While I've seen massive tabletops built of crotches and burls, the instability and poor machining characteristics of such cuts would scare me.

HOW VENEER IS CUT

Thin slices of wood can be taken from a log by sawing, splitting, riving, or slicing. I'm sure that in days of old all these techniques were used. Today, however, all of the veneer I've seen has been sliced with a huge knife. I'm told that that knife can be as long as 17 feet, although I have yet to see veneer slices longer than 12 feet—more often six to eight feet. In many species, it's hard to find a much longer log that's worth slicing.

Preparatory to slicing, the logs are checked with a metal detector. Nails, pieces of wire, and even bullets can raise hob with the expensive and difficult-to-sharpen knife. The logs are "barked" (that is, bark is removed from them), and to accommodate the machinery they may be halved or quartered. They may also be squared up with a saw, providing some lumber from the outer edges, or at least eliminating the need to trim the veneers to manageable sizes and shapes. The logs—or timbers—are then soaked in hot water or exposed to steam for as long as it takes to soften them; often, days are involved in the heating process.

After the log is prepared, it may be taken to different types of slicing machines. Plain-slicing is shown in 1–2. The first few slices produce a figure like that shown in C of the drawing. As the slicing progresses, a different figure will appear called rift (B). And as the knife nears the center of the log, cutting parallel with the medullary rays, a quartered figure appears (A).

The log may also be mounted on a lathe and the knife slowly advanced as it is turned, as shown in 1–3. This technique produces some very wide slices of veneer with a very bold character. These rotary-sliced veneers are extensively used in plywood, for the

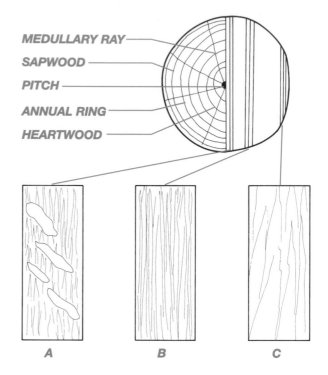

1–2. Plain-sliced veneer. C shows the first slices produced. B shows a rift figure that is produced as cutting continues. A shows a quartered figure.

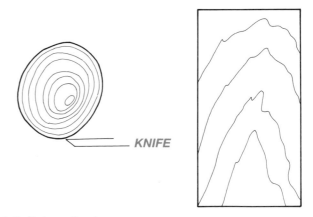

1–3. Rotary-sliced veneer.

process is quick and inexpensive. But some types of veneer can only be achieved by rotary slicing; bird's-eye maple comes immediately to mind.

Logs may also be mounted on a slightly different rotary machine and sliced, as shown in 1–4. Slices produced by this technique are wider than those produced by plain-slicing, and will have a character bold-

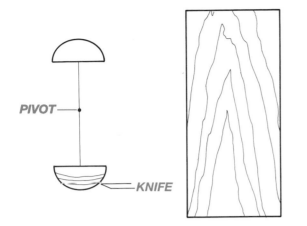

PIVOT

KNIFE

1–4. Veneer produced by a slightly different rotary manner than that shown in 1–3.

LIMB

1–5. Oyster-shell figure.

er than plain-sliced veneer but not near as bold as rotary-sliced veneer.

If the log—more often smaller limbs—is sliced perpendicular to its length, a decorative figure called "oyster shell" is produced (1–5). This particular fig-

ure can be most dramatic if it is sliced from deformed, non-symmetrical limbs.

Parts of a tree other than the main trunk and larger limbs can be sliced to produce veneer, and this can result in very dramatic, decorative figures, as shown in 1–6. Slices taken from the crotches (the area of the tree formed by two branches) not only produce different grain directions, but the compression caused by

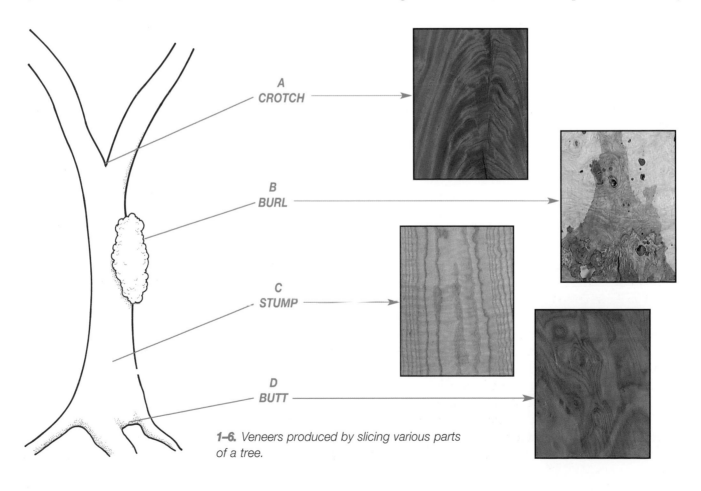

A
CROTCH

B
BURL

C
STUMP

D
BUTT

1–6. Veneers produced by slicing various parts of a tree.

weight concentrated at this area produces a unique wavy pattern (A in 1–6).

Once sliced, those ugly growths on the sides of trees (the burls) render some of the most beautiful figures imaginable (B in 1–6). The wealth of designs that can be found in burls are as wide and varied as those found in clouds.

And let's not forget the stump. The tremendous weight of the tree compresses the fibers of the wood that is located in the first few feet above the ground. This results in a curly figure that is unique (C in 1–6). While slices of stump are not usually more than three feet in length, they can be worked into beautiful designs.

Slicing even farther down into the butt—the base of the tree from which the roots spring—yields a design similar to that produced with burl (B in 1-6).

The foregoing information is somewhat oversimplified, but it should give you some idea of how different figures are derived from different parts of the tree and with various cutting techniques.

CARE AFTER SLICING

After falling from the knife, the individual slices are held flat and sent through drying chambers. At the other end, they are stacked in the order in which they were cut from the log. Keeping the slices in order is extremely important for the purpose of properly presenting and matching grain, as we'll see in the following pages. To ensure that I don't loose the order of the slices, I mark the end with a couple of pencil lines. And, in the case of burls and crotches, I number the slices. Before cutting a slice of veneer—and losing the pencil lines—I mark a squiggle line on one edge; on the underside—beneath the squiggle line—I mark a series of X's.

HOW VENEER IS SUPPLIED

When a species of veneer is ordered from the same supplier, one shipment will come with nicely trimmed slices, all of consistent widths with edges suitable for joints. Other shipments may have slices with the outline of the log; slices that seem rather thick and ragged; or slices that are somewhat thinner and appear to have been sanded. Do you get the idea that wood veneer can be a rather inconsistent

product? Believe me, it's not as inconsistent as it used to be.

Still, mills in various countries have slightly different standards. Some mills are better equipped than others are. Also, some species can't be sliced as thin as others. All of these factors contribute to the irregularities. You must learn to live with them.

Even though veneer catalogues say that the veneer is between $1/28$ and $1/32$ inch thick, don't count on it. The cedar veneer used for the blanket chest described in Chapter 9 measured $3/32$ inch, was twisted, and was rougher than a corncob, while the Benin veneer used for the dining table described in Chapter 11 was substantially under $1/32$ inch, heavenly flat, and appeared to have been sanded. While the catalogue said that the cedar would be three feet in length, it was actually two feet. And while the catalogue said that the Benin would be ". . . up to eight feet in length," it actually measured ten feet, six inches.

Burls and crotches vary dramatically, depending on the species of wood and the type of cut. If you have a specific design in mind, always call your supplier and have him check his inventory for the sizes needed. This holds true for vertical-grain material as well as figured cuts.

PAPER-BACKED VENEER

Veneers are also supplied bonded to a paper backing. Usually they are 8 feet in length and 18 inches wide, but widths up to 48 inches are not uncommon. Narrow strips are supplied in long rolls with hot melt glue on the paper; these strips are to be used for the facing. Wider sheets are even supplied with a peel-and-stick system. While I have used the facing veneer in economy projects, I haven't used peel-and-stick veneer—mainly because of the cost of the material.

CROSS-BANDED VENEER

Cross-banded veneer consists of a face veneer bonded to a less expensive species with the grain running perpendicular to the face. There are several companies that supply cross-banded veneers. Some supply veneers bonded to a plastic-laminate backing sheet. Essentially, you're buying a two-ply piece of plywood. You specify the size and design and the company does all of the cutting, fitting, and patching of the veneer where necessary. These folks do charge for their work, but they can help you produce a magnificent tabletop or some elegant door panels with minimum effort on your part.

VENEER PRESENTATIONS

There are four different ways to show or present the face side of a slice of veneer, as shown in 1–7. These can be demonstrated by considering one single fiber of wood in a slice of veneer. This fiber lies in the slice not quite parallel to the edges—a highly likely situation, as shown in 1–7. If the slice were to be turned over, the fiber would appear as B in 1–7.

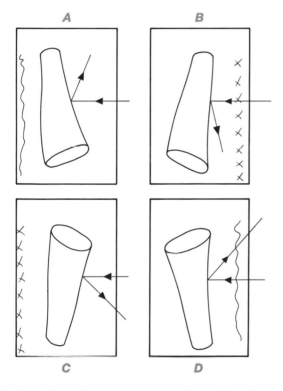

1–7. The light that reflects on a veneer depends on how the veneer is presented.

Turning A end for end would result in C. And turning B end for end produces D.

To prevent confusing these four different slices of veneer, I make a squiggle line on one side of the slice and the X's under it.

So, why should you be aware of veneer presenta-

tion? In many species, this is very important. Wood possesses iridescent properties; that is, it produces lustrous rainbow-like colors that result from light reflection. In some hardwood species this can be very dramatic, and is referred to as the "depth" or "fire" in the wood. The same characteristic is found in softwood species but is not always as dramatic.

Look at 1–7 and observe the lines that represent light coming from a single source. The reflected light in A and D is similar, but not identical. Likewise in B and C. Observe how dramatically the reflection differs between A and B or A and C. Are you beginning to see the color possibilities?

Now, if you were to lay up a panel by slipping several veneer cuts with the same presentation from the top of the stack—creating a "slip match"—the light reflections from all cuts would be the same. This is shown in 1–8. The joints would not be obvious, except for grain-match challenges. With this type of match, the cuts can be slipped back and forth to accommodate the grain, but the method is wasteful (A in 1–8).

If you were to "book-match" the veneers—that is, turn the cuts as if turning the pages of a book or laying out the pleats of an accordion so that they are

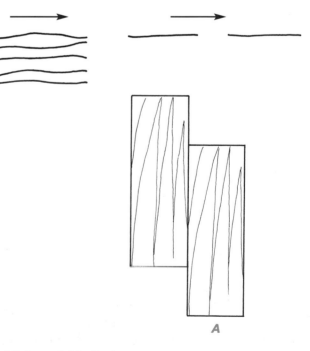

1–8. A "slip-match" effect.

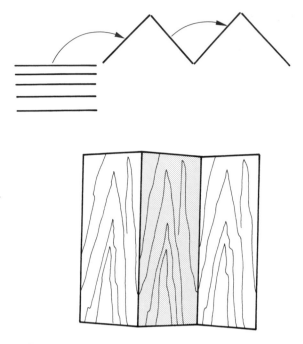

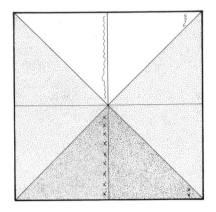

1–10. Diamond design for a tabletop. Compare the effect of this design to that in 1–11.

1–9. Book-matched veneer.

mirror images of each other, as shown in 1–9—the presentation of each would produce opposite light reflections. This type of matching certainly overcomes the grain-matching challenges, but while walking around the panel, you will find that in one position one cut looks light and the next dark. The joints will stand out as the straight lines they are. The finishing process makes the difference even more dramatic.

If you were to lay up a diamond-design tabletop as shown in 1–10, as you walk around the top at one point one diamond shape would look light and the opposite one dark. The other two would fall some-where in between. Laying up the veneers as shown in 1–11 would produce a different effect. Here the oppo-site quadrants of the diamond shapes would reflect light differently.

Burls work the same way. If two slices of a stack of four burl slices were to be flipped, as shown in 1–12, and then the top ones turned end for end, the result would be a "book and butt" match. In this case, the same corner of each slice would touch in the center, and the pattern of the burl would be symmetrical on both sides of each joint. And what about the light? Well, it would reflect the same in opposite quadrants.

By this time, I hope I've made the point that simply laying up veneers in any random manner can be dev-

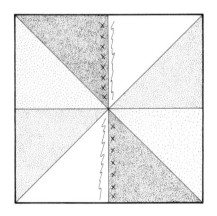

1–11.

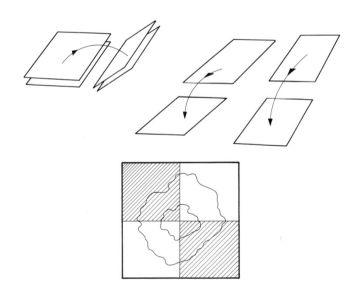

1–12. Burls with a "book and butt match."

astating, but with a little care and planning the effects of light reflection can produce some interesting and beautiful results.

SPECIES CHARACTERISTICS

While many veneers are very similar, some have their own characteristics that will pose challenges. Giving proper attention to these quirks can save a world of troubleshooting and repairs. Below is a description of some of these characteristics and ways to deal with them.

Oils and Resins

Some woods are very resinous. Teak, satinwood, and some rosewoods are particularly troublesome. These veneers can contain so much oils and resin that glue will not stick to them. The degree to which they will repel glue depends on the particular log from which they were sliced. It can get so bad that bonding these veneers is like bonding a piece of waxed paper. And when contact cement is used, the oils will mix with the glue and prevent it from drying, leaving a gooey mess on the surface.

Softwood species such as pine contain pitch around knots that will inhibit the effect of adhesives.

Pitch, resins, and oils can also pose a challenge in finishing because they can bleed through to the surface or inhibit drying. Solvent-based finishes such as varnish, lacquer, and Danish oil will either not dry or dry very slowly on surfaces with these materials. Water-based finishes will dry, but they will float and peel easily. Wax will never harden or, if it does, it will take months. Catalyzed resin finishes won't harden on some species and will remain soft.

I once refinished a game table with a checkerboard in the center. The table had been previously finished with shellac some 50 years earlier. The client requested a poured catalyzed resin coating, and I proceeded according to his wishes. Four days after the finish had been poured, the coating over the white maple squares was hard. The resin over the dark rosewood squares remained soft.

Solution? Before working with these veneers, scrub with a strong solvent such as acetone or lacquer thinner. Don't just wipe off the surface; get out

a brush and scrub. Some craftsmen even recommend soaking the veneers in solvent. I have never had to go that far, but I won't recommend that you don't do it. Soaking would be particularly important when bonding with contact cement. Any oils in the wood will eventually find their way into the glue line, severely weakening it.

End Checks, Splits, and Tears

Rough handling often causes tears or splits along the grain. To prevent these from getting worse, tape them immediately.

Checks pose a different challenge. They appear as a V-shaped void in the end of the cut—a void that may have been in the log from which the veneer was sliced. If the void is less than a quarter inch in width, it is possible to pull the check together and tape it. This will, of course, cause the end of the veneer to cup or bow, depending on which side you are looking at. The stress caused by the cup will have to be relieved. Sometimes this can be done successfully, and sometimes not.

The quickest way to flatten out that cup is to spray the area with a fine mist of water; try to avoid the tape because water will loosen it. Then, with an iron set on medium heat, slowly iron the veneer flat, turning the veneer frequently. Continue until the veneer is dry. If you have met with only moderate success, spray and iron once more.

Another thing to consider is any stain on the sides of the check. These often come from the log and can be permanent. Try sanding or scraping to see if the stain is only on the surface. If the stain is well set, a V-shaped section of the veneer will have to be cut out and a patch of similar grain taped in. (Patching is discussed on pages 27 and 28.) By all means, however, if you can do without that checked end, cut it off and throw it away.

No, don't save that checked end for the project you're thinking of building. Little pieces of veneer can grow into piles, taking up valuable space, to say nothing of the fire hazard. Keep a few of these end cuts for borders or experiments, but dispose of the rest. Give these pieces to a friend who is working on a marquetry mural. And, I've found it useful to keep a few for that guy that wants to "buy" some scraps of veneer. Give them to him—no charge—and show him to the door. If, on the way to the door, he asks how to glue them down, tell him to buy this book.

Thin and Thick Areas and Grain Holes

Veneers sliced parallel with the medullary rays of the log often contain thin spots. Quartered oak and lacewood come to mind as being major offenders. In these species, the thin spots are in the figure resulting from the ray. Holding the veneer up to a strong light will reveal areas that are unusable. Cutting through a thin spot, you'll find that the veneer is only a couple thousandths of an inch thick.

Holding veneer to the light will also reveal coarse, grainy areas that are certain to allow the glue to bleed through. Should these be encountered, think carefully about the glue you intend to use and the manner in which the veneer will be bonded to the substrate. (Refer to Chapter 5 for information on these subjects.) Always be sure to use a cover of heavy paper or plastic if you're using a press. This will prevent the work from sticking to the press components. Also consider the consequences of your finishing technique for the bleed-through.

Thick areas will usually be found in defects such as knots. This is because the veneer has shrunk more than the knot. Compression bands running through stump wood and crotches will often be a little thicker than the surrounding wood. Here, again, uneven shrinkage is the cause.

If veneers with thin and thick areas are bonded with a press, thick areas may be starved for glue while the thin areas can have an overly thick glue line. These challenges are not insurmountable. We'll confront them in Chapter 5.

Mineral Deposits

As a tree grows, it pulls water, and, consequently, dissolved minerals from the ground. In many species, this results only in a unique coloration of the wood. Some deposits are more dramatic. Those dark lines running through some slices of teak are mineral deposits, and they are very hard. I've also encountered this in Brazilian rosewood and koa.

If a cabinet scraper is pulled over some mineral deposits, the deposits often put nicks in the burr of the scraper. And hand-sanding with soft sandpaper will leave the deposits proud or higher than the surrounding wood—to say nothing of dulling the sandpaper quickly. Mineral deposits can leave dull spots in router cutters that are used for trimming—even carbide cutters. How the slicing knife survives them I'll never know.

Color Retention

Almost all wood species, especially when exposed to ultraviolet light, change color to some extent. Walnut fades from purple to warm brown. Mahogany and cherry darken. Oak yellows, the green in poplar turns brown very quickly . . . and the list goes on. The point is: If you have a specific color scheme in mind, be sure the woods will maintain that color scheme in the years to come or make sure the pieces will never be exposed to UV (ultraviolet) light.

Take a small piece of the veneer you intend to use and tape a piece of cardboard or heavy paper over half of it. Leave it in the sun for a week or two. You may be very surprised when you remove the cardboard.

Keeping the pieces out of UV light may sound ridiculous, but many new homes are being built incorporating UV-resistant glass windows.

Holes

Some figured species and burls in particular can be riddled with holes. Olive ash will have holes where knot-like defects have fallen out during handling. Carpathian elm will have voids where no wood was formed in the growth process. If these holes are small, they can be patched with wood putty, but larger holes must be filled with a patch cut from a similar piece of veneer. (Refer to pages 27 and 28 for information on patching.)

Worms and insects also leave behind evidence of their passing. If wormholes can be cut out in fitting and preparation, it is best to do so. Small wormholes in inconspicuous places can also be filled with putty and touched up in the finishing process. Should the patch not be completely invisible and you are questioned by an observer, use my line: "God, in His infinite wisdom, permitted a worm to dine there, and I'm certainly not going to question His judgment."

Wrinkles

Raw veneer is not always supplied in a perfectly flat condition. You may not realize just how wrinkled some slices are until you begin working with them. Figured species are usually distorted in all directions. Don't complain to the supplier. He will quietly reply that the beautiful pleating came at no extra charge. Rather, refer to pages 36 to 38 for information on dealing with this condition.

Surface Compression and Checking

As a piece of veneer is sliced, it is forced to curl away from the parent log and the slicing knife—much the same as a shaving leaves a hand plane. This causes the side nearer the log to stretch, while the side away from it is forced to compress. In some species, it is almost impossible to detect which side is which; in other species the effects are dramatic to the point of defect. The log side can be stretched to the point of checking, and the other compressed to a point that it will repel glue or finishing products.

Fortunately, slicing defect is easy to spot. Gently bend the veneer along the grain in both directions. You will notice that there is resistance in one direction, while the veneer yields easily in the other. If the compressed side is up, the veneer will bend upward easily. If the stretched side is up, the veneer will not be as yielding and cracking sounds will often be heard.

Another method is to examine the veneer under magnification—a photographer's 8x loupe works well. The compressed side will be tight, often to the extent of being shiny. The stretched side will show tiny checks as it is bent away from the loupe.

In application, the compressed side should be up and the stretched side down, allowing the glue to get a firm grasp of the checks. After bonding, the compressed side should be sanded heavily to break any glaze that exists, permitting the acceptance of stain and other finishing products.

Book-matching cuts with slicing defects poses a challenge, but it is by no means insurmountable. Scuff the compressed side with coarse sandpaper so it will accept glue properly. And after bonding, sand heavily to the approximate center of the veneer in order to remove the checks. Only you will notice any defect that remains.

Characteristics of Paper-Backed and Cross-Banded Veneers

Gentle Reader, I have good news and bad news.

First the good news: In paper-backed and cross-banded veneers, you will encounter none of the defects mentioned above. They do not contain oils, checks, splits, holes, etc. The manufacturer has already dealt with these problems.

The glue line between the paper and the wood, coupled with the glazed surface of the paper, inhibits the rapid absorption of glue solvents, be the solvent water or petroleum. In the case of water, this limits the expansion of the veneer, reducing pulling and open joints. In the case of contact cement, the glaze reduces the number of coats needed for bonding.

The paper backing strengthens veneer dramatically. Those delicate burls that will disintegrate easily can be handled as roughly as needed. Vertical-grain species can be handled without fear of cracking. And, both may be cut and fit with little more care than would be given the paper itself.

Now for the bad news: Paper-backed veneers are very thin—at least the wood component is thin. Sanding should be done with extreme care. In some instances, the wood is so thin that the paper and glue can be seen through it. The glue seals the veneer in place, and when a penetrating stain is used, these areas produce blotchy colors.

Paper-backed veneers can vary in thickness from species to species, and even more drastically from manufacturer to manufacturer. This difference in thickness is not as drastic as it was years ago, when the product was first introduced, but it does still exist. Use caution when doing decorative work with a number of different paper-backed veneers, and check all that will be used for consistent thickness.

The glaze on backing paper can cause beading of water-based adhesives. This can be a nuisance when using glues that have been thinned, as in the dry-glue process discussed on pages 68 to 70. It is not an insurmountable challenge. Simply break the glaze using 80-grit sandpaper.

Paper-backed veneers are very attractive—often, too attractive. If you've ever wondered why you can't buy lumber as good-looking as veneer, it's because veneer mills are prepared to pay premium prices for choice logs, so these logs never make it to board form. This attractiveness can get to the point where the veneer looks phony, such as when it resembles plastic laminate.

Suppliers usually roll paper-backed veneers for shipment. One of my suppliers has someone in the shipping department who could probably roll paper-backed veneer around a pencil. This guy is also a "company man." As such, he tries to pack each shipment into the smallest possible container. Paper-backed veneers treated thus have a tendency to stay rolled up, or at least the curve seems permanent.

Should you be dealing with the same supplier, don't call and complain about "Old Sam" down in shipping—the guy needs his job. Rather, roll the veneer loosely in the opposite direction and let it stand for an hour or two. In most cases, the veneer will once again become flat. If not, roll it tighter and let stand longer.

If you intend to work with paper-backed veneer exclusively, you will be limited to the few species available. Oh yes, some paper-backed suppliers have a rather impressive list of species, but it is nowhere as large as the lists provided by suppliers of raw veneer. As my clients browse through my box of veneer samples, selecting the woods to adorn the commission they are presenting me with, they will nine times out of ten pick species that are not available in paper-backed form.

Paper-backed veneers generally cost more per square foot than raw veneers. While they come in sheets as large as 48 x 96 inches, there will be cutting waste just as with the raw material. And there will be leftovers. These are things to consider when choosing the material for a particular project.

CHAPTER 2

Tools and Equipment

CUTTING TOOLS

Veneer is not a particularly hard substance and can be easily cut in a variety of ways. The grain direction and fragile nature of some veneers pose a challenge. In this respect, no cutting method, tool, or technique will work in all situations. I'll describe my experience with various tools and equipment.

Straightedges

Most of the cuts made in veneer will be straight cuts, and for these you will need some kind of guide. This guide could be anything from a very expensive machined, steel straightedge to a ripping from a sheet of plywood. No matter what type of straightedge is used, there are a couple of important criteria it should meet.

It goes without saying that a straightedge must be straight, but it must also be wide enough to be held firmly and safely. Using a narrow straightedge, you will be more prone to hold it by placing your finger-tips too near the guiding edge. At the expense of sounding stupid or reckless, I will mention that I have more than once trimmed a long fingernail or shaved off a bit of fingertip using a straightedge and knife. While a fingernail is of little consequence, regrowing a fingertip takes a long time—a long, painful time. Further, while the fingertip will heal, the bloodstains are sometimes impossible to remove from the veneer. So use a wide straightedge! How wide? At least 2 inches.

In the event that you use a wide straightedge and still nip yourself with a knife, the bloodstains that drip on the veneer can be removed if treated quickly with three-percent hydrogen peroxide—that stuff sold in drugstores as a disinfectant.

It is also important that the straightedge does not slip, for a slippery straightedge will always spoil that most important cut as well as provoke profanity. To prevent my straightedges from slipping, I often place strips of masking tape on them. Masking tape is thin enough that it doesn't interfere with the straightedge, and the rough surface helps immensely. (I once tried

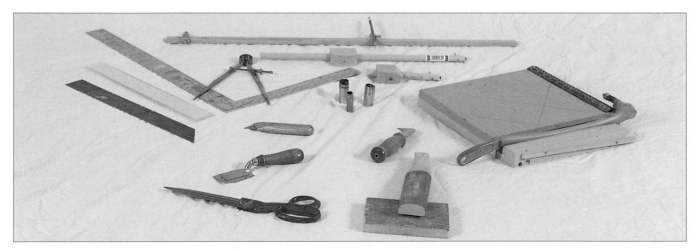

2-1. An assortment of tools needed for veneering.

using double-faced sticky tape, but found it too sticky and too thick.) The masking tape doesn't stay rough forever, but it can be quickly replaced.

In addition to the masking tape, I have drilled holes the exact size of a pushpin into my straightedges. When making long cuts, or cuts in wrinkled material, I tap a pushpin through the holes. The pin not only holds the straightedge in place, it also prevents any movement of the veneer on the benchtop. When using my flexible steel straightedges—through which it is impossible to drill a hole—I place pins opposite the waste side to prevent the straightedge from drifting into the field.

I also use plastic layout tools as straightedges for cutting. Some I equip with masking tape, and all have holes for pins. These have the advantage of letting me see through to the work. They have the disadvantage of not showing up for the camera, so I am not shown using many of these tools in the photos used in this book. See Layout Tools on pages 29 to 32 for more information.

The straightedge does more than provide a guide for the cutting tool; it also supports the veneer. In cutting across grain—or partially across grain—it is important to hold the straightedge down firmly. This prevents the veneer from buckling under the pressure of the cutting tool. When cutting with the grain, keeping firm pressure on the straightedge will help prevent the cutting tool from tearing slivers from the workpiece.

One more thing to consider is that last little bit of cross-grain cut. Keeping firm pressure on the straightedge beyond the veneer will help in preventing the forward pressure of the knife from splitting away that last quarter inch or so.

Knives with Disposable Blades

The mainstay of shop cutting tools is the utility knife. These are readily available, inexpensive, and have disposable blades. Some even have sectioned blades, the tip of which can be broken off as it becomes dull. I don't like them.

The utility knife is fine for making rough cuts, but when precision is required, I always use something else. The reason? The blade flexes too much. And this also goes for single-edge razor blades. This flexing

allows the blade to follow grain without giving me the warning of feeling the body of the knife wander.

I also find a flexing blade objectionable in the smaller hobby knives with disposable blades. By virtue of the wide assortment of blades available, these knives do have a place in delicate marquetry, and I recommend them highly for that purpose. But they are useless for the heavy-duty work involved in veneering.

One other disposable-blade knife worthy of mention is the hook knife. The workhorse of the floor-covering installer, this knife is also useful in wood veneering. Its blade is similar to the utility-knife blade in size and thickness, but rather than a sharpened edge there is a groove cut in the blade and the edges of the groove are sharpened.

I find this knife most useful in making rough cuts—especially rough, curved cuts. While the knife is unpredictable going with the grain, cuts that are partially across grain can be made most successfully. Unfortunately, raw wood veneer does not have the internal strength to withstand the pressures of cuts being made directly across grain.

Hook-knife blades can be found in different sizes. The blade with the smallest groove is best for making straight cuts and curved cuts with a gentle radius. Blades with a wider groove will make tighter cuts, and if you grind off the tip of the blade so that it won't scratch, these wide blades are excellent for edge-trimming.

Linoleum Knives

My all-time favorite knife for cutting veneer is the linoleum knife. Most have a blade that allows little or no flexing, and the shape of the blade allows clear view of the line being cut or the straightedge being followed.

The linoleum knife does need periodic sharpening, but I have found this a minor inconvenience. I often enjoy the break afforded by the necessity to stop and pass the edge over a sharpening stone and strop. I sharpen only the tip of the knife, and go so far as to round off the remaining cutting edge, lest I get my fingers tangled up with that part. The backside of the knife proves most useful in pressing down veneer tape or firming up a joint.

When cutting with the linoleum knife, I never try to make a cut with one single pass. On the first pass, I apply little more pressure than the weight of the knife itself, while holding the knife firmly against the guiding surface I'm using. This is important if the cut being made has a chance of following the grain. With each successive pass, I increase the pressure until the veneer is cut through—five passes are often required. I often think of the linoleum knife as a saw with one tooth and no set.

Spend a few bucks on a linoleum knife and practice a little. If you can't see its worth as a cutting tool, I'm sure you'll enjoy it for smoothing tape and firming up joints.

Veneer Saws

If you don't have a veneer saw, get one. Cutting long joints in most species of wood can be done more accurately with a veneer saw than any other tool—save for a shear. A veneer saw seems to hold up better than a knife in cutting abrasive wood species such as teak or rosewood.

Veneer saws do have some set, and as a result don't always make the smoothest cut. This roughness can also damage delicate veneers. The set is also devastating to the straightedge or to the saw itself. It either grinds away at the straightedge, or if a hardened-steel straightedge is being used, the saw teeth become worn.

One remedy for the effects of the set is to remove it; that is, to sharpen the saw like a knife. This results in a large number of sharp little teeth. The large number of sharp teeth enable a veneer saw to be used far longer between sharpenings than the single "tooth" of the linoleum knife or the single tip of a utility knife. I find this type of veneer saw most useful when making straight cuts in delicate burls and crotches. Refer to Sharpening a Veneer Saw, which follows, for details on sharpening.

I never could get use to pushing a veneer saw, which is what it seems designed for. I rather like to pull a veneer saw through the work. If I'm using a blade with set, this means turning the blade over and remounting it. Some blades are punched to receive a flathead screw. When the blade is turned over, the countersink portion of the punching winds up on the wrong side of the blade, but I've never found this a problem. I just put the screws back in. What does happen occasionally is that the handle falls off when I pull the saw. This can be prevented by filing some

grooves in the tang, filling the handle partially with yellow glue, and gently drive the tang home. After the glue is allowed to dry overnight, the handle no longer comes off.

Sharpening a Veneer Saw

As with general-woodworking saws, you really should have at least two veneer saws—one for ripping and one for crosscutting. (If you have ever tried ripping a board with a crosscut saw—or vice versa—you can appreciate the need for two saws.) Thus it is with veneer. The challenge here: I've yet to see a "rip" veneer saw. But with a file, a vise, and a belt sander—or sharpening stone—a veneer saw can be modified to make rip cuts.

When your crosscut veneer saw becomes dull, buy a replacement blade. These blades can be sharpened and reset, but believe me, folks, it isn't worth it. I do have a saw set and some very fine files. Had I the eyesight and the patience, I still wouldn't sharpen a saw blade that can be replaced that cheaply.

Don't throw away that old blade, however; it can be used to convert a veneer saw to a ripsaw. To do this, I mount the blade in a vise with a small stick backing it so that the jaws won't flatten the countersink screw holes. Then, with a triangular needle file I reshape the teeth (2–2 and 2–3).

2–2 and 2–3 (following page). *Reshaping the teeth on a veneer-saw blade.*

Notice the teeth on the left of the blade in 2–3; these are the shape of the teeth in most veneer saws. They are crosscut teeth, tilting forward. Now notice the few teeth I've reshaped on the right of the blade. They are shaped like equilateral triangles, tilting in no particular direction. These teeth will rip veneer very well; they will also crosscut very well. In addition, they can be pulled or pushed across the veneer with equal cutting action.

2–3. A close-up of blade teeth.

In reshaping the teeth, it's a good practice to keep your thumb on top of the file, feeling the flat area. The cutting angle of the file can then be easily sensed and held in place by the position of the wrist.

To the right of the vise in 2–2 is a loupe. That little magnifier is there to assist me in determining just how good a job I've done. I don't care how good your eyesight; it's always helpful to have some form of magnification handy to critically evaluate any sharpening job.

While I was shooting these photos, I decided to make myself a new stainless-steel veneer saw to be used when working with hot hide glue. The stainless steel won't leave blue stains on the wet surface of the veneer if left in contact with it for any length of time—as will carbon steel—and I continually leave the saw teeth on the veneer.

For the stainless-steel saw, I chose a serrated table knife, rescued from the "super bargain table" at the thrift store—I think I paid a dime for it. After mounting the knife in the vise, I filed its teeth, using the

knife's serrations as a spacing guide (2–4). I have used several veneer saws with these types of blades and I find it remarkable how well they hold an edge. Before investing in a "real" veneer saw, you may wish to consider the economy version.

After filing the teeth, the next step was to form and sharpen the knife-type cutting edge. For this operation, I used a belt sander with a worthless—for wood—belt installed (2–5). (While I now have a very well-equipped sharpening station in the shop—grinder, belts, strops, buffer, etc.—at this point the

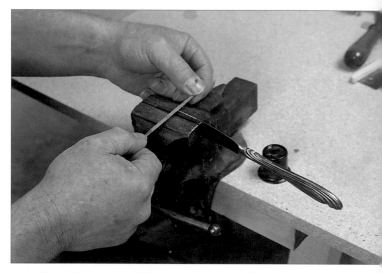

2–4. Filing the saw teeth for a stainless-steel saw.

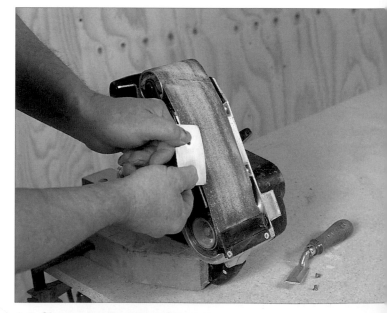

2–5. Sharpening the edge of the saw.

belt sander was all I had.) Even if you don't have a belt sander, a bench stone will work—if you have the time.

The object here is to form a bevel of about 15 degrees. I formed it on only one side of the saw, the side that will be opposite the straight edge. With the saw's blade sharpened thus, the veneer under the straightedge will be prepared for a joint with no need to use a shooting block. Considering the 15-degree cutting angle, even the side of the veneer opposite the straightedge will be ready for a joint with only a pass or two of the shooting block.

Not shown in the photographs is a can of water for dipping the blade into during the sander operation. I was removing quite a bit of metal with the sander, and I didn't want to turn the blade blue, let alone burn my fingers.

On examination with the loupe, I found that I was a little bold with the sander. The saw had a sharp cutting edge, but what started out as pointed teeth had flat spots on the top. So, I returned the blade to the vise and reshaped any teeth with the flat tops. After I was satisfied with my work, I passed a slip stone over the side opposite the bevel to remove any burr that might grind away at my straightedge.

Although a bit unconventional, this type of veneer saw takes no kerf and requires less effort than a conventional veneer saw. It does require periodic sharpening, but it is oh so gentle with those delicate veneers.

Rotary Cutters

I bought my first rotary cutter in a fabric store, but now I see them in office-supply stores, to be used for cutting whatever people who work in offices have occasion to cut. Provided that the rotary cutter is kept sharp and free of nicks, it is not prone to follow the grain, and a cut can often be made in a single pass. It can even be used on freehand curves with a gentle radius. While rotary cutters work best on paper-backed veneer, they will work to a certain degree on raw veneer.

After leaving the floor-covering store with your new linoleum knife, stop by the office-supply store and buy a rotary cutter. They're both good investments.

Paper Cutters

A paper cutter is a fine tool for cutting small pieces of wood. You may have to search to find a paper cutter like the one shown in the project photos—as this type of cutter may have fallen into disfavor with safety advocates, perhaps rightly so, but the search is worth the effort. I must admit that a larger shear would be a far better piece of equipment, but the amount of veneering work I do has never justified the cost.

Sometimes I put strips of masking tape on the table of my paper cutter to keep the veneer from slipping. These are placed about one inch back from the bar to prevent them from padding the action of the knife. There are also a couple of 45-degree marks on the table to help me line up miter cuts.

I must point out that the paper cutter also works well for cutting fingers. If the piece on the table is quite small, I hold it down with a block of wood—guess you could call that a "paper-cutter sissystick." I also hesitate about a half-second before pulling that handle to make sure my fingertips are clear of the shear.

Scissors and Snips

Yes, scissors are a tool that can be used to cut veneer. Heavy-duty scissors work best, and they should be kept sharp. In lieu of scissors, good-quality tin snips will work. Snips will often cut a tighter radius. I have both snips and shears which I use only for veneer and which are kept well hidden from anyone who may enter my corner of the shop. I found out long ago that my colleagues were fond of using my snips to cut sandpaper. While they served that purpose nicely, the cutting edge became well rounded in a very short time.

CUTTING SURFACE

In most cutting operations, the cutting edge, or tip, of the cutting instrument will pass through the veneer and come into contact with the surface that supports the veneer. In order to keep instruments sharp, try to choose a surface that won't dull the cutting instrument. I often use the substrate as a cutting surface—a few fine knife marks won't hurt it. There are times when I find a piece of hardboard useful. The backside of vinyl floor covering is good because it's not slippery. Cardboard will work, but it is spongy and falls apart quickly. Particleboard works, but is just rough enough that it can deflect a knife, causing the cuts to become a little ragged.

My favorite cutting surface is battleship linoleum, a material that is expensive and a little difficult to find. Ten years ago, I was commissioned to re-cover several desktops with plastic laminate. Rather than remove the battleship linoleum from these, I completely rebuilt the tops, saving the originals for myself. I still have three that have not been scarred from veneer cutting to a point that they are unusable. I guard them carefully.

CARVING TOOLS

When working with inlays and borders, it is often necessary to make curved cuts with a tight radius. Wood-carving tools will accomplish this task with little challenge.

Carving tools can split the veneer near the cut. To eliminate this possibility, I usually make a rough cut using a hook knife and then trim to the line using the carving tool. The tool can be tapped with a mallet, but I find that rolling the tool's edge over the line to be cut eliminates the possibility of damage to the surrounding wood. This technique will also permit you to use carving tools with a sweep that doesn't quite match the radius being cut.

POWER TOOLS

Through the years I have seen numerous jigs for cutting veneer with table saws, jointers, and routers—even jigs for planing and sanding with power tools. I once built a jig to hold a number of sheets to be trimmed to size on my table saw, and I sometimes use a router for trimming edges after the veneer is bonded. While I use power tools extensively in my general woodworking, I've found little use for power tools in cutting and fitting veneer.

PUNCHES

As discussed, burls are ugly growths in the sides of a tree. When these are sliced and the slices dried,

defects often fall away, leaving holes in the veneer. These holes need to be patched. A quick and accepted method of patching these holes calls for a "veneer punch." Available in several sizes, this tool punches out an irregularly shaped hole that contains any defect that cannot be worked with. The same tool is then used to punch a patch of similar grain and color from another piece of burl.

A round punch could be used for this purpose, but the irregular shape of the veneer punch makes a less noticeable patch than a perfect circle.

My only objection to the veneer punch is the cost. Now, I would be the last one in the world to deny someone his means of livelihood, but I've never been able to justify several hundred dollars for a set of veneer punches. I use them too infrequently. Rather I have "brewed" my own.

I start by grinding a sharp edge in the end of a piece of thin-wall electrical conduit. Then I clean the burr from the inside with a rat-tail file (2–6). Sometimes this takes several trips from file to grinder and back to form a sharp edge of about 30 degrees.

2–6. Making a veneer punch. Here the burr on the end of a piece of electrical conduit is being cleaned.

After sharpening, I cut about 2½ inches from the prepared end of the conduit and put it in a vise in order to squeeze it into a slight oval. Then with a clamp and a screwdriver, I begin squeezing it into an irregular shape (2–7). I'll also mention that the dainty cross-peen hammer was called into use to produce the irregular shape.

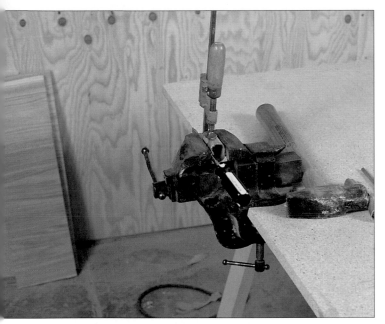

2–7. Squeezing the conduit into an irregular shape.

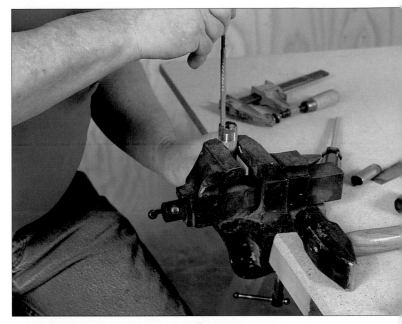

2–9. Deburring the inside of the conduit with a rat-tail file.

After I'm satisfied with the shape, I pass a file lightly over the cutting edge to make sure that it is still flat, again deburring the inside with a rat-tail file (2–8 and 2–9).

Using several different sizes of conduit, I'm able to produce a number of punches that serve me well (2–10). Of course, they don't have the little spring that ejects the punched veneer, but I can push it out using the eraser end of a pencil. My type of punch

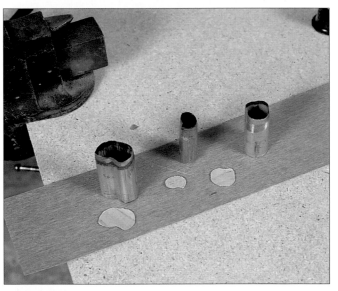

2–10. Shop-made punches.

is not as intricate in shape as the store-bought types, but in a way I consider that a benefit because the punched pieces are not so delicate.

Patching Technique

When I patch a piece of veneer, I don't go after every tiny hole. Most defects will be areas of knots, and small holes can be filled with putty and colored in the

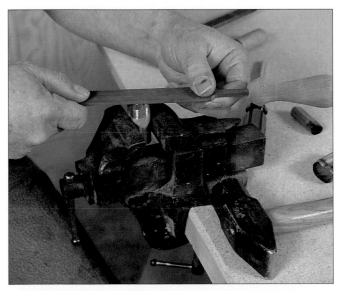

2–8. Flattening the cutting edge with a file.

finishing operation. Any defect over $1/2$ inch I attend to. Before any punching, I tape the area to be worked; this prevents me from doing more damage to the area I'm working on. Sometimes I use perforated tape on the back side of the veneer (2–11), and sometimes I use a stronger solid tape on the face (2–12).

I can usually find the patches I've made in the fin-

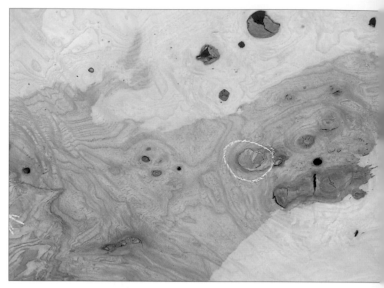

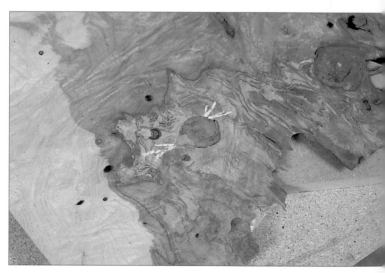

2–13 and 2–14. Veneer patches.

2–11 and 2–12. Patching veneer. Here perforated tape is being used on the veneer back.

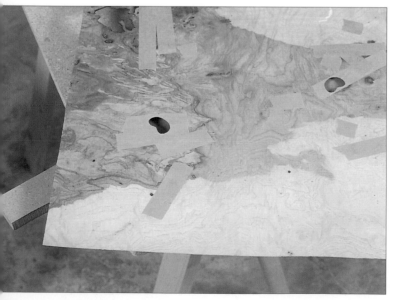

2–12. Using solid tape on the face of the veneer.

2–14.

ished product. If there are a lot of them, sometimes even I can't find them all. In any case, casual observers won't find them unless they are looking closely (2–13 and 2–14).

HOUSEHOLD IRON

Throughout this book, you will see me with an iron in my hand. I consider it an indispensable tool. The one I use most I picked up at a thrift store, and it has been slightly modified so that it will fit into inside curves.

2–15. Modifying a household iron to be used on veneers. Here it is disassembled and the heating element located.

2–16. The shiny area indicates the tip and edges that have been rounded off.

To modify the iron, I first disassembled it to locate the heating element (2–15). Then I rounded off the tip and part of the edges—shown as the shiny areas in 2–16. (If all you're able to find is a steam iron, be careful to avoid the steam jets.) I rounded the edges with a disc sander, but a file will work equally well. Just be sure that the rounded area is sanded smooth so that it won't damage the veneer.

GLUE CONTAINERS WITH SPREADERS

Cleaning glue-spreading tools after a project can be time-consuming, and it's just one of those things that I don't like to do. Solution? I don't clean my spreading tools. For white and yellow glue, I have a plastic container—I believe it was sold as a container for lettuce (2–17). In the container I keep a 4-inch paint roller with the handle cut off. Usually I have about 1/2 inch of glue at the bottom. Left for a week or two, the glue does deteriorate, but I use this glue continually for edge-gluing as well as for spreading veneer.

To the right in 2–17 is a clean gallon can I

2–17. Glue container with spreaders.

bought at my local paint store. In the can is a brush. The bottom of the can contains no more than a quart of contact cement. I replenish the contact cement from a gallon or a five-gallon container. Yes, sometimes I get a dab of contact on my fingers from the brush that remains in the can, but I'm a big boy; I can take it.

LAYOUT TOOLS

One thing I have found very handy for veneer work is some see-through layout tools and straightedges. When trying to match figure and grain patterns, it is oh so nice to have transparent marking tools. You'll only see a few of my see-through tools in the photos in this book because they just don't show up well. As a matter of fact, I often spend time looking for a triangle or a straightedge that's right under my nose.

Just as with drawing-board layout tools, I have a number of different sizes of 45-degree triangles, some 30/60-degree triangles, and a couple of different isosceles triangles with 22$\frac{1}{2}$-degree angles—I do a lot of work with octagons. In addition, I have quite an assortment of different lengths of straightedges in assorted widths—2, 2$\frac{1}{4}$, 2$\frac{1}{2}$ inches, etc. These I use extensively for laying out and cutting borders.

Most of my see-through tools are made of $\frac{1}{8}$-inch acrylic or polycarbonate sheet. Some are $\frac{1}{4}$ inch thick, and the polycarbonate sheet is by far the strongest. I have had to pay for a lot of these materials, but my friend at the glass shop has often given me small pieces, especially strips to make straightedges from. He has even given me large pieces which have been around for a long time and which have protective paper that is almost impossible to remove. These I douse in mineral spirits, and the paper does come off eventually.

Both types of plastic sheet may be cut on the table saw using a carbide blade. This is often dangerous because the plastic often overheats and binds, causing a kickback. I've found it far safer to rough-cut the plastic on a band saw and then fasten it to a bench with a straight, smooth edge using a few flathead screws (2–18). I then trim it to final dimension with a router and flush-trim bit with the pilot riding on the edge of the bench (2–19). Sometimes it's just as easy to screw the whole sheet to the bench and cut it with the router (2–20).

2–19. Trimming the plastic sheet with a router and flush-trim bit.

2–20. Trimming the plastic sheet with the whole sheet attached to the workbench.

2–18 to 2–20. Cutting plastic sheets. A close-up of the rough-cut plastic sheet fastened to a workbench.

I have drilled holes in all of my plastic layout tools to accept a pushpin. This prevents them from wandering. Sometimes I have wanted a few extra lines on my layout triangles, turning them into a protractor of sorts. The lines were easily scribed with a knife or the point of a pair of dividers (2–21). The scribed line soon fills with dirt, making it easily visible.

2–21. Scribing lines on a layout tool.

Scribing Dividers

I do a lot of fitting by scribing, and for this a good pair of dividers is a must. I think that the most important criteria for scribing dividers is that they have a hardened steel needle that can be either sharpened or replaced. To the right in 2–22 is a pair of dividers designed for drafting. I have two objections to these: First, I tend to move the adjustment wheel unknowingly. Second, in tight spots, the body of the instrument gets in the way of the scribing. But they do have replaceable needles and they work in most applications.

To the left in 2–22 is my favorite pair of dividers. These are nothing more than an inexpensive pair that I took to a machinist to grind off the tips and bore holes to receive the needles. I buy the needles at either a drafting-equipment supply store or a supplier that sells tools to floor-covering mechanics. With one drop of CA (cyanoacrylate) adhesive, the needles stay in place until I heat them and pull them out for replacement.

Also shown in 2–22 is a slip stone; I keep it with the dividers to sharpen the point.

2–22. Scribing dividers.

Edge Scribes

My two favorite edge scribes are shown in 2–23. The one on the top is a "home brew." The scribing "needle" is a piece of $1/8$-inch drill rod that has had its end ground to one side at about a 20-degree angle. It is locked in place by a drywall screw driven into the end of a $5/8$-inch dowel. (I run the screw in to establish the threads, withdraw it, and grind off the sharp point to keep it from marring the drill rod.)

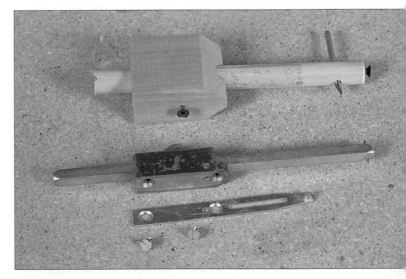

2–23. Edge scribes.

The body of the scribe is a simple block of wood drilled to receive the dowel; another drywall screw—with the tip ground off-locks it in place. Note that the front of the body is tapered to allow it to correctly follow tight, inside curves.

Below the home brew is a needle scribe used by floor-covering mechanics to scribe joints. I pulled off the joint hook to give it a deeper reach in order to scribe the border for the kidney-shaped desk described in Chapter 10.

When used carefully, both scribes will cut veneer as well as scribe a line.

Circle Devices

Shown in 2–24 are my favorite circle devices. On top is another home brew, similar to the edge scribe described above. Here the bored block that slides along the dowel has a #3 finishing nail driven into it; the head of the nail is clipped off and the remainder filed to a sharp point.

Beneath that is a pair of store-bought trammel points. The beam for the points can be of any length that is convenient. And that pencil can be replaced with a hobby knife or a scribing point.

Smiling from the bottom of 2–24 is a simple pair of 8-inch dividers. Slid over one leg is a piece of 1/2-inch

copper pipe. The pipe is slightly squashed to form an oval, and two brass nuts are soldered to it to receive the two stainless-steel locking screws. To solder those nuts on, drill the pipe and insert the screws with the nuts threaded on. You will find that the solder sticks well to the brass nuts and copper pipe, but it doesn't stick to the stainless-steel screws, which will keep the solder from the nut's threads.

VENEER HAMMERS

Gentle Reader, I have a confession: I have never owned a "real" veneer hammer. I keep telling myself that it's one of those things I have to buy just to look professional, if nothing else. But I have yet to get around to it, because my shop-built contrivances work well for me.

The top contrivance in 2–25 is nothing more than a handle turned from 1 3/4-inch-square stock. I would have whittled it if the lathe had not been available that day. The metal thing stuck in the end of the handle is a brick chisel. I bored the hole in the handle slightly undersized for the chisel's octagonal shank. After rounding off the cutting edge and corners of the chisel, I pressed into the bore, which had been swabbed with hot hide glue. After ten years and a lot of use, it hasn't come loose.

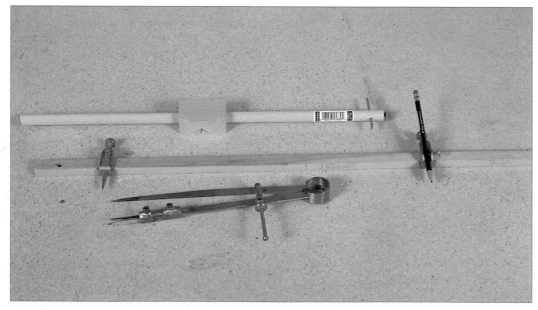

2–24. Circle devices.

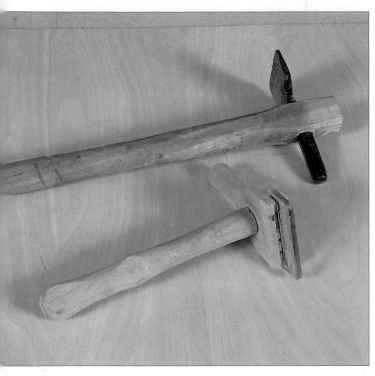

2-25. Shop-made veneer hammers.

Below that rests another piece of lathe work. In the working head, I cut a slot and inserted a small piece of 1/4-inch polycarbonate sheet. The plastic piece has had its edges and corners rounded off, and it's held in place with CA adhesive. The plastic-edged contrivance has the advantage that it does not leave a blue stain if left sitting on a piece of wet veneer.

Either hammers are a must for hot hide glue, but they also work well for putting down contact cement.

ABRASIVE DEVICES

If you have discovered the convenience of wrapping a piece of sandpaper around a stick or a block of wood for some special sanding job, carry this one step further: Glue the sandpaper to the stick and call it a tool.

I have a large number of such devices scattered all over the shop (2–26). Some are simple, flat blocks; some have varied radiuses; others are wedge-shaped. Some have crudely formed handles, and some are simply pieces I pulled out of the scrap barrel. In all cases, I bond industrial-grade sanding cloth—usually

80 grit—to them with contact cement. (Many companies that manufacture sanding belts sell their remnants by the pound. Seek and ye shall find.)

I bond the first piece of sandpaper tightly to the stick. When it's time for a replacement, I bond a new piece over the first. This one doesn't stick too well, so when it's time to replace it, it's easy to peel off.

You'll see these abrasive devices used often in the following pages; the flat ones are used for shooting straight joints, and the curved ones for shooting curved joints. Both I use for final trimming.

2-26. An assortment of shop-made abrasive devices.

CLAMPS AND OTHER EQUIPMENT

When working with contact cement, dry glue, or hide glue you are bound to have a spot or two in a piece of veneer that refuse to stay down and need a little clamping or a weight to hold them for a time (2–27). Spring clamps work great around the edges. Out in the field, sometimes a weight will work. I have a couple of pieces of square steel plate, and that silver thing shown in 2–27 is a piece of babbitt ingot; if I rebuild one more old machine, this ingot will disappear from my veneering equipment. A deep-reach screw clamp is always handy, and if it won't reach far enough, it's a simple matter to fasten some extensions with a few drywall screws. If all else fails, you can span the surface with a stick, put a block under it over the offending spot, and clamp both ends (foreground).

No matter what, make sure to keep on hand some paper to prevent any glue from sticking to the weight or clamps. Also have available a few handy blocks of wood to prevent the clamps from marring the veneer.

The orange cup shown in 2–27? That's for you. Fill it with your favorite beverage, take a sip now and then, and enjoy your work.

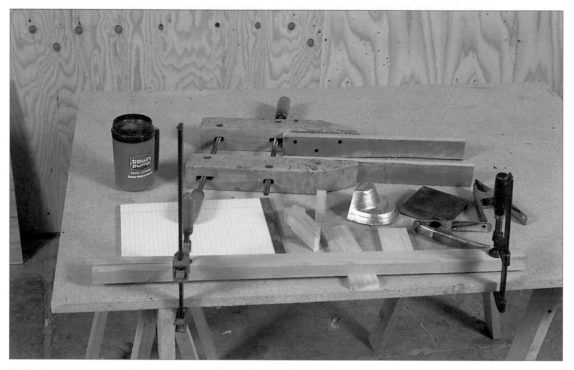

2–27. *An assortment of clamps and weights that includes spring and deep-reach screw clamps, steel plates, and an ingot.*

CHAPTER 3

Preparing and Cutting Veneer

PREPARATION

Right from the unpacking of the shipment, veneer does need some care. Should I unpack a shipment and discover damage, I first mark one end on the face side (3–1). This way, I'll have a reference for proper presentation. Then I repair all damage using perforated tape (3–2)—just in case the tape winds up in the glue line.

If the veneer is not damaged, I tape the ends to prevent the veneer from getting damaged through my own rough handling. I tape one end with brown paper tape to keep the face and end located (3–3) and the other I tape with perforated tape so that I won't confuse the two.

Long slices I either return to the shipping box or I construct a short tube of Single-Side or cardboard.

3–2. Repairing damage to veneer using perforated tape.

3–1. Marking one end of the face side of veneer.

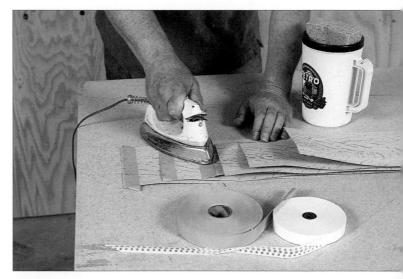

3–3. Taping the end of veneer with brown paper tape to help locate the face and end.

3–4. This shipping envelope provides a storage container for short slices.

Short slices I store in the shipping envelope after cutting off the ends so that it will lie flat (3–4).

Flattening Techniques

One of the frustrations of using raw veneer is that it's not always flat. This is especially true of figured cuts—burls, crotches, stump wood, etc. Some of these cuts are wrinkled to such a degree that an attempt to force them flat in a dry state will cause severe breakage. Even vertical-grain veneer, if not properly stored, can have waves or be cupped to a degree that it will split if forced flat. Cutting, fitting, taping, and bonding of wrinkled veneer is all but impossible. Irregularities must be dealt with before any work can be done.

I have often pondered the reason for such distortion. After all, the veneers were flat when they were sliced. I reasoned thus: When veneer is sliced, it is usually in a saturated warm condition. Various sections of burls and crotches are of vastly different textures and densities, with grain running in different directions. As the slice dries, different areas shrink to various degrees, accounting for the wrinkled condition.

The first stage in any flattening process is to render the veneer as pliable as possible, or plasticize it. This will permit some areas to stretch and others to compress when the veneer is eased into a flat condition.

One effective method of plasticizing wood is to expose it to gaseous ammonia under pressure. The drawbacks to this method are that the equipment required is expensive, the ammonia is dangerous, and the discoloration resulting in some species is impossible to reconcile.

Also on the list of plasticizers are such common products as fabric softener and hair conditioner. When mixed with water, these products do an excellent job of plasticizing wood. Their drawback is the residue left behind. The silicone in fabric softener, for instance, will render the veneer almost impervious to many bonding adhesives, and, if that's not bad enough, any surface coating applied to the veneer will orange-peel and fish-eye to a most unacceptable degree. Hair conditioners are not as bad as fabric softener, but I always worry about the long-term effects of the residues. I mention these products only to point out that I have not had much success with them . . . so on to more ancient techniques.

Water alone will plasticize wood to a great degree. Water mixed with glycerin works even better. And added alcohol makes the mixture even more effective.

Wood that has been heated to 150 degrees Fahrenheit or higher is far more pliable than wood at room temperature. Heat alone will relax the fibers of wood, allowing it to take on a new shape and keep it.

Time is another factor. Wood can be encouraged to change dimension, but this encouragement must be applied gently and lovingly over a period of time. Pretend you're a piece of veneer for a moment. If you were forced to change your existence in an instant, you would rebel—perhaps to your own undoing. However, slowly encouraged and accommodated, you might more willingly accept change.

Now that I have attempted to instill in you an empathy for the material you are working, I'll go on to recommend specific techniques that I have found most successful for flattening veneer in the small shop.

Minor Flattening

If the veneer is not seriously wrinkled and the bonding agent used will be hot hide or "dry" glue, little flattening is required. About a minute after the hot hide glue is applied to the veneer, it becomes as limp as a dishrag. This is true even of large mahogany crotches. Invariably, however, and in full conformity with Murphy's laws of inevitability, there will be a couple of spots about the size of a quarter that will refuse to go down. For these little annoyances, I keep some deep-reach clamps or sandbags handy.

Flattening Veneer with a Household Iron

If you are using adhesives other than hot hide glue—and the material is not seriously wrinkled—pressing with a household iron works well. A steam iron is effective, but I find a spray bottle and a standard iron more versatile. (Don't knock the concept. It works for wrinkled clothes.) In addition to figured species, the iron can also quickly flatten vertical-grain slices that are too cupped to work with. It is also useful in restoration work to put down small, loose spots and heavy grain that has been raised in the stripping and washing process. Put an iron on your shopping list.

To flatten with an iron, spray both sides of the veneer with warm water. Then give a second coat to concave areas of figured cuts or the concave side of vertical-grain cuts; this begins the flattening process by expanding the "short" side. With the iron set on medium, slowly apply heat while supporting most of the iron's weight. Turn the veneer frequently and work both sides. As the veneer becomes flatter, more and more of the iron's weight can be applied to it. Pressing continues until the veneer is thoroughly flat and dry.

When using a steam iron, as the veneer becomes flat turn off the steam and continue ironing until the veneer is dry.

Remember those words I used above: "slowly," "lovingly," "encourage." Never forget them; never force the iron when flattening veneer.

Flattening Veneer with a Hot Press

Refer to Bonding Using Mechanical Presses on pages 71 and 72 for a complete description of flattening with a hot press.

Flattening Veneer with Glycerin

Another method—and perhaps the most time-honored—is to spray the veneer with a mixture of water, glycerin, and alcohol. Here, water is the plasticizer. Glycerin serves as a wetting agent and its hygroscopic properties (ability to readily absorb moisture from the atmosphere) will force the wood to hold some moisture, keeping it pliable. The alcohol speeds drying.

One large veneer supplier recommends this formula: one gallon water, eight ounces glycerin, eight ounces alcohol. I've used this concoction frequently, finding it very effective.

Some authors suggest mixing in such things as flour and glue. These components will add some strength to the veneer and help keep it flat, but I've seldom considered the added mess worth it.

Although the water will work by itself, if you live in a warm, damp climate and drying will take many days, add alcohol. It will act as a disinfectant. Without it, you may find all kinds of "stuff" growing in the veneer. Mushrooms may even sprout from the drying stack.

Caution: Should you apply heat to veneers with residues of glycerin or alcohol—either from an iron or from the steam process described below—there will be generated some very interesting fumes, none of which are beneficial to the human body. Work in a well-ventilated area and at the first sign of discomfort, open all doors and windows and leave the area until the fumes have cleared.

In practice, I spray both sides of the veneers to be flattened with a heavy coat of the water/alcohol/glycerin mixture (3–5). These are then placed between two pieces of 3/4-inch-thick particleboard. The coated varieties favored by kitchen cabinet manufacturers are especially useful because the coating prevents the water from penetrating to the particleboard and eventually destroying it. Weight is then placed on the stack in increasing amounts as the mixture disperses, penetrates the veneer, and the

3–5. Flattening veneer using a water/alcohol/glycerin mixture.

veneer begins to flatten. Finally, I place several clamps around the edges of the particleboard and a deep-reach clamp in the center (3–6). All of this takes place over a period of an hour or more. Depending on the tenacity of the veneer, I often leave the stack clamped overnight.

Clamping as soon as the veneer is reasonably flat is important because it limits the movement of the veneer, causing compression rather than expansion. Many woods will compress up to 20 percent without failure, while expansion of as little as five percent may result in splitting.

Flattening Veneer with Steam

Steam works great for flattening veneer. If you've used steam for bending wood, I don't have to convince you that it will plasticize to a high degree. Two methods for generating steam are mentioned in Chapter 6. Carefully consider these, as steam has many uses in the small shop.

The veneers to be flattened are sprayed with warm water on both sides, stacked, and moderate weight is placed on the stack for an hour or so. This provides for some initial flattening and allows the water to disperse throughout the veneer.

The veneers are then placed—usually no more than two at a time—in a shallow box constructed of lightweight exterior plywood at the top and bottom, and with 3/4-inch-thick material screwed to the plywood, forming the sides (3–7). Veneers are spaced from the bottom of the box—or each other, if I have stacked several slices in a box—with small cubes of 3/4-inch material, permitting free circulation of the steam. The steam box rests on a piece of foam insulation. This, in combination with another piece placed over the lid, helps substantially to raise the temperature of the box. Steam is introduced into the box at such an angle that it will flow in a circular fashion.

After three to five minutes in the steam box, the veneer becomes quite limp. The heat also drives some of the moisture from the veneer. It is important to not oversteam the veneer, since my experience has shown that this makes it brittle.

3–7. Shop-made steam box for flattening veneer.

Remembering the burns I received the first time I used a steam box, I wear a light jacket and gloves to remove the heated veneer, while keeping my face well clear of the box. Although there is little steam pressure involved, a large volume of hot steam is released when the lid is lifted.

The veneer slices are then quickly placed between pieces of particleboard and clamped or weighted heavily until cool. After cooling them, I proceed with a drying process.

3–6. Clamping procedures when flattening veneer.

Drying Technique

After flattening, veneers must be dried before using. Many recommend placing the veneer between layers of newspaper, weighting the stack, and periodically changing the newspaper. Not wanting to periodically change newspaper between veneers—on the bottom of the birdcage, beneath the cat's litter box, or any other place—I have discovered a product called Single-Side. This is a corrugated cardboard with paper applied to only one side of the corrugations. It is relatively inexpensive and readily available from those engaged in the packing and shipping industry.

(I'll tell you the real reason I don't like drying veneer between sheets of newspaper. I once set some veneer to dry between the pages of a freshly printed newspaper. Several days later, I found that the residual alcohol in the veneer did a fine job of softening the uncured printer's ink, carrying it deep into the veneer. Were it not for a lot of scrubbing with lacquer thinner and a prodigious amount of sanding, the newspaper's headlines would have been immortalized in the tabletop I was about to veneer.)

I place each cut of veneer between two pieces of Single-Side with the corrugations against the veneer and all corrugations running in the same direction (3–8). In the case of burls and crotches, rather than stack them in order I rotate each 180 degrees, providing more evenly distributed pressure as the material dries and tries to resume its wrinkled condition.

I then place the stack of veneer between the particleboard pieces and clamp them with moderate pressure, in no way flattening the corrugations of the Single-Side cardboard. Clamps are important, because there is nothing more frustrating than to see the stack expand as it will if there is only a single, lightweight object on it. Believe me, it can happen. The cumulative pressures exerted by those thin little slices of wood can be tremendous.

To speed the drying, I situate a fan so that it blows air through the corrugations of the Single-Side cardboard (3–9); I leave the fan in place for one to three days. (The exact time will depend on the ambient humidity. The times I give are related to the very dry climate of northern Utah.) On the last day, every hour or so, I blow hot air from a hair drier through the stack. (I avoid hot air initially because this will

3–8. *Placing veneer between corrugated cardboard.*

cause too rapid a drying, which causes excessive checking and splitting.) When I disassemble the stack, if I feel that any of the veneer is still moist, I reassemble the stack and continue the hot-air-and-fan treatment for another day or as long as it takes.

It is extremely important that the veneer be dried to as little moisture content that the ambient humidity of the area will permit. Otherwise, after bonding, the veneer will shrink, opening joints. Unfortunately, this shrinkage can occur weeks, even months, after the veneer has been bonded, causing all manner of embarrassment and profanity.

Commonly Asked Questions

There are some questions concerning the flattening of veneer that I'd now like to address:

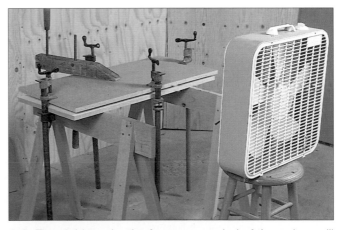

3–9. *The air blown by the fan over a period of three days will speed veneer drying.*

1. Does the veneer wrinkle again if not kept under weight? Sometimes. This usually happens when the veneer is not completely dry before removing it from the weights. In all cases, I have not had veneer wrinkle as bad as it was originally. Just to be safe, I store flattened veneer horizontally in envelopes of cardboard with a weight on top.

2. Can the veneer be treated several times?

Not only can it be, but sometimes several treatments are required. When using water/glycerin/alcohol, delete the glycerin on the second and subsequent treatments, as there will be plenty left from the first try.

3. Will the veneer wrinkle again when using water-based adhesives?

Yes, but here again the wrinkling will not be as severe as it was originally, for certain areas of the veneer have been encouraged to stretch and others to compress. These dimensional changes tend to be permanent.

4. Does the veneer crack, split, and check during the flattening process?

Sometimes. This depends on the type of slice and the wood species. Fortunately, I've found that the crack or check occurs in the same place on each successive slice. When matching veneer figures, this can be used to advantage, and I usually try to accentuate these defects rather than hide them.

5. How do you know when the veneer is dry?

Through experience and "feel." All right, this answer may seem like a cop-out, but it's true.

If you have a moisture meter, use it, but don't depend on the reading. Take readings periodically and consider the veneer dry when the reading stabilizes. When using a moisture meter, remember that the meter does not measure moisture; it measures the electrical conductivity of the wood, which should be related to moisture content.

If you have an accurate scale, weigh the veneer before and after drying it. Consider the veneer dry when its weight stabilizes, remembering that if you have used glycerin, there will be some residue.

Dry veneer will not have that cool feeling of moist veneer. In the dry climate where I work, dry veneer is quite brittle and has the feel of a fresh corn chip. I always keep in mind that if the veneer was treated with glycerin, it will feel slightly more pliable than veneer treated with water only or with steam.

Strengthening Veneer

There will be those times when you encounter a piece of veneer that is just too delicate to handle—some exotic burl or piece of highly compressed stump that looks as if it will fall apart if sneezed at. These pieces can be so delicate that the pressure required to tape their faces effectively could destroy them. Don't take a chance on ruining them; take a little time to strengthen them. The strengthening process can also be used to flatten the piece, thereby killing two birds with the one proverbial stone. It can consist of taping the piece, "sizing" it, or bonding it to paper. Each is discussed below.

Taping Technique

Veneer tape will impart great strength to small areas. Splits and checks should be taped to keep them from getting worse. Knots that look as if they are about to fall out should be covered with tape. I often place tape over fragile veneers in places that will be cut for joints. And I routinely tape the edges of fragile veneers while unpacking them.

For this type of reinforcement, I'm very partial to perforated tape. It allows me to see the grain through the perforations. Often, when taping these areas, I have not yet determined which side of the veneer will be the face. Thin perforated tape can be left in the glue line. It shouldn't be, but I often leave it and as yet have had no problems.

Sizing

"Sizing" refers to the process of giving the veneer a coat of glue and letting it dry. This can be incorporated in the flattening process. If you're using the dry-glue process (described on pages 68 to 70) or contact cement, sizing is incorporated in the process. But for other bonding techniques I proceed thus: I mix hot hide glue in the proportions of one part glue to five parts water (the proportions may vary). After the added water has come up to temperature, I quickly brush a thin coat on both sides of the veneer and stand the piece up to let any excess run off.

After the veneer has had a chance to dry for about a half hour, I place a piece of fiberglass window screen on each side of it and proceed with the drying operation described above. The window screen is a must, for it prevents the fresh glue from sticking to the Single-Side cardboard.

Liquid hide glue may be used in the same manner, but it's always seemed to me that it dries softer and will clog sandpaper to an extent. Of course, if you live in a damp climate, hot hide glue remains soft to an extent.

Pieces sized with hide glue may be bonded with contact cement or urea-formaldehyde. I don't recommend using the dry-glue process to bond pieces that have been sized with hide glue because the PVA glue used in the process and hide glue are not completely compatible.

Before sizing, consider the finishing technique you intend to use. The residue of the hide glue can be sanded from the face of the veneer, permitting it to accept stains properly, but it remains in the pores, sometimes partially filling them. This will make paste filler difficult to use and often cause a blotchy pore pattern. Experiment with the wood species you intend to use.

Bonding Veneer to a Backing

If sizing alone won't do the trick, the veneer may be further strengthened by bonding it to a backing of some sort—essentially making your own paper-backed veneer. Of course, that backing will make for a thick glue line, so I have always used the thinnest paper I can find. Each Christmas, after unwrapping those ties I will never wear and the shirts that are too small, I save the tissue paper for strengthening veneer.

Using a soft brush, I give the veneer a light coat of thinned, liquid hide glue—about one part water to three parts hide glue. (White or yellow glue will also work—about one part water to three parts glue—but has far less open time.) It is necessary to spray a fine mist of water on the face side to keep the veneer from curling due to the moisture of the glue. Then I carefully lay the tissue over the veneer, working it down with a soft, dry brush.

After the tissue is completely down, I place a piece of fiberglass window screen over both sides of the veneer to prevent any bleed-through from sticking, and then proceed with the drying operation described above.

Dyeing Veneers

Your project may call for a border of bright red or yellow, or even blue or green. These are not colors common to wood, but wood can be dyed. Aniline dyes used as stains in finishing work well; even fabric dyes from the variety store will work. Some experimenting will be necessary to determine how much dye to mix to get it to the strength described in the manufacturer's directions. (In the case of fabric dye, don't use the salt.)

Soak the pieces to be colored at least overnight. Check to see that the dye has penetrated clear through the veneer. This is done because you may need to sand the finished piece, and you don't want to sand through the dye that is only on the surface.

After the experimental pieces are dried, check to see what the topcoats will do to the color and make the necessary adjustments. Also check to see if there is significant "bleed" into the topcoats. You may wish to apply a thin coat of shellac to act as a sealer in order to prevent the dye from bleeding into surrounding areas.

Pre-Forming Veneer

When veneering curved surfaces, pre-forming the veneer is often in order (3–10 and 3–11). Even when using the dry-glue or hot-hide glue methods described in Chapter 5, some pre-forming will eliminate the "fight" in getting the pieces down. In any instance where the veneer will break during bonding, pre-form it.

An iron can be used to pre-form veneers and, if the pieces are narrow, a "hot pipe" can be used—much the same as a musical-instrument maker forms the veneers used in instrument bodies. A hot piece is about two inches in diameter. The flame of a torch or steam is passed through the pipe, to heat it. Pieces of veneer are passed over the pipe to heat them and are bent slowly around the pipe to form a convex curve.

The bombé chest described in Chapter 12 presents some ideas on pre-forming.

CUTTING VENEER

I don't mean to insult your intelligence by providing instructions on how to use a knife or saw,

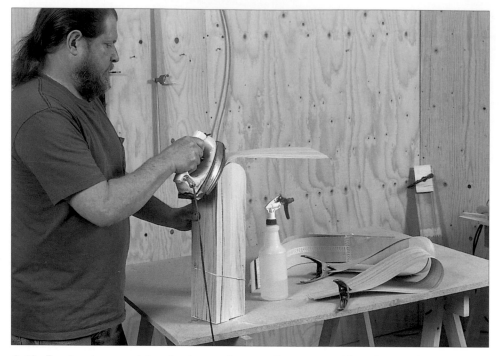

3–10. Pre-forming consists of using an iron on the veneer. After the pre-forming, the veneers are spread with glue and placed in a vacuum bag.

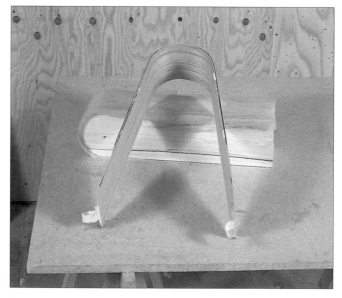

3–11. The pre-formed pieces after vacuum-bonding.

but let me point out some things that may not have been considered.

Any cut that is made is likely to be part of a joint. For economy of time, the cut should be made as carefully as possible, in the exact place it should be.

There should be no tear-out, and the cut must be made perpendicular to the surface.

That word "perpendicular" is important. It may seem logical to undercut. Then the joint can be given a little pressure and the mating pieces squeezed tightly together—right? Wrong! If pressure is applied to any joint, the edges will be forced to meet each other. If the edges are undercut, this meeting point will force the edges of the veneer above the surface of the substrate. Yes, you may be able to force the joint back down, but then it is very likely that it will overlap. That's why it is important to make all cuts perpendicular to the surface.

One thing to consider when using a knife is the cutting angle of the blade. The knife blade removes no material. It severs the fibers of the wood while compressing material in a V shape to both sides of the blade. If the knife blade is held perpendicular to the surface, very critical examination of the cut will show that the veneer appears slightly overcut, and, if a guide is being used, the finished cut will be away from the edge of the guide by half the thickness of the blade. Therefore, it is best to tip the knife slightly to the waste side and slightly into the guide.

I always try to place my straightedge or other guide opposite the waste. Should the cutting tool wander—which does happen—it wanders into the waste. Often I find myself cutting joints after a piece has been partially bonded; this is no place for a cutting tool to wander into the workpiece.

It's always best to cut with the grain, but, taking many things into consideration, this is not always possible. Cuts made against the grain are very possible, provided a sharp cutting tool is used. With a sharp tool, you'll need take little notice of the grain direction.

Cuts don't always come out perfect. A veneer saw will often leave the edge a little too ragged for a joint. Often a slight sliver will be torn from the workpiece. A miter cut in a border piece might not fit as well as anticipated. The straightedge may have drifted slightly while a cut was being made. In these cases, slight adjustments can be made to a cut with a process called "shooting." This consists of running a hand plane over the edge of the veneer to truc it, just as you would run a plane over the edge of a sawn board. Many craftsmen do this as a matter of course. I try to keep my tools sharp, eliminating this step and the time it takes—resorting to the process for adjustments and the removal of small defects.

I once read a magazine article in which the author had built a "shooting board." This was a jig that held the veneer securely and provided a guide surface to hold a hand plane square and true. I thought, wow, that's the way to go! I built the jig and played with it for an afternoon. I found that on some species, the plane, even though razor sharp, had a tendency to tear the edge. Burls and crotch tore even more. Stump wood? Forget it. Veneer with burls, crotches, and stumps and unique species of veneer are what I use most frequently, but I was not about to abandon the principle involved in using a shooting board. I substituted a hand plane with a block of wood with 80-grit sandpaper glued to it; this eliminated the tear-out. Later I found that it was just as well to let the veneer hang slightly over the bench—or substrate—and support it with a straightedge for shooting with my sandpaper block. That eliminated the need for a shooting board.

Shooting a piece of veneer that is hanging over the bench takes a little practice. Remember to keep the overhang to a minimum, hold the block for a square cut, and apply pressure exactly perpendicular to the edge of the veneer. Try this method and you won't have to clutter your shop with yet another jig.

TAPING VENEER PIECES

Once the pieces are cut, you may find it necessary to tape several together before bonding. Gummed paper tape works very well for this purpose. Gummed paper veneer tape can be found in many woodworking supply catalogues. If you're lucky, you'll find two different kinds: a smooth tape about an inch wide and a much thinner perforated tape. Avoid tape with strong adhesives such as masking tape. This tape has an adhesive that can pull fibers of the veneer from the surface as it is removed. If you are using a hot press or iron over the tape, the heat will make things worse. If masking tape must be used, remove the tape while it is still hot or use the more expensive "detail tape," which is a masking tape with a not-so-sticky adhesive. You'll find detail tape in many paint stores and also automotive supply stores that deal in paint products.

The smooth tape is good for all taping operations. After the tape is moistened, it is applied to the veneer. I highly recommend getting the tape as wet as possible without dipping it in water. I place a sponge in a cup and fill the cup almost to the top of the sponge. Lots of water completely activates the adhesive and, as the tape dries, it shrinks and pulls the pieces of veneer tightly together.

Veneer tape should be used on the face side of the work. If it is in the glue line, the bond will be no stronger than the adhesive on the tape. And remember that a bond is reversible with water. I also recommend putting the tape down with a warm iron. This not only secures the tape quickly, but makes the bond as complete as possible, just in case a piece winds up in the glue line.

In many operations, different pieces of tape on different joints may overlap. If the veneers are to be pressed, I have a rule: no more than two layers of tape in any spot. Much more than that will concentrate the pressure of the press over the tape and leave the area starved for glue, while the area surrounding will have an overly thick glue line.

Perforated tape can be treated differently. It is much thinner and, therefore, may be overlapped for several layers and left in the glue line, because the bonding glue can reach through the perforations. Those perforations will also permit you to see the joint being taped—which is often very handy. Though not as strong as solid tape, when ironed down perforated tape holds most simple joints very well.

Veneers are taped in the blanket-chest project described in Chapter 9.

CHAPTER 4

Substrates

Veneer has to be applied to something. This material, which I shall hereafter refer to as the "substrate" or "ground," can be solid wood, plywood, or any of the various composition materials that fill the market these days (4-1). If the appropriate adhesive is used, wood veneer can be applied to almost any smooth, clean, stable surface—including steel, glass-even drywall.

I once saw a fine job of wood veneering over a steel, fire door. The innovative creator of this work of art was clever enough to apply a thin coat of contact cement to the door before applying the peel-and-stick veneer. I've passed through this door for years as I visit my dentist. After opening the door and entering the office, I chuckle a couple of times, and then, as the automatic closer pulls the door shut, I tip my hat and salute.

The proper selection of a substrate is important, as it will affect the longevity of the veneer work. All substrates are not created equal, but each has application in this most wonderful craft. Each possible substrate has certain properties that should be considered. Below I describe some of the many types of material that can be used as a substrate and point out one very important thing to watch out for: pull.

PULL

In all cases where a water-based adhesive is used, the substrate will be subjected to a condition called "pull." This condition develops because of the different expansion and contraction characteristics of the veneer versus the substrate. Pull must always be considered when choosing the veneer, substrate, and adhesive.

When a water-based adhesive is spread on any substrate, the moisture causes the side with the adhesive to expand, resulting in cupping of the opposite side. In many tenacious substrates this cupping is almost unnoticeable, because the dry bulk of the material resists the expansion of the side. When the adhesive's

4-1. An assortment of substrate material.

moisture gets to the veneer, because it has little volume, the veneer can expand to almost the full extent of its capability. After the veneer/substrate bond is complete and the moisture begins to escape, the substrate will shrink slightly, but the veneer will shrink dramatically, pulling the substrate into a cupped condition.

You wouldn't think that a thin piece of wood could undergo such a powerful reaction, but it does. Because of moisture content, wood can expand and contract dramatically. In quarrying operations, for centuries pieces of dry wood have been driven into cracks or holes drilled into the face of mountainsides. When these pieces of wood are soaked, they expand, and the wood splits away some very impressive pieces of stone from the mountainside.

Dealing with Pull

Pre-Cupping

In days of old, large pieces of solid wood to be veneered were intentionally expanded on the side to be coated with adhesive, by bringing them into contact with wet sawdust, paper, or rags. When the substrate was cupped to the proper degree—this degree being determined by the veneerer—the veneer was laid with hot hide glue and a hammer. When the whole assembly dried, it would be flat . . . hopefully. I've tried this method several times with several different types of substrate, and it does work. I must admit that on a couple of occasions my calculations were a bit off and I had to use dry heat to encourage the assembly into a flat condition.

Sizing

One method to limit the amount of pull is to "size" the veneer and substrate, that is, to give both a thin coat of glue and allow it to dry thoroughly. This partially seals the surfaces and will slow the absorption of moisture from the glue used in bonding, thus limiting, for a time, the dimensional changes. If the dimensional changes can be held in check until the bonding glue grabs, pull is reduced or eliminated.

Veneering Both Sides of the Substrate

Today's standards call for veneering both sides of the substrate. This pulls both sides in the same manner, provided that they are covered with the same species of veneer—which is, in some respects, a little costly. The costs, however, can be minimized by using a veneer of inferior grain pattern on the underside of the substrate. And, often a less costly species of similar texture can be used on the underside, i.e., birch under bird's-eye maple, rift oak under quartered oak, etc.

TELEGRAPHING

Another thing to be mindful of is "telegraphing." Irregularities in the substrate can appear in the surface of the veneer, sometimes weeks or months after the veneer is bonded. In some instances, this can be a desired thing, but in most cases it is something to watch for.

WOOD SUBSTRATES TO AVOID

There are two types of substrate to be avoided: rotary-cut fir plywood and waffle board (or flake or chipboard, or whatever it's called in your area). This latter material is composed of chips or flakes rotary-cut from softwood logs. These are mixed with knots, sand, rocks, broken machine parts, assorted floor sweepings . . . and glue. This concoction is pressed into a very stable building board that is wonderful for floor, roof, and wall sheathing.

Although waffle board and fir plywood are relatively cheap and lightweight, they have one glaring disadvantage: Their grain patterns telegraph to the surface of the veneer. The reason this happens is because the winter and summer wood of the logs are of vastly different textures. Residual moisture in these products, coupled with dimensional changes caused by moisture from the bonding glue, affects summer and winter wood to different degrees. When these woods have dried out, these changes become obvious and can even be felt—which can make for a lot of unnecessary sanding.

Now, if for some reason, you would like the effect of the telegraphed appearance that occurs with these substrates—it could look great in a contemporary piece with a funky finish—proceed as follows: Select very fresh plywood or waffle board, even a little on the wet side. Sand the surface with a random orbital sander with a soft pad. This will tend to cut away the soft spots, leaving the hard areas high. Veneer the surface using a vacuum bag and a water-based adhesive, or use a blanket between the mechanical pressing surface and the veneer. This will press the veneer into the low spots. Using hot hide glue and a hammer will leave a buildup of adhesive in the low spots. If care is not taken, this will dilute the effect.

Imagine a maple veneer with the texture and grain pattern of fir plywood or waffle board.

SOLID WOOD

Solid wood is an acceptable choice of substrate, but if not thoroughly cured, it can present some of the same telegraphing problems as fir plywood. Knots and other defects will usually telegraph. If all the boards in a particular glued-up substrate are not of equal moisture content, one will shrink more that another, and this difference will telegraph. Any glue joints in solid wood will telegraph if not permitted to dry for several days before sanding or when otherwise preparing the substrate for veneering. And, if the veneer and solid-wood substrate are of vastly different texture, expansion and contraction due to normal seasonal changes can buckle or pull the veneer loose.

The disadvantages of a solid-wood substrate can be overcome by a technique called "crossbanding." Here, an inexpensive veneer such as poplar is bonded to the solid wood across its grain, on both sides. Then the face veneer is bonded to the poplar with the grain running in the same direction as the substrate. An alternate technique is to bond the crossband to the face veneer and then bond the assembly to the solid wood. With either technique, the solid wood forms the thick core of a piece of plywood.

Solid wood that has been crossbanded and veneered forms a very stable panel. Telegraphing of defects and glue lines is minimal, and seasonal changes have little effect on it, even if the underside is not sealed. This technique came into extensive use around the turn of the last century and remained popular until some of the man-made substrate materials gained acceptance.

Even with crossbanding, in some of the antique tables I have restored I've noticed telegraphing of patching material. In some of these pieces, poor-quality lumber was used in the core. Holes from missing knots were filled with what appeared to be plaster—I even ran into one that appeared to be filled with sand and Portland cement. Often the core would shrink, but the plaster would not. This would leave a bump in the tabletop. When the center of the bump was tapped with a fingernail, it sounded tight, but tapping around the bump produced a hollow sound.

If you are building an authentic antique reproduction, by all means use veneer over solid wood. Softwood that is not thoroughly dry would be an excellent choice. As for defects, choose material with tight knots—spiky knots will be particularly interesting. If the wood is thoroughly dry, sand around the knots using a soft pad beneath the paper. This will cause the knots to stand proud of the surrounding ground. Of course, these knots will telegraph to the surface, and this is to be expected in an antique piece. Veneer over only one side using the pre-cupping method described above, and be sure to refer to the bombé chest described in Chapter 12 for more ideas and details.

MAN-MADE BOARDS

During the twentieth century, man's knowledge and ability have led him to "improve" on nature and produce some very fine building boards that can be used as substrates. Man-made boards are relatively inexpensive, and some have a definite resistance to pull, which is discussed on pages 44 and 45.

One interesting product that I have seen used in the damaged furniture I repaired through the years comes from Europe—I see it mostly in German pieces. One day, out of sheer curiosity, I closely examined a broken piece of this board. Separating the particles and examining them under magnification, I discovered that the bulk of the particles were wood of some kind. I also discovered a piece of something that appeared to be a corn husk and particles that appeared to be ground plant stalks of some sort. Also, there were soft particles that, after discovering the corn husk, I guessed to be ground corncobs.

This material is less dense and far lighter than American particleboard. The veneers used over this product are a little thicker than I'm use to seeing, but it seems to veneer well, with little or no telegraphing of its coarse texture. The material is not very strong and has poor fastener-holding properties. Edge-banding with solid wood requires a long tongue-and-groove joint for best results. As its only advantage is its light weight, I'm inclined to stick to other, more substantial, substrates and pass the shipping costs along to my clients.

Veneer-Core Plywood

Plywood composed of thick softwood-core veneer with hardwood-face veneer—called "veneer-core" plywood—is a good choice for a substrate. Veneers can be bonded to it either across or with the grain. Hardwood-face plywood is somewhat susceptible to pull (described on pages 44 and 45), so both sides should be veneered if you're using a water-based adhesive.

Another characteristic to take into consideration is that hardwood-face plywood varies in thickness from sheet to sheet; take care when cutting dadoes to fit a piece of veneer-core plywood. Also, the surface can be somewhat rippled due to the softwood core. While this ripple would go unnoticed on a cabinet side, on an area such as a highly polished tabletop the effect is less than attractive. Veneer-core plywood is used for the blanket chest described in Chapter 9.

Lumber-Core Plywood

Essentially, lumber-core plywood is two pieces of $1/8$-thick hardwood-core plywood bonded to the face and back of a solid-wood core of about $1/2$-inch thickness. The material is tenacious (it holds stubbornly to its shape) and very stable. Though comparatively expensive, I have found that it is not very susceptible to pull, and I've been known to veneer only one side using a water-based adhesive.

Bender Board

This wonderful product has only been generally available for the last few years. It consists of a very thin veneer with two much thicker veneers—usually luan—bonded cross-grain to either side. The thick outer veneers appear to be severely knife-checked or stretched. What do you do with it? You bend it. When bent with the grain, this material is pliable enough to bend around a pencil. Well . . . maybe not a pencil, but $3/8$-inch bender board can be easily bent around a five-gallon bucket.

As I do a lot of curved work, I've found this material to be the greatest thing since front-wheel drive. Before bender board, I had been making up curved panels with six layers of $1/8$-inch-thick plywood. Two pieces of $3/8$-inch-thick bender board, though not as structurally sound, make for a terrific savings in cost and are far more flexible. If somebody would just invent a bender board that would bend in both directions, I could forget about $1/8$-inch plywood forever.

Particleboard

This is a product composed of wood particles about the size of coarse sawdust—some refer to it as "sawdust board." It has good stability and is suitable for veneering. When you are using water-based adhesives, minor difficulty may be experienced with telegraphing, as the particles may be of far different densities. This can be resolved by waiting several days until the adhesive is completely cured and thoroughly dry before sanding the finished product.

I stated that particleboard is composed of wood particles, but I'm convinced that another ingredient is anything that may fall into the mixing vat. As it dulls saw blades and router cutters with a vigor unknown to solid wood, I'm sure that sand is important to the manufacture of particleboard.

Once I was cutting a hole in a particleboard vanity top for a basin, prior to veneering with plastic laminate. At one point, my saber saw stopped and no amount of force could encourage it forward. Turning off the saw and withdrawing the blade, I discovered that it was devoid of teeth. After installing a new blade, I followed the line in the opposite direction. About an inch from the place my saw stopped the first time, it stopped again; of course, the blade was once more relieved of its teeth. After I broke the cutout from the hole, I discovered a chunk of broken cast iron, smiling at me from the center of the particleboard. This cast piece, about the size of a dried apricot, appeared to have come from a chip breaker or guard used in the wood hog that ground the particles.

Incidences such as this are not uncommon. I have often seen small pebbles basking in the surface of particleboard. These pebbles had been sanded smooth with the surface. Suffice it to say, use caution when working with expensive blades and cutters on particleboard.

MDF (Medium-Density Fiberboard)

Probably the finest veneer substrate that has been developed to date is MDF (medium-density fiberboard). This product is composed of wood reduced to its fiber state. The fibers are mixed with a suitable bonding agent and the mixture pressed to form a stable building board that is as smooth and flat as a pool table. As a matter of fact, it has replaced slate in many low-cost pool tables.

MDF is a tenacious material. It holds fasteners reasonable well and it glues well not only to itself but also to edge-banding materials without the need for a tongue-and-groove joint.

MDF may, of course, be edge-banded to receive a decorative shape, but I have seen a great deal of recently manufactured furniture in which the shape is cut into the MDF itself. This molded edge is then painted with a gesso and a wood grain is glazed on—definitely unnoticeable to the unaware.

While I could sing the praises of MDF for several more paragraphs, I must here point out the reason I am often reluctant to use the product. I am no longer man enough to handle a sheet of it by myself. It's heavy. As I often work alone, I have the deliverymen stand the sheets lengthwise against the shop wall. When I'm ready to cut a sheet, I tip it over onto sticks placed on the floor, rough cut the pieces needed with a handheld circular saw, and then trim them to exact size with a router and straight bit. I suppose I should be ashamed of my out-of-shape condition.

Rather than do something about it, I've found it far easier to admit it and blame it on my advanced years.

Fasteners and Water

Both particleboard and MDF have two pronounced enemies: fasteners and water. Screws driven into the face of these products do hold rather well—especially those with coarse threads. However, putting hardware screws into the edge of either of these products requires faith in God; for only He will be able to keep them there under any stress. Great claims are made for "knockdown" fixtures specifically designed for particleboard and MDF. Are these claims founded? I'm not the guy to ask, as I've been in the repair business too long. My only comments would be derogatory. Any time I build with particleboard or MDF I add solid wood to the face of any edges that are to receive screws for hardware and the like.

Water leaking from a houseplant can damage a veneered tabletop in a very short time, even if the veneer was bonded with waterproof glue. If the substrate is solid wood or plywood, often the top can be repaired or reveneered. If it is particleboard or MDF, repairs are usually impossible. The moisture causes these products to swell dramatically, and even after they are dry, the swelling remains.

Tops are often faced with solid wood after veneering, and sometimes a slight, decorative groove is cut at the joint to disguise it. Water—and it doesn't take much—seeping into that groove will cause both the wood and substrate to swell. When things dry out, the wood shrinks; the substrate doesn't.

In the repair and restoration section of our operation, I have seen this time and time again. If the swollen area is small, I've had moderate success with rewetting the spot and putting it in a press, using a hydraulic jack; sometimes this works, sometimes it doesn't. It hurts to tell a client that there's nothing that can be done short of replacing the top.

I use both particleboard and medium-density fiberboard extensively, but I keep in mind the use of the final product and the tendency of my client to care for the product when determining which substrate material to use.

OTHER SUBSTRATES

Metals

I was once commissioned to veneer a steel filing cabinet with oak. I used contact cement and paper-backed veneer. And while I could generate little enthusiasm for the project, it did provide a savings for my client over a solid-wood filing cabinet.

Glass

I have seen strips of veneer bonded to window glass to simulate muttons and mullions. One contractor told me, "I just stuck that stuff on there with Krazy Glue (cyanoacrylate)." Another pontificated on the virtues of contact cement. While the windows looked okay from the face side, from the rear the ones bonded with contact cement looked . . . ah . . . less than attractive.

Drywall

While visiting a client's office while under construction, I watched workmen bonding pieces of oak veneer to the drywall. These pieces they framed with pieces of solid oak a half-inch thick, and over the top of this "wainscot" they placed a chair rail. It did look good, and I'm sure it was economical.

LAYOUT TECHNIQUE

Layout is essentially drawing in full scale. For the most part, I like to do my layout drawing and planning on the substrate. I lay out the location of joints, grain direction, and often the presentation of the veneers being used. Why waste paper or some other medium when you have a big, clean surface to work with? In instances where I'll be cutting patterns from the layout, I'm very partial to #15 roofing felt. Some of the projects described in Chapters 8 to 12 were veneered using layout techniques on the substrate and on roofing felt.

While it's always useful to lay out the location of joints, borders, etc., on square and straight-line work, I'll not take up space with this, as it is so straightforward. Rather, below I point out some useful ways to lay out irregular shapes.

Circles

Circles are very easy to make on the drawing board using a compass. A compass has one leg with a point and a leg that holds a pencil. Just place the point leg on the center of the circle and swing the pencil throughout the desired radius. If you are drawing in full scale—say for a 48-inch round tabletop—large compasses can be used. I watched a carpenter use a compass for laying out some large circles for the concrete forms he was building. He constructed the compass out of two eight-foot-long rippings, whittled the ends to a point, and then nailed the other ends together. Then he nailed a third, and shorter, ripping, to the center of these two pieces, fastening them together. The most remarkable thing was not the instrument itself but the dance performed by the maker in using the instrument.

If you have thought of drawing a circle with a pin, pencil, and sting, forget it; string stretches too much. If you must use this technique, use wire instead of string. Fine wire used for hanging small pictures works very well.

More effective for drawing large-diameter circles—and sections of such circles—is a pair of trammel points. Trammels clamp to a stick of any convenient length and usually consist of one point that can be set in the work and another that will hold a pencil, knife, or scribing device. The fact that a knife can be substituted for the pencil can be very useful for cutting either patterns or the veneer itself. In Circle Devices on page 32, I present some ideas on building your own very economically.

Ovals

An oval is a planar circle that has been tipped. There are ways of mathematically plotting an oval, but that's more math than I want to go into. I do recall passing trigonometry, but I don't recall exactly how I did it.

So, if an oval is a circle that has been tipped, a quick way to make a small oval is to draw a circle and tip it. Make the circle with a diameter of the maximum dimension of the oval, out of a substantial material—cardboard, plastic laminate, thin plywood, etc. Lift an edge of the circle until the base of a right triangle formed by the circle as its hypotenuse equals the second or smaller dimension of the oval. Use this as an "eyeball" guide for drawing. Note: There is another way to draw an oval, so before you use this method to lay out a 60 x 40-inch dining table, please read on.

In the second method, given the dimensions of the oval, on the substrate draw line AB to equal the length and CD to equal the width (4–1), intersecting perpendicularly at the center of each; call this point E. With a compass or trammels, draw an arc from point C which has a radius equal to AE and which will intersect AB—call these intersections F and G. Drive small nails at F, G, and C. Stretch a loop of fine wire around the three points and secure the ends. Then remove the nail from point C, insert a pencil, and draw the oval.

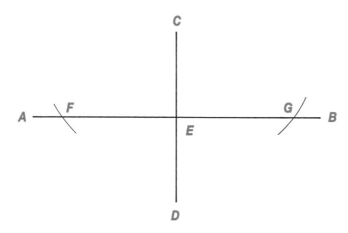

4–1. Method for drawing an oval.

Irregular Curves

There may be a time when you will have to draw curves of specific dimensions. Drawing curves freehand will work, but often the lines are not smooth and flowing. In such instances, lay out all the fixed dimensions. Then draw the curves desired freehand, as best you can. To check the drawings, drive a number of small nails along the curved lines. Then bend a flexible straightedge along the nails—band steel is my favorite for this purpose. Any irregularity will be shown in those places where the straightedge doesn't contact the nails. Use the bent straightedge to draw the final line. This technique is used for the kidney-

shaped desk and the bombé chest described in Chapters 10 and 12.

EDGE TREATMENTS

Veneered panels which are to become table or cabinet tops and which use particleboard, plywood, or MDF as a substrate will need some sort of edge treatment. Even the edges of panels that form frameless cabinet sides need edge treatment. Molded tabletop edges and veneered raised panels will need some form of solid wood to receive the shape.

In some instances, the face veneer may be rolled and formed over an edge in one continuous piece. Even molded edges may be veneered by "upholstering" them with the face veneer. This process is tricky and requires considerable skill and knowledge of the veneer being worked. I love the concept, because those familiar with veneering will look at the finished product and ask, "How did you do that?" This technique is used on the lamp and blanket chest projects described in Chapters 8 and 9.

Solid Wood

If your project calls for veneering over solid wood, no special treatment may be required, provided that the substrate and veneer have similar characteristics, e.g., oak veneer over a poor-quality oak substrate. The caution here is to be careful to avoid defects that will appear at the edge. A beautiful, vertical-grain face veneer flowing into a knot on the edge ruins the effect. And, if the edge is to be molded, you don't want to be running a shaper or router through knots and other defects that are likely to cause tear-out.

Many finishing techniques will disguise the character of the wood in an area as small as an edge. If your finishing ability is such that you feel unable to disguise the edge, there is the option of gluing a narrow piece of the chosen species to all edges that are sufficiently wide to accept the decorative molding.

In gluing pieces around a panel that has a solid-wood substrate, consideration of the end grain is important. A narrow board glued lengthwise across end grain is a poor choice. Movement of the substrate across the grain will be far greater than the movement of the narrow board glued to it lengthwise. Within just a few seasonal changes, the substrate will tear the narrow board loose. If this doesn't happen, the narrow board on the end can cause the substrate to check, usually also causing the veneer to check at the same time. Although I've seen this done with cross-banded veneering, I shy away from the practice.

The alternative is to glue a narrow strip of wood with the grain running in the same direction as the substrate. Here, a tongue-and-groove joint can be used for added strength. Making that tongue-and-groove in a narrow piece of end-grain material can be dangerous, but it can be done. If you are working with a rare, exotic species, it is all worthwhile, but it's a high price to pay for simple economy.

Plywood and Composition Boards

If the panel is to receive a decorative edge, plywood and composition boards should be edge-faced with solid wood. Even if they are not going to receive a shape, facing with solid wood is a good choice. If veneer is glued directly over the edge of plywood, the various bands of end and flat grain can telegraph to the surface of the veneer. Also, a careful examination of the edge of particleboard will reveal that the density of the face sides is greater than the center. This can telegraph, leaving a slight cup in the facing veneer. The edge of MDF may be directly veneered, but if the piece is to receive very rough use, consider edge-banding with solid wood.

When working with plywood and composition boards, all edges may be treated equally. Seasonal, dimensional changes will be the same for the substrate as the face material. The face may be glued directly to the substrate or a joint of some sort may be used. A tongue-and-groove joint works well, and even a spline is adequate.

In facing without a joint, narrow strips of wood are spread with glue and clamped to the face of the substrate. Bar clamps that will span the substrate are always good to use. In instances where a bar clamp is impractical, edging clamps may be used. When using edging clamps, be careful not to mar the surface that will be veneered—the marred areas will need to be patched.

In practice, I've used glue joints only when there is a lot of facing to do. The joint is used more to locate the facing rather than for strength—I have great faith in glue. I run the facing sticks through a molder (an automatically fed machine that is capable of cutting all four sizes of a board or stick at once) that sizes them and cuts a tongue. The groove in the substrate I cut with a router set so that the facing will stand a couple of thousands of an inch above the substrate.

If you may not have the luxury of a molder and will be using a shaper or router to form the tongue, I have some suggestions: First, face the boards that you will be taking your cuttings from. It is important that they be as straight and flat as possible to start with. This may seem counterproductive in that the pressures in the wood may distort the facing strips as they are ripped from the board; but if the boards are not originally flat and straight there is no chance that the stumps will end up flat and straight.

Plane the boards to a thickness that is about .010 inch thicker than the substrate—about the thickness of a matchbook cover. (Note: Plywood thickness can vary dramatically throughout the sheet and from sheet to sheet. Measure in several places.) Next, using a router or shaper, cut the tongue—or other glue-joint shape—in the edge of the full-width board. Then rip off the desired width of facing. This method is far safer than attempting to run narrow sticks through a shaper or router.

For cutting the groove or matching glue-joint shape in the substrate, I highly recommend a router, it being far more accurate and easier to handle than trying to "muscle" large pieces of substrate through a shaper or table-saw dado. Set the depth of the router cut very carefully, using scraps to make test cuts. Also, especially when using plywood, run the router on the side of the substrate that is to be veneered. This will ensure that the facing stands proudly from that side.

The facing at the corners may be butted or mitered—the choice is yours. Should you decide to butt the corners, I recommend that the end pieces be installed so that they extend slightly past the substrate edges. Then, with a jointer or hand plane, carefully trim them true with the remaining edges. Be sure to "blind" any joint in the side pieces so that the glue joint won't show on the ends or on any shape.

In all cases, the facing should be at least 1/2 inch in width. When facing to receive a shape, the facing should be of sufficient width to accommodate the shape plus about 1/8 inch. For edges that will be scalloped and shaped, the facing should accommodate the scallop and shape plus about 1/4 inch.

Where the facing is sufficiently wide to accept a scallop, special attention should be given to the corners. These should be reinforced with a spline, dowel, or even a biscuit to prevent up-and-down movement at the extreme end of the joint. Even though you have made a good miter or butt joint at the corners, a sharp blow could knock the joint loose. Further, a slight dimensional change in the facing could loosen the corner joint—especially a miter. Take the time to reinforce those corners, making sure that the reinforcement is blind and, therefore, will not interfere with any shape to be used.

Round, Oval, and Other Irregular Edges

Dealing with facing on round, oval, or other irregular panel edges can pose a challenge, but all that is required is a little more time and precision.

Facing for irregular edges may be formed by steam bending. If you have the equipment and are proficient in the craft, go for it. Steam-bent facing has no joints to contend with and can be a one-step operation. My only caution would be to make sure that you let the bent facing dry thoroughly. Keep in mind that any dimensional changes in the facing will telegraph to the veneer.

If you may be thinking of a kerf-bent facing, forget it. All of the patching and sanding of the voids left by the process would not be worth the effort.

An alternative to bent facing is a sectioned facing. Here a circle, oval, kidney shape, or whatever shape is needed, is carefully laid out and its periphery reduced to a number of straight sections. To the edge of each straight section pieces of solid wood are glued and carefully joined to each other with a reinforced joint. These boards are of sufficient width so that the periphery of the irregular shape may then be cut.

Facings Thicker Than the Substrate

Often it is desirable to have a facing that is thicker than the substrate. This is particularly true when weight is a consideration. Basically, all of the techniques mentioned above may be used to produce a thicker facing; just make the facing board thicker.

Applying Facing After the Substrate Has Been Veneered

It should go without saying that a facing can be applied with some "show" wood after the substrate has been veneered. The techniques mentioned above would apply in this case. There is, however, one added technique I should mention: Where the facing meets the veneered substrate, you can leave an incised groove. This will break the continuous plane of the veneer and facing, just in case one is slightly higher than the other. The groove will permit a slight variation that will not be noticed. Even a hand passing over the top will have a hard time feeling variations as great as 1/32 inch.

That groove can collect spills. Even though the piece has received a good finish, a little water standing in the groove can find its way to the substrate. If the substrate happens to be particleboard or MDF, it will swell, and even when the water dries out, the swelling will remain. Although the groove is very effective in hiding slight inaccuracies, it can be the seed of destruction within your project.

Hinges, Locks, Etc.

If the veneered panel is to become the side of a frameless cabinet or chest, keep in mind any hardware that may be fastened to it. The facing should be wide enough to accommodate mortises for locks, hinges, lid stays, etc., along with the screws that accompany them. Remember that composites—even plywood—are not the best at holding screws and other fasteners.

Shaping Composites

It is possible to run a mold on the edge of plywood, particleboard, and especially MDF. In the finishing process, this shape is painted with a heavy gesso and sanded smooth. A wood grain is then added to it, using glazes. I have seen recently manufactured tables with shaped MDF edges painted a brown color—usually a little darker than the color of the wood top.

In shaping particleboard and MDF, you will need to use a carbide cutter. Contamination in the substrate will dull a steel cutter in no time.

As far as longevity goes, be aware that the edge of any tabletop is subject to a great deal of abuse, and the edges of particleboard and MDF are not durable. If you intend to spend a lot of time and expense for veneers, please consider a solid-wood edge treatment.

With regard to shaping composition boards, I have one further comment: Please keep the craft of woodworking a craft. Don't cut so many corners that your work cannot withstand the test of time.

Trimming and Repairing Faced Substrates

Once the facing has been applied, it will hopefully stand slightly above the substrate. This slight excess will have to be trimmed off, but before even thinking about trimming consider this: The moisture in the glue used to secure the facing has caused both the facing and substrate to swell at the glue line. If any trimming or sanding is done before this moisture has left the assembly, it will cut away this swelled area. When the moisture does leave completely, it will leave behind a valley that will telegraph to the surface of any veneer applied over it.

There may be some defects in the faced substrate. A ding or two that you put in while applying the facing, or perhaps a miter joint that fits less than perfectly, will need to be patched. Normally, I avoid any water-based patches, as these will need to dry for several days. The moisture from the patch will cause swelling of the surrounding wood, and, if the panel is processed immediately, telegraphing can occur much the same as with the glue line described above.

I also shy away from nitrocellulose putties. They just don't seem to stick as well as they should.

I rely, rather, on auto-body putty. This catalyzed filler sets quickly, sticks well, doesn't shrink, and is very hard. Try it; you'll like it.

FINAL PROCEDURES

Once all glue and patches are completely dry, trim any facing flat with the surface of the substrate. If the difference between the facing and substrate is small—say the difference of a matchbook cover or less—a sharp scraper is all that is needed. A sharp hand plane may be needed if the difference is greater. If the facing is narrow, a router and a flush-trimming bit will work, or, if you feel proficient, use a belt sander.

In days of old, substrates were "toothed"; that is, they were passed over with a small hand plane with an iron ground to resemble saw teeth. This was done to provide small reservoirs to hold the hot hide glue that was to be used. I have never owned a toothing plane. (I do have a plane that I once loaned to a friend; when it was returned, the iron did somewhat resemble the iron of a toothing plane. This plane has become my permanent "loner.") For substrates on which I intend to use hide glue, I drag the teeth of an old saw across the substrate—this works for me.

Even if I'm not using hot hide glue, as a final step I completely scratch the surface with 60- or 80-grit sandpaper. This will remove any mill glaze that may exist on wood and remove that very hard and shiny surface on MDF.

The substrate is now ready for the veneer.

CHAPTER 5

Bonding Veneer to the Substrate

Back in the 1960's I had a T-shirt inscribed: "LSD! Better Living Through Chemistry." While I can't attest to the "wonders" of LSD—honest—I can attest to the fact that chemistry has produced some wonderful woodworking adhesives. At the beginning of the twentieth century, the mainstay of the woodworking industry was hide glue, an adhesive that had been used for centuries. Since then, chemistry has provided us with numerous adhesives, some good and some not so good. All have their own unique properties and should be used with attention paid to those properties.

For veneering, essentially any adhesive that will stick to wood may be used. By that definition, such things as rubber cement and wallpaper paste are serviceable. However, there are so many adhesives and so many techniques that describing them all could take up volumes, so here I'll concentrate on the most applicable and the most readily available, not forgetting economy (5–1). But first I describe adhesive properties and their effect on the veneering process.

ADHESIVE PROPERTIES

Strength of Bond

Any adhesive used for veneering should exhibit a strength-of-bond at least as tenacious as the veneer being used. This is a property easily tested. Apply the adhesive to two pieces of wood—according to the manufacturer's recommendations. After the glue is dry, pry the pieces apart. At least some fibers of the wood must remain attached at the glue line.

This test will quickly remove rubber cement from the list of acceptable adhesives.

Penetration

Some adhesives penetrate deeply into the wood, while others simply remain on the surface. It would seem that deep penetration is generally a most desirable characteristic, but not always. While good penetration is most desirable at the glue line, should the adhesive find its way to the surface of the veneer through holes, open grain, spills, or squeeze-out, it can seal the wood, posing challenges in the finishing process.

Shock Resistance

Many adhesives are not extremely shock-resistant, but this characteristic can be beneficial. Glue blocks for many years have been secured with hot hide glue

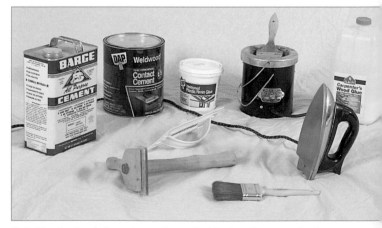

5–1. The tools and equipment needed to bond veneer to the substrate.

to hold table slides in place. These blocks cannot be pulled loose with a team of horses. Yet one sharp rap with a hammer will free a block in its entirety, with little or no damage to the table, table slide, or block. It sure makes it easy for the restorer who wants to disassemble a table for refinishing. Let's hear one for hot hide glue! Don't put your hat back on; we will be cheering hot hide glue more before this chapter is complete.

A gluc's shock resistance should be considered when veneering edges—an area most susceptible to shock. A client once brought me a table with the edge veneer loose in many spots, a condition that seemed to have been caused by the back of chairs bumping into it. To remove the veneer that was intact, I went around the edge of the table with a hammer, tapping lightly. The veneer was easily freed. To repair the piece, I cleaned off the old glue—which appeared to be hide glue—and reinstalled the veneer using yellow glue. I haven't seen the table since.

Hardness

Adhesives used for veneering should not form a pad beneath the veneer. A panel veneered with a hard spccies such as maple will loose a great deal of its durability if padded with a soft adhesive. If you have ever torn a cushioned floor covering with refrigerator feet, you are quite familiar with the dangers of a pad beneath an otherwise durable surface. While adhesive hardness can be of little importance on vertical surfaces, it is something to consider on tabletops.

Glue-Line Thickness

Most adhesives work best when the adhesive thickness is held to a minimum. In all cases, any veneering process should attempt to hold the glue-line thickness to a minimum. The finishing process will reveal a thick glue line on an edge—especially if the adhesive is of the deep-penetrating type and seals a small area—inhibiting the penetration of stain. Durability of the surface will be affected by the glue line, as described in the section on hardness, above.

Are you beginning to sense that adhesive properties are interwoven? Wait until we get to the end of the list.

Clamping Pressure

It is important that the materials being bonded be held in tight contact during the time that the glue takes to set. The amount of pressure required is often related to the viscosity of the adhesive, as excess glue should be squeezed from the glue line. While generating such pressure may be of minor importance in a plant using a hydraulic prcss and microwave drying equipment, it is something to consider when working in the cool garage with the mere aid of a few clamps. Most of the readily available woodworking adhesives will work using moderate clamping pressure, but as there is a large surface to be considered in veneering, the more pressure the better.

Gap-Filling Properties

Yes, there are gaps in veneer that need to be filled. I find this most prevalent in veneers where the medullary-ray pattern is displayed on the surface. Gaps are also to be found in veneers where the density of the wood varies greatly, such as in burls and crotches. In such veneers as quarter-sawn oak and lacewood, the ray area may be substantially thinner than the surrounding wood. Here, an adhesive that will fill this gap is of great value, for it will permit the successful use of veneer that may have to be otherwise rejected.

Shrinkage is so closely related to the gap-filling properties that I'll not mention it separately, but will point out that an adhesive that fills gaps and then shrinks dramatically can pose challenges.

Open Assembly Time

Open assembly time refers to the time permitted between the application of the glue and thc application of the clamping process being used. This is an important characteristic if the assembly of the veneers is complicated or if getting the assembled panel into clamps or a press involves several steps.

Open assembly time may be greatly extended working in a cool area or by spreading the adhesive with a toothed trowel rather than with brush or roller. Here, beads that are formed by the trowel will squeeze out fresh adhesive when the assembly is pressed. There is good news and bad news with this process. The good news is that there will be fresh adhesive available. The bad news is that if the beads have set sufficiently to overcome the pressures of the press, they will telegraph to the surface, leaving the pattern of the toothed trowel in the veneered surface.

Initial Adhesion or "Tack"

Some glues, like urea-formaldehyde, have little or no initial adhesion. These will permit the veneer to slide all over the substrate unless it is held in place with tape or pins. They would be unworkable in any type of process involving hammering the veneer to the substrate. A glue like hot hide glue is initially tacky and becomes even more tacky almost immediately upon being used. This is the ultimate glue for a hammering process. Yellow and white glues have little initial tack, but a few minutes after they are spread, the tack develops to a great degree.

Setting Time/Drying Time

Setting time refers to the time it takes for the glue to "get a hold" on the veneer; that is, the time it takes to render the veneer difficult—but not impossible—to remove from the adhesive. Drying time refers to that time it takes for the adhesive to reach full strength; it does not refer to the time it takes for all the moisture to leave the adhesive and wood.

Setting and drying times are usually set forth in the manufacturer's directions. With regard to veneering, keep in mind that these can vary depending on whether the adhesive sets and dries through the evaporation of a solvent, a chemical reaction, or a combination of the two. If evaporation is involved, and the adhesive is contained in a vacuum bag or under a press, setting and drying times can be considerably longer than if left in the open, as the moisture has nowhere to go but into the veneer and substrate.

Ambient temperature also affects setting and drying times. Heat not only accelerates chemical reactions, but it aids in dispersing a solvent—water included—into the air as well as into surrounding dry wood.

Susceptibility to Heat

A table with a dark finish that is placed in front of a sunny window can become very warm. A hot serving platter set on a dining table can transfer a great deal of heat to the tabletop, even if it is set on an insulating pad. While I've never considered building something that will survive the heat of a fire, the two examples mentioned have always caused me to ponder the heat susceptibility of any adhesive I use.

An adhesive that can be activated by heat can be very useful. These adhesives are investigated in Dry-Glue Bonding on pages 68 to 70. I've also used heat to encourage the complete bonding of contact cement when building the kidney-shaped desk and round dining table described in Chapters 10 and 11.

Creep

Some glues permit slight movement at the glue line even after they are cured. PVA glues are notorious for this, while urea-formaldehyde and hide glue do not permit creep. This is an important property to consider, because a glue that permits creep can be responsible for joints opening days or weeks after bonding.

Reversibility

The action of some glues can be reversed. In other words, these glues can be encouraged to release whatever they are holding and then hold it again. Liquid hide glue can be reversed by soaking the glue joint with water. Hot hide glue can be reversed by soaking the glue joint with water and applying heat. Contact cement can be reversed by soaking the glue line with the appropriate solvent—usually lacquer thinner—and then the bond can be destroyed with methylene chloride. Heat can also release contact cement.

While reversibility can be of great value in repair work, in the overall process of building veneered furniture it can create challenges. One should have the entire process in mind, along with the intended use of the finished product, before choosing an adhesive.

Susceptibility to Solvents (Including Water)

A panel veneered with hide glue—a reversible adhesive—and then drenched with a water-based stain can come apart. Veneer bonded with contact cement can be loosened if colored with a stain and a finishing process using lacquer thinner. Even mineral spirits can weaken a contact-cement bond.

The bond of nonreversible adhesives can often be weakened by solvents. White and yellow glues cannot be reversed, but their bond can be weakened with water.

Usually, a glue's susceptibility to solvents depends on the length of its exposure to the solvent, the strength of the solvent, and any pressure that might exist within the veneer. Flat veneers bonded with contact cement may be finished with lacquer, especially if the initial coats are light and permitted to dry thoroughly between coats. A wrinkled burl that has taken considerable pressure to put down could loosen if given a lacquer finish. And the same applies to water-susceptible glues used in conjunction with water-based finishes.

Susceptibility to Rot, Mold, Mildew (and Other Creepy Stuff)

In my career as a furniture restorer, I have rarely encountered a situation where some microscopic life attacked only the glue line. One encounter was dramatic enough that I'll take a couple of lines to describe it.

A client, while on vacation, purchased a pool table and had it shipped from a very damp climate. When the table arrived, he noticed loose veneers on one of the rails and brought it to me for repair. I found the veneers easy to peel from the rail, and there was evidence of glue in only one small area. Rather, a white powder covered both the rail and the veneers. After a few moments of handling the powder-covered pieces, my eyes began to water and I had a violent sneezing attack, followed by nausea. I immediately left the area and washed my hands and arms thoroughly.

When I returned to the scene, I was prepared for a space walk—hat, goggles, respirator, and elbow-length rubber gloves. I scrubbed powder from the rail, veneers, and surrounding area, using warm water and chlorine bleach. After everything dried, I experienced no more distress from the white powder.

Many modern adhesives that could be susceptible to "creepy stuff" contain a biocide of some sort, and a dry climate gives the adhesive further protection. Should you ever encounter a disintegrated glue line in restoration, I highly recommend washing it with water and bleach—about 1/4 cup bleach to 1 gallon of water.

TYPES OF ADHESIVE

Hot Hide Glue

> *Hot hide glue, hot hide glue.*
> *How much do I love thee?*
> *Let me count the ways.*

Do you get the impression that I think highly of hot hide glue? I do. For the mass-production shop, it's all but worthless. However, in the hobby shop, small woodworking shop, and custom studio, it is a most valuable adhesive when used properly (5-2).

This centuries-old adhesive is made by rendering the hides, hooves, and bones of animals. It is supplied dry, in flake form, and also ground to about the consistency of coarse cornmeal. In adding cold water to the amber-colored, dry product, it soaks up

5-2. Veneering molding using hot hide glue.

the water and each flake or granule turns to a rub-ber-like glob; the water does not dissolve the glue, it brings it to life. When these globs are heated, they melt and turn into a very thick, sticky liquid.

Hot hide glue is nontoxic. I suppose that in a desperate situation you could eat it. But we have different types of dry hide glue stored in several places in the shop, and the rats and mice that the neighbors seem to breed in profusion have never touched it. If the rats won't eat it, neither will I.

Hide glue does not penetrate deeply, and relies on surface adhesion rather than deep penetration for bonding. It will stick even to glass. A process in the decorative-glass industry consists of spreading hide glue over glass that has been scuffed by light sanding or sandblasting. When the glue dries, it shrinks but holds to the glass with such tenacity that it fractures the surface, creating a design called "glue chip." Needless to say, a product with that tenacity will hold two pieces of wood together.

Hot hide glue dries quite hard. (It is possible to cut oneself when handling the fractured flakes.) This hardness, coupled with the fact that the glue does not penetrate deeply, makes sanding a breeze. The glue does not readily clog sandpaper, and little sanding is required to remove every trace of it from the surface of the wood. I should mention that it does fill the pores of open-grain woods to an extent. If your finishing process calls for filler, it's a good idea to remove all of the hide glue from the surface of your project using warm water and a stiff brush.

As it is a dense liquid that dries hard, hot hide glue is a good gap filler. The only problem here is that it does shrink when drying. The percentage of shrinkage can be observed when preparing the glue. Note how much volume the flakes or granules gain as they absorb the cold water; this should give you an idea of how much the glue will shrink.

If you smoke cigarettes, be very careful when working with hide glue. No, it's not flammable, but a finger with the tiniest bit of hide glue on it will stick instantly to a cigarette, tearing the paper as it is pulled away. Hide glue on the cold end of a cigarette will adhere well to the lips, removing large patches of skin when an attempt is made to remove the cigarette. What's more, a tiny speck of hide glue on the body of cigarette can be enlightening. When the hot

end of the cigarette burns down to the speck, the smoker is in for a real treat. If you think that the taste of the filter in that last drag is bad, wait until you get a hit of burning hide glue!

Hide glue may be applied to the work using a coarse bristle brush or a toothed glue spreader. I've never had any luck with a roller because the glue is just too sticky. Whatever spreading system you use, work quickly because the glue must be spread and the veneer set in place before the glue cools. The length of the open assembly time is dependent on the temperature of the substrate and the air in the surrounding shop.

This wonderful adhesive is unique in that it presents two opportunities for sticking to the material. When the glue is first spread and is hot (150 degrees Fahrenheit), it is moderately tacky. As it cools, the tack increases continually. When it cools to a point that it gels (about 90 degrees Fahrenheit), this is when the glue can first stick to the surface; and the strength of this bond increases as the glue cools more and begins to dry. With effort, the initial bond can be broken, but the glue sticks well enough to hold a flat veneer in place very tightly.

Wrinkled veneers coming in contact with the moisture and heat of the glue become quite pliable, making them much easier to work with. This does not mean that the veneers to be used should not be pre-flattened, but the flattening need not be as extensive. The pliability created by heat and moisture makes hot hide glue an excellent choice for curved surfaces, permitting the veneers to be applied with little or no pre-forming.

After overnight drying, the bond is complete, provided that there are no thick areas of glue. These will take longer to dry.

A hide-glue bond is not susceptible to solvents used in finishing. Alcohol can soften it slightly, but the exposure must be of long duration—days or weeks. The bond is susceptible to water, but here too exposure must be lengthy.

In my younger days, I set about removing the ink-stained veneer from a turn-of-the-century buffet top that I was restoring. At the time, I thought that hide glue was not a very good adhesive and was susceptible to water, so I scraped the thin finish from the top and covered it with wet rags. I could return in an hour and peel the old veneers from that top effortlessly—right? Wrong! I left the wet rags in place overnight. The next morning some of the veneers were loose, but the bulk remained intact. It was afternoon before I got the idea to heat the wet rags with an iron. Then, and only then, were the veneers easy to remove. Just as an experiment I placed a small piece of veneer back in place and weighted it with a heavy scrap of wood. The next morning, the piece was firmly bonded. It was then that I decided to learn more about hide glue and its wonderful reversible properties.

Hide glue, being a rendered animal product, does have some nutritional value to mold, mildew, rot, etc., and, as a result, is susceptible to these fungi. I have found that woodworms also seem attracted to hide glue; their holes are far more prevalent in and around joints that have been made with hide glue. In most cases, I've discovered that creepy stuff growing in the hide-glue joint is also growing in the surrounding wood—save for the one instance mentioned above. Furthermore, in all cases, I've noted that the item in question has been exposed to a condition of high moisture—Western woodworkers, take heart.

Preparing Hot Hide Glue

Place the dry flakes or ground glue in a container and add about twice the volume of cold water. Stir the mixture to ensure that the water comes in contact with all surfaces of the glue particles, and let the mixture stand. After about an hour—two hours for flakes—the hard glue will become soft and will have "grown" substantially. It will not, however, dissolve in the cold water. Pour off the excess water and heat the glue.

Hide glue may be heated in a glue pot especially designed for this purpose. It may also be heated in a double boiler placed on a hot plate or range. Or, I've found that the heating plate of a coffeemaker makes an excellent hide-glue heater. (My coffeemaker holds the temperature at 150 degrees Fahrenheit—a good temperature for hide glue. You can check yours with a candy thermometer.) Here, place a small pan on the coffeemaker's warming element and in the water place a container for the glue. Make sure that the glue container is not iron or steel, as any acids in the glue will dissolve the iron and discolor the wood that it is applied to.

No matter how you heat it, never overheat hide glue; not only will it destroy the glue, the smell is quite unpleasant.

As the jelly-like particles of glue heat, you will notice that they melt and form a thick, sticky liquid. This is a starting point for the glue. I usually let the glue "cook" until the volume is reduced by about ten percent before using it. If I am to be working in a very warm shop with warm substrates and can tolerate a more viscous glue, I may let the glue reduce further. The less water in the glue, the better. A scum will form on the glue, but it can be broken up and stirred back in. If I intend to be using a lot of glue, I will have another container full of glue soaking so that I can gradually add it to the pot.

To test the glue, apply a drop to the pad of your index finger and squeeze it firmly with your thumb. Hold the fingers in place for about a minute, and then pull them apart slowly. This should give you a good feel for the adhesion of the glue.

Cleanup

When I work with hide glue, I have close at hand a bucket of warm water and a wash cloth. Hide glue cannot be wiped off hands and tool handles with a dry cloth. It cannot be wiped off using a cold, wet cloth, but a warm, wet cloth cleans it up easily. A washing machine will remove it from clothing, and a hot shower will remove it from a beard and hair— don't laugh; it can happen.

An Experiment with Hot Hide Glue

If you are skeptical as to the value of hot hide glue and are reluctant to make an investment of your hard-earned money in an unknown product, pick up a package of unflavored gelatin at the grocery store. This will cost a mere buck or so.

In a water glass, mix a couple of packets of the gelatin with cold water at the rate of one part gelatin to two parts water; let this mixture stand for at least fifteen minutes. Then place the glass with the gelatin/water mixture into a water bath heated at

150 degrees Fahrenheit. You can do this on a range, but I find that the heating plate of a coffeemaker works best because it is thermostatically controlled at about 150 degrees.

The gelatin won't be very sticky at this point and will need to cook for several hours. As the gelatin cooks, a scum will form over the top that should be stirred back into the liquid, which will be taking on a slight amber color. Liquid dripping off the stirring device should eventually fall as a drop with a long tail. At this point, try the thumb and forefinger test mentioned above. Also try sticking postage-stamp-sized pieces of veneer coated with the glue to a substrate, holding them with your thumb for a minute or two.

You can let the gelatin cook even longer, adding a tiny amount of water if necessary. The longer it cooks, the stickier it will get.

After overnight drying, try pulling the experimental pieces loose. If you are the least bit satisfied with the results of the experiment, remember that hot hide glue has far more bonding power than the refined gelatin.

Refer to the bombé chest described in Chapter 12 for specific techniques on using hot hide glue.

Liquid Hide Glue

Liquid hide glue is hot hide glue that has an additive—usually salt or urea—to keep it from gelling at room temperature. While the additive prevents it from jelling, it also seems to weaken the glue and causes it to remain somewhat soft; liquid hide glue will clog sandpaper. Although we do have liquid hide glue around the shop, I use it rarely for veneering. I do like it for assembling French windows or door sash with large numbers of muntins and mullions. Its long, open assembly time is heavenly, and it can be cleaned up with water several days later. But, for the most part, it is relegated to the paint shop for creating crackle finishes.

PVA Glues

Today polyvinyl-acetate glues are the workhorses of the general woodworking industry. In addition to the ones on the shelf at your neighborhood store, there are a great number of formulations available for specialty applications.

PVA glues are advertised as nontoxic. This is true in that contact with the skin is basically harmless. However, as many of these products contain a biocide to inhibit the growth of molds and mildew, I wouldn't consider a taste test.

These nonreversible glues cure by the evaporation of their water base—with the exception of the water-resistant type that also cures through chemical reaction. The strength of bond is more than adequate for all veneering operations. And they also have a unique thermoplastic property that we'll discuss in Bonding Techniques on pages 64 to 77.

Below I describe two popular types of PVA glue: white and yellow glues.

White Glue

White glue (sometimes referred to as white vinyl glue) reigned as the best all-around woodworking glue until it was replaced by a cousin, aliphatic resin glue—which I refer to as yellow glue. It still has a place in the woodworking industry and is useful in veneering. White glue penetrates well, has a moderate open assembly time, sets quickly, and cleans up with water. I don't care for the fact that it dries clear, and have at times put a drop or two of food coloring into the glue so that I can see the spots missed during cleanup. Any residues of white glue left on a surface inhibit the penetration of stains.

White glue dries soft. A thick glue line can have a padding action beneath the veneer, forming a pad beneath any veneer. This softness also accounts for the fact that residues are difficult to sand off and usually clog sandpaper. Also, white glue permits considerable creep.

Yellow Glue

Yellow glue (also referred to as aliphatic resin glue) is nothing more than a superior formulation of white glue. It has greater bonding strength, is harder when dry, and sets more quickly. It also has a quicker open assembly time and permits less creep.

Water-Resistant Yellow Glue

This product is a superior form of yellow glue that has additives that cause it to form a water-resistant bond as it cures over a period of days. If a water-resistant bond is needed, consider urea-formaldehyde, described below.

PVA Cleanup

All PVA glues can be immediately cleaned up with water. After they've dried, water will soften them so that they can be scraped off more easily or peeled from the skin. A washing machine will remove most PVA glue stains from clothing. If you're working with the water-resistant type, be sure to get that clothing into the washer within 24 hours.

Urea-Formaldehyde

Also known as "plastic resin glue," urea-formaldehyde is a two-part adhesive. It is supplied either as a liquid with a separate liquid catalyst that must be mixed in before use or as a powder that must be mixed with water before use. In the case of the powder, the included catalyst is activated by the water. After mixing, the glue has a limited pot life—about 2½ hours.

On the plus side, urea-formaldehyde has a long open assembly time—about ten minutes or more, depending on conditions. Once cured, it produces water-resistant bonds. (I tried a couple of experiments by bonding with urea-formaldehyde and then soaking and steaming the bond. These experiments indicate that it is waterproof.) It is not affected by heat or finishing solvents. Rot and mildew are not a problem, and joints made with the product are not susceptible to creep.

This glue produces a very hard glue line, and any gaps that it might fill become very hard. Its squeeze-out is also very hard when dried. Wear safety glasses when scraping off any squeeze-out, and watch for sharp edges—they cut very well.

On the minus side, urea-formaldehyde is toxic. It has been discovered that formaldehyde causes cancer—mostly in laboratory rats, which seem to be very susceptible to cancer of every type and description. It is unfortunate that this information was not available back in the 1960's. I could have presented it to my biology teacher, and it might have relieved me of dissecting all manner of frogs, worms, rats, and other creepy critters that are known to be preserved in this toxic chemical.

If you're mixing powdered urea-formaldehyde, be aware of the dust. Either hold your breath—as I do—or wear a mask. Work in a well-ventilated area, and be sure to read all of the cautions on the package.

Urea-formaldehyde's dark color can be hard to contend with when bonding light-colored woods. Immediate cleanup can be done with water, but this can wash the dark glue into the pores of the veneer.

This glue is slow to set and cure. That's great for open assembly time, but the instructions on the container I have before me suggest that, at 70 degrees Fahrenheit, glued assemblies should be allowed 14 hours to set and if there is any stress in the joint, it should be clamped for 24 hours. At 100 degrees, that set time decreases to 3½ hours.

I have found that in veneering operations using my hot press—at about 180 degrees—I can remove panels in about 15 minutes, and herein lies an advantage. The glue has a firm hold of the veneer before much moisture has left it. As urea-formaldehyde is not susceptible to creep, this limits joints opening due to shrinkage of the veneer.

Mixing Technique

Always mix urea-formaldehyde in accordance with the manufacturer's directions (5-3). After be-

5-3. Mixing urea-formaldehyde glue.

coming familiar with the product, you may want to vary things a little. I like mixing in flexible plastic containers. After the leftover glue dries, a little flexing and a sharp rap clean the container.

Cleanup

Cleanup attempted after the pot life of the glue is exceeded becomes impossible with water. Scraping at this point is recommended, but after the glue cures, scraping often tears out large chunks of wood. Sanding off urea-formaldehyde residue is far more difficult than sanding hide glue, but, like hide glue, urea-formaldehyde residue does not clog the paper.

Keep urea-formaldehyde off your hands, other body parts, and clothing. While it's fresh, it can be washed off with cold water, but after it begins to cure there's no hope of removal. It will peel off skin if soaked in warm water, allowing oils and perspiration to break its bond from beneath. It will not come out of clothing once it is cured. While I've never worried about the cosmetic appearance of my work clothes, those hard, crusty patches of dried glue—depending on location—can be downright uncomfortable.

Never dispose of urea-formaldehyde into your sewer system while it's in a liquid state. Not only is it against the law, but the glue can settle in low places in traps and pipes and harden like a rock. Rather, wait until it's hardened and dispose of it in the trash.

Contact Cement

I'll tell you straight away my main objection to contact cement: It's too quick and easy to use. I use other, harder-to-work adhesives. And since misery loves company, everyone should work as hard as I.

Well, that's probably part of my objection to contact cement, but there are more sound reasons to avoid it in certain instances.

Contact cement is very susceptible to heat and solvents. It will hold down flat, regular veneers, but if there are any pressures in the veneers and they have to be forced down, heat from sunlight shining through a window can soften contact cement to a point that it will turn loose. A hot serving platter set on a padded tabletop can cause contact cement to loosen its hold. These conditions can occur months after the contact cement is supposedly cured.

Solvents used in finishing can destroy a contact-cement bond. Lacquer thinner is especially effective. While mineral spirits will not dissolve contact cement, they will soften it. Finishing systems using mineral spirits usually expose the contact-cement bond to the solvent for long periods of time, making matters worse. Due to the glue-line barrier that exists in paper-backed veneers, solvent exposure is minimized, but it should still be considered.

Should a veneered piece ever need to be refinished, the methylene chloride in the stripper is especially effective in breaking a contact-cement bond. If a water wash is used after the stripper, it causes the veneer to swell, pulling the veneer loose in spots.

I once unwittingly stripped a buffet top that had been reveneered with paper-backed veneer and contact cement. I noted a couple of loose spots as I was stripping. When I washed off the stripper using warm water, distinct bubbles began to appear. By the time I was finished, it looked as though the top had been attacked by a thousand hornets. I gave the top another coat of stripper and in about a half-hour I easily peeled off the sheet of veneer. The sheet could not be reused, because there were also some separations between the paper and the veneer.

The above is just one of many stories I could tell regarding the use of contact cement.

I also have concerns over the longevity of this glue. Contact cement is basically rubber, and rubber deteriorates quickly. I have removed many plastic laminates bonded to countertops with contact cement. Though a lot of these required much heat or solvent and prying and praying to remove, there were those plastic laminates that could be lifted up with a little pressure from a large putty knife.

I'm not saying don't use contact cement. I've used it on wood veneer many times, and that's to say nothing of the hundreds of gallons I've spread over plastic laminates. Although there are certain applications where I would definitely shy away from using it, it's a good adhesive when properly used in situations for which it is suited. Several respected furniture manufacturers use contact cement in curved applications where pressing is cost-prohibitive or impractical.

One of my first experiences with contact cement and wood occurred when I veneered curved doors on a large back bar I had built. (A back bar is the cabinetry behind a drinking or serving bar.) These doors, about 36 x 20 inches, were veneered with paper-backed, book- and butt-matched walnut burls as a field or the center of the panel and were surrounded by or bordered with red oak. Giving all veneers and substrates two careful coats of contact cement and letting the glue dry completely, I installed both field and raw borders without incident. The next day, I gave the doors a generous coat of Danish oil. The oil produced several loose spots in the raw veneers, but about two days later I was able to put these down with a hammer and a few choice words.

About twelve years later, I was called on by the bar's new owner to level the cabinet in its new location. I had a chance to carefully examine the veneer work and found all the veneers intact save for a couple of new loose spots in the border veneers—unnoticeable to all but me.

More recently, I was working freelance in another's shop and was directed to veneer the tops of two end tables. The substrate was two layers of 3/4-inch particleboard. The top veneers consisted of mahogany crotches that were to be arranged in a sunburst with zebra borders and facing. All were raw veneers.

I was directed by the boss to use contact cement as he was in a hurry to finish and ship the tables, and I was given a contact cement formulated for leatherwork; this glue was a very heavy-body product. After flattening the veneers as quickly as I could, I glued them into place with this contact cement.

I was amazed at the way it grabbed and held the still somewhat wrinkled veneers. My concern began to grow as the tables were carried to the spray booth and the boss began to coat them with a lacquer-thinner-reduced-aniline dye. He applied so much dye that it dripped off the edges of the tops. I cringed.

An hour later, as the boss was preparing sealer, I peeked into the booth to examine the tops. They were in good condition, with no loose spots. I watched him spray the sealer. I use the word "spray," but he couldn't have applied the sealer more heavily had he spread it with a trowel. I cringed once more.

I was able to examine the tops two days later, just before the shipper loaded them; they were still in good condition. Conclusion? That leatherwork contact cement is one terrific product, for I know that contact cements designed for plastic laminates would not have withstood the boss's finishing technique when coupled with the pressures of the wrinkled crotches.

If contact cement is going to be your choice of adhesives, let me provide a list of do's:

1. Use flammable-type contact cement. Water-based contact cement can cause the veneer to curl. I have had poor experiences with nonflammable contact cements and plastic laminates, so I've never considered them for veneer. If you are concerned with the health hazards of the flammable products, read the precautions on the nonflammable products. I'd say it's a toss-up as to which is safer to use.

2. Read the fire-hazard precautions on the container of flammable contact cement, and follow them explicitly. Remember always that the flammable fumes of contact cement are heavy and will settle to the floor. You may not smell enough fumes to think there is any concentration at all, but your water heater's pilot light will sense the concentration. If the explosion doesn't kill you, the burns you will receive may make you wish you were dead.

3. Use a heavy-bodied contact cement. After that experience I described above, I've come to use contact cement formulated for the leather industry. Barge is my favorite brand of contact cement to date. Weldwood—formulated for woodworking—would be a second choice.

4. Give the veneer and substrate two coats of contact cement, reducing the first coat 10 to 30 percent with the manufacturer's recommended thinner or acetone. Lacquer thinner can be used, but the retarder in even cheap lacquer thinners will slow the glue's drying and leave behind residue that will render the adhesive softer than it should be.

5. Bring the surfaces into complete contact using heavy pressure. A roller is okay, but it should be a small roller that will concentrate the weight of your body on every square inch of the surface. A store-bought or shop-built veneer hammer also works well. In cases where the veneers are wrinkled, a warm iron will smooth them and also aid in the bonding.

6. Let the work bonded with contact cement cure for several days before exposing it to heat or finishing products.

7. Work with very dry veneers. Contact cement permits considerable creep. Any shrinkage in the veneers will cause open joints.

Cleanup

Keep contact cement off skin, clothing, and the veneer's face. On clothing, it will find a lifelong home. It can be dissolved with lacquer thinner or acetone. These products will tend to drive residue into the veneer and are also not the best thing for the skin. Rather, clean up the veneer using a rag dampened in mineral spirits. Rub the rag vigorously into the glue. The mineral spirits will not dissolve the contact cement, but will cause it to soften and "ball up." For the hands, use baby oil or hand lotion; this too will cause the glue to ball up and will not hurt the skin. Better still, volunteer to do the dishes. The warm, soapy water will soften the contact cement and cause the hands to perspire, forcing the glue from the skin. It could also score some points with your mate.

More ideas on using contact cement are presented in the kidney-shaped desk and round dining-table projects described in Chapters 10 and 11.

Other Adhesive Possibilities

There are other adhesives that can be used: epoxies, cyanoacrylates, hot-melts, polyurethanes, and peel-and-stick adhesives—even products designed for the floor-covering industry. I can't tell you much about these products, for with the exception of white linoleum paste, I never used them for veneers. As I've always been confronted with making a living at what I do, cost has always been a major factor in my choice of material and supplies. I have yet to come up with better all-around adhesives than those I've described above.

BONDING TECHNIQUES

Once the veneer has been laid out and cut to the needed dimensions, the substrate has been prepared with all treatments necessary, and the glue has been mixed to the proper consistency, its time to bond the veneer and substrate.

I have read articles wherein the author offers his bonding method as a panacea—good for all that ails you; able to leap tall buildings; the greatest thing since sliced bread; and, of course, guaranteed not to rip tear, bind, or cause warts. Gentle Reader, I don't believe in panaceas. I do believe there's a place for every technique—there are even several places for every technique. In the following section, I describe several ways of sticking the veneer to the substrate with what I consider a minimum of cost and effort.

Using a Hammer and Hide Glue

Right up front, it should be known that you don't pound on anything with a veneer hammer. Think of the veneer hammer as a small squeegee with a stout handle. If you wish to forego the cost of buying one, there are a couple of ways to make your own, described in Veneer Hammers on pages 32 and 33.

If there is any one bonding method that approaches being foolproof, it is the technique of using a veneer hammer in conjunction with hot hide glue. Used for centuries, this technique has produced some very fine works that have withstood the test of time. Hammer and hide glue produce a bond that is of completely adequate strength. The bond is impervious to finishing solvents and, in many cases, resistant to water damage. The technique lends itself to working with single pieces of veneer—cutting and fitting as you go—rather than taping all components together and risking tape failure in the bonding step.

Many of the things that can be done with hide glue can also be done with dry glue or contact cement. If you are a hobbyist and want to bond the material as was done in days of old, hot hide glue is the way to go. And if you're a professional, you'll find that hide glue is quite convenient for certain applications.

Because hide glue is a water-based adhesive, pulling can be expected. Today's solution to the problem of pulling is to veneer both sides of the substrate with similar veneers—a great technique that's foolproof. However, I have had the honor of working on many antiques that had only one side of the substrate veneered and on which no pulling seemed to have taken place.

In days of old, there was another way to prevent pulling. This was to "pre-cup" the substrate in the direction opposite to which the veneer would pull. This is easily done by wetting the side of the substrate that is to receive the veneer and watching it expand. When the substrate is sufficiently cupped, the veneer is applied and the assembly set to dry so that air can reach all surfaces. As the assembly dries and approaches a flat condition, it is either clamped between heavy timbers to hold it flat or it is fastened into place in the piece of furniture.

The concept of pre-cupping works not only for hide glue, but also has applications for other water-based adhesives. It will not, however, work on man-made substrates that have been edged with solid wood. I tried it once and wound up with a distorted mess. It is also not completely reliable with figured veneers whose grain runs in all directions.

I would imagine that the practitioners of old experienced a little trial and error in determining just how much to pre-cup the substrate. Having little time for trial and an ego that will not permit me to admit error, I use pre-veneering experimentation to determine the amount of cup required.

I save an end cut of the substrate material. This I veneer without pre-cupping. After the test piece has dried for several days, I can see how much pulling has taken place. With this bit of information, I'm able to proceed and pre-cup the substrate.

It should be added that if the veneer is to be bonded to a very heavy substrate such as a small piece on the square top of a chair or table leg or even the three-inch-thick side of a bombé chest, distortion from pulling will be minimal—even unnoticeable.

Hammering down veneer, though simple, does require some skill, practice, determination, and an appreciation of the materials being used. That in mind, I must insist that you not practice on your project. Save small pieces of veneer and substrate material, or buy some inexpensive material on which to practice. Experiment with different consistencies of glue and try pre-heating. Start by bonding small pieces, and don't work on large cuts until you are completely confident.

Work in a warm shop. I prefer a minimum of 72 degrees Fahrenheit, although 80 feels oh so good on my arthritic bones and keeps the glue fluid longer. If the substrate feels cool to the touch, I often heat it with a hair drier to a point where it feels slightly warm.

Do you have a bucket of warm water, a rag, and a towel handy? If you don't, you didn't read the information on hide glue in Types of Adhesive on pages 57 to 64. Go get the bucket, rag, and towel—I'll wait.

There should also be a household iron handy for warming areas that congeal before you get to them. It should be set to a heat that is uncomfortably warm to the touch. Set the warm iron in a shallow pan with about 3/8 inch of water in it. To ensure that the water gets to the bottom of the iron, I set a piece of aluminum window screen in the bottom of the pan. This will facilitate cleaning off any glue that may accumulate on the iron.

Depending on the species, it is a good idea to wet the veneers before beginning. Using a spray bottle, I mist one or both sides and let the veneers stand for at least five minutes. Open-grain woods will expand dramatically when they come into contact with hot hide glue. If not pre-wet, the veneer will curl around the edges and the joints will tend to buckle. Out in the middle of the veneer, tiny areas will rise and refuse to go down. In addition to spraying beforehand, sometimes I spray after the veneer is set in the glue and even dribble some glue on the surface. In addition to preventing curl, the glue and water lubricate the hammer.

Does all of this wetting and expanding, etc., cause the veneer to pull? Read on for the answer. If you are veneering both sides of a panel, use the same technique for both. And you need not veneer both sides the same day.

One of my first projects using hot hide glue and a hammer was to veneer two particleboard door panels with book-matched mahogany crotch. I set the first cut in dry and hammered it down. All went well initially . . . or so I thought. After about ten minutes, the edges began to curl and bubbles began to appear in the center of the cut. I hammered some more, but to no avail. I wet the surface as blobs of glue were beginning to dry and hammered some more. By this time, I feared that there were some glue-starved spots under the veneer. I wet the whole thing again, heated it with an iron, and lifted the veneer from the panel. After spreading fresh glue, I hammered the wet, sticky mess down once more.

At that point, there was so much glue on my hands that I couldn't let go of anything. There was a blob of glue in my beard and a dab on one eyelash, preventing me from blinking. I looked at the hot end of a burning cigarette stuck to my left hand and decided that before it reached the skin, I'd better clean up.

When I returned some 15 minutes later, lo and behold, the veneer was still stuck; but there were no bubbles, curls, or buckling. It was smiling up at me, and seemed to say, "Thanks for doing it right . . . dummy."

I moistened the second veneer cut and let it soak a while before hammering it down. It too smiled, but said nothing.

The next morning when I walked into the shop and viewed my masterpiece, I noticed it was a bit bowed. A bit? The center of this 3-foot-long panel was standing a good inch off the bench. I prayed. Well, it wasn't exactly prayer, but some of the words I uttered might be used in prayer.

Knowing that the panel was a lost cause, I decided to do a little experiment and veneered the back side with some oak stump veneer. Two days later, the panel was as flat as a pool table.

The message here is that some pull can be expected when the veneer is wet. But enough story! Now on for some information on preparing the joint.

Step-by-step hammering directions are given for the bombé chest described in Chapter 12.

Preparing Butt Joints

Once the first cut is firmly bonded, gently scrape up the squeeze-out, which should by now be congealed. If the squeeze-out is not contaminated with fibers of wood, return it to the glue pot.

With a straightedge and knife, prepare the joints. You will find that cutting veneer that is wet, warm, and bonded is a complete pleasure, especially after working with the dry, wrinkled stuff. You will also notice that there is no worry about distortion of the straightedge due to wrinkles being pressed out of the veneer, because the veneer is already in place and smooth.

I usually let the first bonded piece set while I'm preparing the joints on the second cut. Not being in too big a hurry to bond the second piece is always a good thing. It gives the glue a chance to set a little and the veneer a chance to dry slightly, the drying being beneficial to tight joints.

The second cut I prepare by carefully preparing a straight edge for the joint and shooting it with a sandpaper block. Then I hold the prepared cut against the bonded piece to make sure the joint fits properly. If it doesn't, a little touch-up with the sandpaper block is in order. Minute open areas are of little concern, for as this next piece is bonded, it may be pulled and stretched slightly. If you have ever hung wallpaper, you'll know what I'm talking about.

After the first veneer cut has set for a quarter to a half-hour, it's time for the second cut. Spray the veneer, spread the glue as before, and place the veneer, using care to see that the joint is tight.

Now, starting at the joint and with heavy pressure, begin squeezing out the excess glue. On the first pass, let about half of the hammer ride on the first cut. Stop for a second and check to see that the joint is tight. If not, with your fingertips push the joint so that it is closed; there should be enough slip in the glue to accomplish this. Then continue to hammer down the second cut.

After the second cut is bonded, I usually make firm passes across grain toward the joint to ensure that it fits tightly. Then I make a firm pass or two down the joint to make sure it's level and there is a minimum of glue on the surface of the veneer.

Double-Cut Joints

Joints may also be double-cut. Here, place the second piece of veneer so that it overlaps the first by at least one-half inch. Hammer down the second cut, avoiding the joint area. If the hammer gets too close to the overlap, it can tear the second piece. Then place a straightedge down the center of the overlap and cut carefully with the knife blade held perpendicular to the surface.

By this time, the glue will probably be cooled and congealed. Heat the joint area with an iron and carefully lift back the second piece so that you may retrieve the waste from the first. Spread a little more glue along the joint area; buckle and fold in the lifted edge, and carefully hammer down the joint. Some glue will be escaping through the joint, so work carefully.

Borders

If a border is to be used to encircle the center slices or field (the large portion in the center of the design), now is the time to hammer it down. Trim the field on all sides. I don't recommend trying to double-cut joints in which the grain of the veneers run in different directions. Short cuts of end grain are difficult to retrieve, and the opposing grain in combination with the small pieces being used in a border can be more trouble than it is worth. Butt the joints of the border. Different techniques are shown in Chapters 9 to 12.

Final Procedures

Once the panel is complete, trim all edges using a straightedge to support the fresh veneer. Don't be tempted to let the panel dry before trimming. The overhanging veneer will dry far more quickly than the bonded material. This can cause checking that can find its way into the panel. In addition, glue squeeze-out can be very difficult to remove when dry.

As the panel dries, some shrinkage of the veneer can cause it to pull back from the edge of the substrate. So, I hope you are working with a slightly oversized panel.

Whether butt joints or double-cut joints are being used, they should always be taped. This will prevent them from parting as the panel dries and shrinks. I usually watch the joints for about an hour before taping. If they begin to buckle because of further growth, I clamp them down. If they begin to open, I wet the veneers and, after they've expanded together, I tape them immediately. If they begin to curl, I wet and hammer them lightly. If they stay put, I smile . . . and they smile. If there are no smiles, I clamp them.

Usually, I use heavy veneer tape rather than the perforated type. Instead of moistening the glued edge, I dip the tape in water. This soaks and expands it. Hopefully, as the tape dries and shrinks, it will pull the joints together.

Most of the time, a single piece of tape down the joint is all that need be used, but sometimes paranoia sets in. On these occasions, I place two-inch-long strips across the joint at two-inch intervals. Then I put that single strip down its length.

An alternative is to spread a thin coat of glue down the joint and place a piece of wet, heavy paper—about two inches wide—over it. Then hammer down the paper. This must be done carefully, because the hammer can tear the paper to shreds.

The glue on the paper—or the tape—will dry far more quickly than the glue beneath the veneer, and it will hold the joint together.

When the panel is thoroughly cured, the paper may be easily removed by moistening and scraping it off. Any residual glue or tape may be removed by sanding after it has dried.

Hammering with Other Adhesives

If you have a small area to veneer, adhesives other than hide glue can be used in the hammering process. Essentially, any glue with good initial tack may be used, but yellow glue is my favorite. The veneer in question should be flat enough that the initial hold of the adhesive is not required to flatten it. Paper-backed veneer is my veneer of choice for this type of operation. Here, there will be no glue mixing, no hot-glue pot, and no bucket of water for washing.

To hammer with yellow glue, spread a thin coat of the adhesive on the substrate; then quickly place the veneer on the substrate and touch it with the hammer to transfer glue to the veneer. Next, remove the veneer by carefully peeling it back and set it to one side. This allows the glue to dry slightly and "tack up." If the squeeze-out is excessive, spread it out with your fingers, trying not to disturb the little mounds of glue on the body of the veneer that were formed when the veneer was peeled back. These will hold fresh glue that will help in the final bonding.

Observe the veneer and the substrate as they set in the open. Depending on the shop humidity, in a minute or so the glue will begin to take on a transparent look. Testing with a fingertip will prove that the glue has become substantially more tacky. At this time, place the veneer back on the substrate and hammer it. If the edges are curling up because of the moisture from the glue, moisten the face of the veneer with clean water. After the curling subsides, hammer it one final time. Set the work aside for a few minutes before trimming it.

This technique takes a little practice, but it's well worth it. Small pieces can be bonded far more quickly than with contact cement, and it goes without saying that the bond will be better. I've used this method for years and recommend it highly for small pieces. If the work is over a quarter-foot square, however, I'd heat up the glue pot or choose another technique.

Hammering Irregular Shapes

Hammering lends itself to the veneering of all kinds of irregular shapes. In many cases, the veneer should be pre-formed to the irregular shape before the process (see Pre-Forming Veneer on pages 41 and 42), and often the conventional veneer hammer will have to be substituted with a slightly different device. In all cases, the work can be successfully done without the investment in forms, clamps, jigs, vacuum pumps, or vinyl bags. It requires only you, the substrate, the veneer, a hammering device, some glue and, well, maybe just one clamp to hold the substrate in place.

Dry-Glue Bonding

Another method of installing veneer with a minimum of equipment is by a process I call "dry-glue" bonding. Here, white, yellow, or waterproof PVA glue is spread on both the veneer and substrate. After the glue is dry, the veneer is set in place and heated with a household iron. The heat reactivates the glue and bonds the two surfaces.

White glue is the easiest to use. It requires less heat—about 180 degrees Fahrenheit—and the bond is more complete. Its disadvantage is that it leaves a soft glue line that can act as a cushion under the veneer. This is something to consider in veneering a tabletop that is to have heavy use.

Yellow glue leaves a harder glue line, but it requires more heat—about 250 degrees. And as it is not as fluid when warm, more pressure from the iron

is needed to complete a good bond.

Waterproof PVA? I only tried it once as an experiment. I found that it takes even more heat—350 degrees—and still more pressure. Knowing that the pieces I build are not meant to soak in water, that the finish will protect my work from casual wetness, and that if the veneered piece did get wet for any extended period, there would be other damage, I have never gone to the extra trouble to use waterproof PVA in any of my work.

As the water has left the glue before bonding takes place, pulling is almost nonexistent. This aspect of the process is the most appealing to me.

I once veneered a seven-foot-diameter tabletop using this technique. I could only detect 1/8 inch of cupping in the seven feet, and this could have been easily caused by irregularities in the bent skirt. A year after that, I veneered a 42-inch x 12-foot tabletop using the dry-glue process. Chatting with me some ten years later, the client said, "Warped? You could shoot pool on that table."

I don't consider this method useful in all applications. It can be resorted to in instances where the work is of such magnitude that presses, pre-cupping, or veneering both sides of the panel are impractical. The technique permits veneering with one piece at a time, cutting joints as you proceed. It lends itself to making compressed joints that have no tendency to open. Dry glue can be used on curved as well as flat surfaces and is nowhere as messy as hot hide glue. The process does require some skill, practice, and a good feel for the materials, but it is well worth considering.

Preparation

The substrates used for dry glue should be prepared as are those for any other veneering process, but be sure to scuff the surface with 80-grit sandpaper-especially the surface of MDF-to remove any glaze that may have formed. Glaze will often cause the glue to bead up or become "fish-eyed" as it is spread. Also, I have found that the dried glue tends to separate from glazed surfaces when warmed.

In preparing the veneers, the paper on paper-backed veneers should be scuffed to prevent fish-eye. Wrinkled veneers should be flattened. This will seem redundant as the work progresses, but believe me, starting with reasonably flat veneer is important.

Until after the glue is spread and dried, keep the veneer in as large a piece as you can practically work with. You will find that veneer is far easier to handle and cut with that coat of dried glue on its back reinforcing it.

I prefer to thin the glue with water and give the surfaces two coats. Thinned glue is much easier to spread evenly. This ensures good coverage. Thinning also lessens the thickness of the glue line. The amount of water added depends on the glue. White glue requires less water than yellow, and glues from different manufacturers are of different consistencies. In any event, the glue should be the consistency of heavy cream.

I prefer to spread the glue with a brush, so that the liquid can be worked thoroughly into the surface. I take the same approach to this job as I would painting the eves of my house, which take a 20-foot ladder to reach. As I don't want to climb that ladder any more than necessary, I also don't want to have to lift a piece of veneer to put more glue under it.

Spreading the substrate is simple, but the veneer can present challenges. When the wet glue hits the veneer, it will expand one side, making it curl up like a cinnamon stick. To prevent this, I keep my trusty spray bottle handy and spray a water mist on the face side of the veneer just prior to spreading the glue. If the veneer still curls, I spray more water. I continue to watch the veneer as the glue dries, spraying a mist of water whenever necessary. This is a part of the process you have to stay with—don't spread the veneer and go to lunch.

Some distortion of the veneer is to be expected. If the distortion causes the glue to flow into puddles, spread them out and don't apply the glue so heavy the next time.

To aid in drying, I set the veneer on sticks so that it will get airflow on all sides. And to get that air to flow, I place a fan across the room, setting it so that it gently blows on the veneer and substrate. Drying time is completely dependent on the temperature and the ambient humidity. In the dry climate of northern Utah, drying takes about a half-hour. In southern Florida, it could take hours—perhaps days. After the first coat is dry to the point where it has

lost its opaque look, I apply the second coat. Because the first coat has sealed the veneer, I find that spraying a water mist on the face side is often unnecessary.

When the glue has dried, I put the veneer between sheets of coated particleboard to help flatten it and hold it flat until it's bonded.

Material that has been spread with white glue can sit around almost indefinitely before it is ironed down. Material spread with yellow glue should be bonded within a week. If waterproof yellow glue must be used, bonding must take place within 72 hours. In all cases, try to keep the spread materials as dust-free as possible.

In cases where the veneers have become terribly wrinkled—as happens so often with figured cuts—I pass a warm iron over the faces to help flatten them. If they're too wrinkled for the iron, I heat them with a hair dryer. Then, while they are still warm, I place them between the sheets of particleboard.

Prior to bonding, I pass a block with 80-grit sandpaper lightly over the substrate and, if possible, the veneer. This cuts the top off any dust particles that may have settled in the wet glue. Then I wipe the surface with a damp cloth to remove any dust. The tiny amount of moisture thus imparted seems to have a positive effect on the bonding.

Bonding Techniques

With the glue dry on both the substrate and veneer, bonding can begin. After I set the first piece in place, I usually tack it in a couple of spots to keep it from moving. If the veneer is wrinkled, I pick low spots and, with the tip of the iron, heat areas about the size of a penny. Then, I begin to pass the iron lightly over the surface of the veneer. The warmth thus imparted will soften the veneer and the glue, helping to reduce any wrinkles. I increase the pressure until the veneer begins to stick. At this point, the surface should be uncomfortably warm to the touch if I'm using white glue and hot if yellow. When the veneer is flat and seems bonded, starting at the center, I work with the tip of the iron, passing over every square inch of the veneer.

How much pressure do you use? Don't break the iron's handle. The hot glue is somewhat fluid, and firm pressure will cause the surfaces to mix—which is the desired effect. Working with the tip of the iron will concentrate the pressure and also accommodate any differences in the thickness of the veneers.

If there is trimming to be done after the veneer and substrate are bonded, avoid heavy pressure in the areas that are to be cut away. Bonding that may accidentally occur from light pressure can usually be parted with a chisel or putty knife. Should the bonding be complete in the areas that are cut away, the chisel work will be more difficult and the substrate will probably need to be reglued.

Joints

Joints may be double cut using the dry-glue process. Simply avoid bonding about one inch from the joint area. After both cuts are bonded, double-cut the joint, gently lift the top veneer, and remove the waste. Then, firmly bond the joint area.

I don't recommend double cutting. Although the glue and veneer are "dry," there exists in the veneer and glue some residual moisture—more moisture than ambient conditions would dictate. When this moisture finally escapes—and it could take weeks—the joint could open, as PVA glue does permit some creep. Experiment. If in your climate double cutting works, do it. In the dry climate of northern Utah, I've experienced only moderate success with double-cut joints.

Compressed Joints

A far more reliable method than double cutting is compressing the joints. Bond the first veneer and trim the joint. Trim the joint of the second veneer and make sure it fits the first. Then place a 1/8-inch metal rod about an inch away from the first bonded slice and lay the second slice over it, butting the slices together. Tack the joints down with a couple pieces of masking tape if necessary. Bond the second veneer (except for the area two inches from the joint) with the metal rod under it. Withdraw the rod and iron down the buckle that it caused. Forcing that buckle down establishes significant pressure at the joint—enough to counteract considerable shrinkage.

I even use the compression technique when installing border components. If there is a small inlay strip in the border, it cannot, of course, be compressed. But the next component can, and this will force the inlay strip tight. With small components, the metal rod is impractical, but these small pieces can be buckled with the hand. Or, sometimes I start ironing from the edge opposite the joint, forcing any wrinkles toward the joint and causing compression.

The blanket chest, round dining table, and bombé chest described in Chapters 9, 11, and 12 present some ideas on dry-gluing techniques.

Contact Cement

I'm not a big fan of contact cement for veneer. It does have a place. It's great for on-site plastic laminates. It works well for installing cabinet skins. It is the recommended adhesive of the paper-backed veneer manufacturers. Because of its waterproof properties, I'm sure that if I ever get a commission to veneer a boat, it will be my adhesive of choice.

Okay, if you must use it, I'll give you a few pointers: Spread the contact cement evenly over the surfaces to be bonded. Blobs of contact cement will show through to the surface, and that also goes for any foreign stuff such as wood or other particles. If you're using a thin paper-backed veneer, you won't be able to sand them out. Two light coats of thinned contact cement are far better than one heavy one. It's not only easier to spread and covers better, thinned contact cement is also less likely to form clumps.

Let the contact cement dry thoroughly. Do a little experimenting and you'll see the importance of complete drying. Spread contact cement on something and observe it as it dries. As the glue develops a skin, which will make it appear dry, test it with your finger periodically. At one point, you'll find that the skin over the glue sticks to your finger and pulls completely away from the material on which it is spread. The glue may look dry, but isn't. When you place your hand on the contact cement and press firmly, it should not transfer to your hand or separate from the material.

If the contact cement gets too dry—say it was left to dry for a day or two—it will be difficult to get a good bond. The surfaces may be glued again or wiped with lacquer thinner or acetone. If the surfaces are dust-free, warming the veneer with an iron once it's in place will help immensely.

Some folks recommend using heavy paper to hold the two surfaces apart until the veneer can be properly positioned. Don't use paper! It can stick and when you pull the paper out, it can tear, leaving sections under the veneer. Strips of plastic laminates about three inches wide and as long as necessary are a far better choice. Placed four to six inches apart, they will hold the two surfaces apart very nicely. Oh yes, they can stick too, but a sharp rap with a hammer will free them.

Rollers work well for bringing the surfaces together. A veneer hammer works even better. The thin edge of the hammer concentrates far more pressure on a particular area than a roller. One paper-backed veneer manufacturer recommends rubbing the veneer with the edge of a block of wood that has had its sharp edges sanded off. Never pound on veneer with a rubber mallet as you would plastic laminate. It can mar the veneer.

Compressed joints work well with contact cement. Use great care when pressing down the buckle because the veneer has more of a tendency to wrinkle and double up. (The kidney-shaped desk described in Chapter 10 presents further ideas on working with contact cement.)

When carrying your masterpiece to the finishing shop, remember that the mineral spirits in stains and varnish can soften the contact cement. Work quickly with the stain. Don't allow it to soak in any more than necessary, and be sure it dries completely before applying any topcoats.

Lacquer works better than varnish over veneer that has been bonded with contact cement. Even though the solvent in lacquer is stronger than that of varnish, the exposure to the solvent is far less because it evaporates much more quickly. Spray the lacquer in thin coats and allow complete drying between coats.

Bonding Using Mechanical Presses

So you want to invest some real money and set up a veneer press. I did too at one time, and I designed a beauty. Then I started adding up the cost of the press

screws, timbers, bolts . . . and abandoned the project. Besides, where would I find the floor space? A couple of years later, I had a real need for a press, so I redesigned. This time my design incorporated clamps rather than press screws, because I already had these on hand. My second design can be found in the following chapter, which deals with mechanical presses in depth.

Veneering with a press is much the same as edge-gluing boards. You're just working with larger surfaces. You spread an appropriate adhesive and clamp the pieces together.

Press Criteria

The press surfaces must be flat and smooth. Should you contrive some type of bench press or clamping arrangement and it is a little twisted, whatever panel put into the press is likely to conform to the twist of the press.

The pressure exerted by the press should be even. Otherwise, it is very likely that pockets of glue will form. These will dry slowly and can cause buckling. They will also shrink, pulling the veneer down but usually in an uneven manner. It is also very convenient if the pressure of the press can be applied to the center of the work first. This will force excess glue to the outer edges.

How much pressure is required? Essentially, all that is needed is enough to flatten the veneer and hold it in close contact with the substrate. Also, the pressure should be sufficient to overcome any pressures exerted by the veneer as it is moistened by the water in the glue. And that can be a lot.

The press must also be convenient to use. If you have to go through contortions to load the press and apply the pressure, you will wind up with spoiled work. True, some glues have a long open assembly time, but open assembly time is directly related to drying time. If you would like to press more than one panel a day, make the press convenient to use and use a faster-setting glue.

Things to Be Aware Of When Using the Press

When the press is loaded with veneer and pressure is applied, the veneer can slip and slide all over the substrate. Always be sure to secure the veneer in position with paper tape. You can also use masking tape, but it will stick firmly because of the pressure and is likely to damage the veneer as it's removed. To prevent this, gently heat the tape before trying to remove it, and when removing it pull it back across itself.

In the pressing operation, glue will be forced from the panel. This will definitely occur around the edges, but glue may also be forced through the grain or undetected cracks. You may also have inadvertently transferred a speck or two to the face side of the veneer or the back side of the panel. In all cases, this glue must be kept from sticking to the plates of the press. I keep glue from the press plates by covering them with a sheet of plastic film; even a sheet of heavy paper helps.

When the veneer comes in contact with the moisture of the glue that is spread on the substrate, it will begin to expand immediately. Very often, the glue will grab around the edges, giving this expansion nowhere to go except the center of the veneer; this causes wrinkling. The wrinkles can become so severe that when the pressure is applied the wrinkles will fold over. The folded wrinkles will be bonded firmly, surrounded by pockets of glue. A spoiled panel is the result.

On the other hand, if the glue has plenty of open assembly time and it doesn't grab quickly, the veneer can expand excessively. As the moisture dries, the veneer shrinks, causing excessive pulling and even checking.

Suffice it to say that the panel must be loaded and pressure applied quickly. If you are veneering both sides of the panel in two separate steps, consistency is also important. Spread the glue in the same density and take the same amount of time getting the panel into the press. The veneer should expand the same amount on both sides so that the pull on the back will be equal to the pull on the face.

The Effects of Heat

All glues set more quickly when warm. Heat, therefore, can be an important factor when using a press. The substrate, the veneer, or the press components may be heated.

Heating the substrate will decrease the open assembly time of the glue, and if that is tolerable in your situation, do it. The temperature of the substrate can be raised considerably by wrapping it in an electric blanket—don't let your mate catch you taking it off the bed. You can also go over the substrate surface with an iron or hair dryer.

Heating the press components works better in most cases because it doesn't affect the open assembly time of the glue. The substrate may even be cooled to extend the open assembly time. The press plate that contacts the veneer may be heated with an electric blanket, iron, or hair dryer. I've even heated the plate with a large propane torch that I use for installing linoleum; I've also scorched press plates.

Don't think about leaving the electric blanket in the press under pressure. It will be devastating to the little safety thermostats. In addition, the tiny coils of heater wire could be squashed together, causing shorts and setting the blanket on fire.

Do think about using a heated metal plate. Steel works best, because it's cheap and holds heat longer than aluminum. It does need a sheet of plastic film between it and the veneer, to prevent staining. If your press is small, the plate can be put in the oven and heated. On a sunny day, the plate can be wrapped in black plastic and set in the sun for a time. When you go to unwrap the plate, wear heavy gloves or oven mittens; you'll be surprised how hot it can get.

I do have an MDF press plate with grooves cut in it for copper tubing so that I can heat the press continually with steam. An aluminum plate distributes the heat evenly across the surface. See the following chapter or more information.

In the earlier discussion of veneer itself, I mentioned that it could vary in thickness—sometimes dramatically. The flat press plate will hold the veneer against the flat substrate, and the thicker places in the veneer will be held tightly to the substrate. Because there is little or no pressure applied to the thinner spots, they will float above the substrate. Hopefully, the voids between the thin spots and the substrate will fill with glue. But what if they don't? In this case, you have an area or spot that isn't bonded, a loose spot, a spot that sounds hollow, or a spot that will be very noticeable under a good finish. What to do? What to do?

When I press veneers that exhibit inconsistencies in thickness, or if I'm pressing a taped-up piece of "artwork" that is likely to have pieces of different thickness, I use a "blanket" between the press plate and the veneer. This blanket consists of a piece of outdoor carpet—that felt-like stuff that's about an eighth-inch thick. The carpet is spongy enough that it takes up the differences in thickness of the veneer, yet is firm enough that it won't permit buckling.

Cauling

Curved work may be veneered with the use of cauls. These are forms which are constructed to match the curvature of the piece being veneered, and which can be thought of as curved press plates. With the hot-hide glue and dry-glue processes at our disposal, it seems to me a waste to expend energy and material to prepare a set of cauls for one-time use. I've resorted to cauls only when faced with a large amount of repetitive production work.

Cauls Made from Waste

There are times, however, when the cauls are already part of the work process. Waste cuts can be saved from curved work and used as one side of a caul gluing arrangement. The beauty of saving the waste cuts for veneering purposes is that the width of the kerf removed by the saw blade is the approximate thickness of the veneer, so the piece removed will fit the work perfectly. Further, because the sides of the waste cut and the substrate are parallel, clamping challenges are eliminated. Also, if the curves to be veneered are gentle, pre-forming can be eliminated.

'Tis true that the waste cuts may have thin spots with little or no strength, but these places may be reinforced by screwing or gluing the waste cut to a flat board or piece of composition material. In instances where the waste may not be complete, a blanket can be used to take up the slack in the void areas.

One thing to remember when using curved cauls: The ideal clamping pressure is at right angles with the tangent of the curve. Varying more than about

20 degrees from the tangent clamping pressure may not be sufficient in bringing the veneer into good contact with the caul and holding it flat, let alone squeezing out excess glue. Here, relief cuts in the caul combined with some creative clamping may be necessary.

The lamp project described in Chapter 8 contains some ideas on cauling.

Molded Cauls

There are times when a caul is appropriate, but it is too much trouble to make one. In some cases, simple auto-body putty can come in handy. I used this technique to veneer the knobs for the desk described in Chapter 9.

For this desk, my client requested zebrawood knobs to match the borders of the drawers. Not having any zebra lumber lying around to turn knobs from, I veneered the face of some store-bought maple ones.

To do this, I first constructed a small form and filled it with body putty. After placing detail tape over the face of the knob, I set it in the fresh putty and allowed it to harden (5-4).

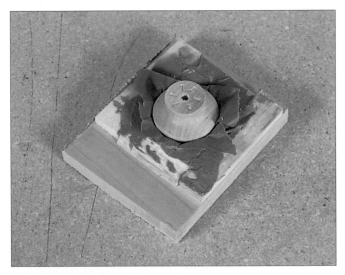

5–4. A shop-made molded caul.

After a little trimming of the mold, I heated the veneer in boiling water, set it over the mold, then clamped a knob spread with glue over it (5-5). Simple, quick, and definitely economical.

5–5. The caul was used to veneer drawer knobs

Once, I used this technique to veneer some shallowly scooped chair seats with olive ash burl. I thought my client was out of his mind for specifying veneered seats, but they were very attractive and quite unique—even though there was quite a bit of patching in places the veneer wasn't capable of stretching the required amount.

Bonding Using a Vacuum Press

I have a confession: I'm not a big fan of using the vacuum press for veneering. I have a vacuum press that I use, but I've found it more helpful for working bent laminates than for the veneering of those bent laminates. I must admit that it is not as fine in quality as the variety found in various woodworking catalogues. I've drooled over that equipment, but have always found a better place to invest the 500 to 1,000 dollars.

For simple, flat work, my little mechanical press has served well. On occasion, a couple of pieces of MDF and a handful of clamps took care of a "make do" situation. Most of the very large tabletops I've veneered I prefer to work a piece at a time. These would not fit into commercially available vacuum bags, and my "home brews" have never seemed adequate. Besides, the thought of spending two or three days taping up the veneer and having something go wrong in the pressing operation makes me cringe.

I have found that if everything is perfect—as can potentially occur with paper-backed veneers—a vacuum press works well. Unfortunately, most of my work is with difficult veneer species, and a vacuum-pressing job in which all conditions are ideal is just fantasy.

Early in my career I did use a vacuum press for veneering a large conference table. The table was made of 4 x 16-foot particleboard veneered with eighth-inch diamond-matched oak plywood. It was quite an operation. Yellow glue was spread on the substrate with a towel. The components were quickly set in place and held with masking tape. A large sheet of plastic film was placed over the plywood and sticks were nailed along the edges to hold it down—this took a crew of six. The air was evacuated from beneath the plastic film with a shop vacuum cleaner through a hole in the border area. (The border was to be installed later.) I got the idea from a RV manufacturer who was using the technique to bond skins, insulation, and interior finish for the sides of motor homes.

Sandbags were employed to hold down any spots that wouldn't be flattened. When we ran out of sandbags, we sat on the remaining loose areas or held them down with a foot or a hand. It looked as if we were playing Twister. Realizing that we were going to be there for a while, we sent out for pizza. As I observed the look on the face of the pizza delivery guy, I realized that the crew and I could go on to form a great circus act . . . or an act that the Three Stooges would've been proud of.

With that experience, I lost some enthusiasm for vacuum-veneering. Then I discovered that this could be a great way to work bent laminates and curved veneers. All I had to do was build some type of form to bend them over. After crushing several forms, I lost enthusiasm again. I didn't realize that the forms had to be stout enough to park an airplane on. By the time I built that stout a form, I could have executed the project by other means. I resorted to building the forms only for repetitive work, where a form could be used for a number of pieces.

Once more, I tried some flat veneering with vacuum, but by this time I had a decent bag and an improved pump. I taped up some very nice quartered oak veneer about 18 x 60 inches for a buffet top. I spread yellow glue on the substrate, placed the veneer on it, slid the whole thing into the bag, and turned on the vacuum. I was ecstatic because everything had gone so well. I was finally going to be able to do veneering without all the mess of hide glue or the expense of a press.

Then the job went awry. The moisture in the glue caused the veneer to expand. Ripples began to form all over the surface, and the vacuum didn't have enough pressure to hold them down. What could I do? I cried a little, and then I loudly referred to the unsavory character of the veneer's mother.

The story has a happy ending. After several hours, I removed the tabletop from the bag and ironed out the ripples, saving the top. And this, Gentle Reader, is when I began my experiments with the dry-glue process.

The next time I tried flat vacuum-veneering, I placed a cover sheet of 1/4-inch-thick plywood over the veneer. This held down the ripples. I calculated the pressure on that 2-foot-square panel: 6,912 pounds—over three tons! Then I got out my bathroom scale and a couple of clamps and did some more calculating. Though my calculations were rough and perhaps flawed, they showed that I could have developed that pressure with four clamps.

Since I don't consider myself an authority on the process of vacuum-veneering, I'll not go into any great detail on the subject, but will present some ideas on how we use vacuum equipment in our shop. You may want to try out some of these ideas before spending any serious money on commercial equipment.

I have never had a real vacuum bag. All of mine have been prepared from eight-mil plastic film. After cutting a piece of film to the size required, I spread a thin three-inch-wide coat of contact cement on the two edges. When trying this in the workshop, you will find that the film starts to curl almost immediately. Don't get excited and try to keep it from curling; you'll get glue all over your fingers. Just make sure that the contact cement is spread thinly, and the film will uncurl when it dries.

Next, using whatever I have on hand for slip sticks and weights and something to hold the spread surfaces apart until I get everything in place, I fold the film over and bring together the edges spread with contact cement (5–6). As a precaution, I spread another three-inch-wide band of contact cement down the edges of the bag and, after it's dry, I fold the edge over to make a double seal (5–7).

5–6. *Making and using shop-made vacuum-veneering equipment. Here plastic film is being folded over to form a vacuum bag.*

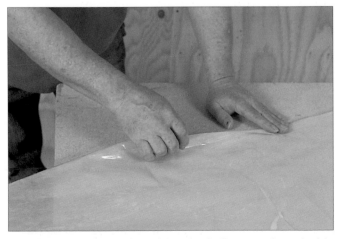

5-7. *Folding over the edge of the plastic film to make a double seal.*

The first job for this particular bag was to bend and veneer a replacement for a chair seat. I spread two pieces of 1/8-inch plywood with glue along with the top of the seat frame (5–8). That seat frame rests on a piece of ³/4-inch plywood. If I were to put the frame in the bag without the ³/4-inch plywood, the pressure of the bag would be exerted on both sides of the ¹/8-inch material and it would stay flat. Because I wanted the seat to be pulled down in the center, the ³/4-inch plywood base was a must.

5–8. Spreading the glue.

I then slid the assembly into the bag, stuck the vacuum hose in the middle of the seat, and closed the bag by wadding it around the hose and tying it with a piece of bailing wire—nothing fancy here. Once the vacuum was turned on, it pulled the bag even tighter against the hose, reinforcing the seal. In some instances, I've found it necessary to use a hose clamp in order to seal the bag to the hose or I wrapped the mess with a long piece of rubber cut from an inner tube; but those instances have been rare.

Despite the pressure of the vacuum, there was one spot that needed a little extra help, and a clamp was called into service. That clamp, incidentally, has pads of outdoor carpet on the jaws to prevent it from damaging the bag.

That thing shown on the left in 5–9 is not a vacuum pump; it's an air compressor. For an air com-

pressor to compress, it has to suck the air from somewhere. So I fastened a block of wood over the intake of the compressor and screwed a hose fitting into it. After opening the drain cock on the air tank, I had a vacuum pump.

When I first tried this stunt, I carefully watched the compressor, to make sure that it didn't overheat. Because the compressor is old, there probably is enough leakage in the piston-to-cylinder fit to prevent this from happening. Also, there may have been enough leakage in the bag and closure to help. Suffice it to say, if you try this in your workshop, keep an eye on the compressor.

Does this atrocity produce the "oomph" of the real equipment? Well, I tried putting a bathroom scale in the bag. Before the bag crushed the scale, it maxed out at 500 pounds. Later I placed a stiff spring in the bag with a square block of wood on top of it. I measured the amount of compression to the spring with a ruler. Then I removed the spring from the bag, placed it on another bathroom scale, compressed it to the dimension measured above, and noted the reading on the scale. My calculations revealed a pressure of 12 pounds per square inch. This is the best that can be expected from "real" equipment.

The fact that my "shop-built" equipment may have shortcomings is irrelevant. It worked, and another project was completed (5–10).

BONDING CHALLENGES

Murphy said it. In his first law of inevitability, he boldly states, "Anything that can go wrong, will." This is the case in any veneering operation.

The biggest challenge you will face is bubbles or loose spots. These can be caused by insufficient pressure on a press or when bonding with contact cement; insufficient heat and pressure when bonding with dry glue; or insufficient spread of glue. The exact reason for the loose spots can be irrelevant when they are found. More important is how to fix them.

Detecting Loose Spots

After the glue is dry, loose spots can often be detected by passing the edge of a thumbnail over the entire

5–9. *Using the bag and a modified air compressor to form and veneer a chair seat.*

5–10. *The completed chair seat.*

surface and listening for a hollow sound. I find that the points of dividers work even better. Once a loose spot is detected, tapping with a fingernail will confirm your findings.

Another method is to wet the completed panel and carefully examine it under different conditions of lighting. The wetting will cause the veneer to expand, and any loose spots will form some rather dramatic bubbles or wrinkles. Holding the panel up to a light source will show the defects more dramatically and, if the panel is large, a flashlight can be used.

Fixing Loose Spots

If the only loose spots are around the edges, you are truly blessed. Carefully lift the edge with a putty knife, spread more of the bonding glue under the veneer, and clamp the veneer back down. This will even work with contact cement.

If you have used dry glue, hide glue, or contact cement and you find a bubble in the center of the panel, heat is the answer. Heat will not only reactivate the glue to an extent, it will also relax the veneer should there have been pressure that caused the loose spot. In the case of hide glue, you may have to wet the spot and let the dampness soak through to the glue.

If none of the above works or the veneer was bonded with urea-formaldehyde, some fresh glue will have to be added under the spot. Cyanoacrylate can be injected with a hypodermic needle and syringe; a piece of plastic film should be placed over the spot, along with a block of wood that should remain clamped for a time. Other glues will have to be thinned to make it through the needle.

If the bubble is adjacent to a joint, the veneer may be gently lifted with the tip of a knife and glue forced under it. The bubble may also be slit along the grain and glue forced through the slit. Both of these techniques make a mess.

No matter what method is used, consider the fact that any glue that reaches the surface of the veneer will seal it and will have to be sanded off before finishing.

Repairs After Finishing

Couldn't happen, could it? How could the project make it through the sanding and finishing operations with you not noticing that bubble? It happens. Refer to Murphy—Law #3, as I recall.

Almost anything you could do will likely damage the finish, so the first thing is not to get too excited. Let the finish cure. I once noted two small bubbles in a tabletop I had veneered with dry glue as I was wheeling it out of the paint shop. I couldn't attend to any repairs for several days, and when I did get back to the top I couldn't find the bubbles. The finish had shrunk and pulled them back down. I've had the same experience with panels bonded with contact cement.

Had the bubbles persisted, in the case of contact cement, I would have warmed the area with a hair dryer, being careful not to overheat and spoil the finish. Then I would have placed my thumb over the spot, applying all of the pressure I could. I've repaired a lot of contact-cement bubbles like this, and the procedure has yet to fail.

In the case of dry glue, there's no way to heat it hot enough to reactivate the glue without spoiling the finish. In these instances, I've poked a couple of holes into the bubble with a pushpin. I poured a few drops of water over the holes and pushed them into the holes with my thumb. Usually, a bubble will begin to stick as I'm forcing the water drops through. Just to be sure the bubbled areas stays down, I clamp a block over them with a pad beneath it.

Rather than water, you can use a solvent that will dissolve resins and not hurt the finish. The only such product I know of is Brasive, supplied by the Mohawk Finishing Products Co. It does work very well, but if you're in no mind to be ordering things and waiting for their arrival, try water.

Open Joints

Considering all of the gymnastics I go through to ensure tight joints—compression, taping, etc.—I have rarely been challenged with open joints. When building the blanket chest described in Chapter 9, I did place a tiny sliver in an open joint. That was for the purpose of demonstration as much as anything. I rarely have a joint open that much.

In cases where I intend to use a similar-colored grain filler, I let the filler take care of the joints. If I intend to use a contrasting grain filler, I patch open joints with nitrocellulose putty before finishing, letting the putty pick up the color of the stain. Usually my open joints occur in border areas where two contrasting woods or grain patterns meet. Here the putty is unnoticeable except on very careful examination.

I must interject here that if there is a critic who wants to find defects in your work, he will. As he bends over the project, magnifying glass in hand, examining the newly completed tabletop, look at your right foot. You'll know what to do.

On a couple of occasions, a joint has opened that neither filler nor putty would have corrected to my satisfaction. In these instances, I forced yellow glue into the joint from a glue bottle with a tiny tip. After carefully scraping all wet glue from the surface, I wet the veneer on both sides of the joint with a brush and water, being careful to avoid the joint on both sides by about $1/8$ inch because I didn't want to dilute the glue. As the veneer expanded, the joint components tightened; this was evident by the glue that was being squeezed out. I kept the veneer wet for about an hour and then said to myself, "Self, that's all you can do."

The next day I examined the joint components that now fit together tightly. The glue held. All that remained was to scrape off the squeeze-out.

CHAPTER 6

Shop-Made Veneering Equipment and Miscellaneous Techniques

MECHANICAL VENEERING PRESS

In my shop, space has always been at a premium, and the month always seems to always outlast the money. Therefore, any useful tool or fixture that can do double duty is always welcome. It was with this in mind that I built the mechanical press described in this section. The clamps that apply the pressure have myriad other uses, and the press bench can also double as a stout workbench—if you take special care not to mar the top.

Dimensions

Top

I chose to make the table, or bottom fixed-plate, of this press 24^1/$_2$ x 72 inches—the 24^1/$_2$-inch width being what I could get by ripping a sheet of 49-inch MDF in the middle. This would let me veneer tall cabinet sides and doors as well as buffet and credenza tops. In addition, it would permit me to veneer one-half of a 48-inch dining table—a size very popular with my clients.

Economy was also a consideration. Buying two sheets of MDF, I was able to get four pieces that were 2 x 6 feet. Three of the pieces were for the table and one for a full-length cover sheet. In addition, I had two pieces that were 2 x 4 feet; one was to be used as a shorter cover and the other as a heater. These are described later.

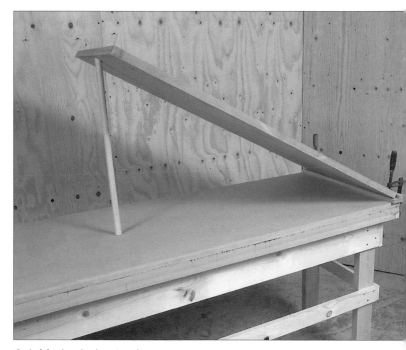

6–1. Mechanical veneering press.

Base

I built the base out of the cheapest stuff I could think of. The legs and spanners were made from 8-foot-long 2 x 4's. Eight-foot-long 1 x 6 common pine was used for the rails and stretchers. Normally, I would have substituted plywood rippings for the pine, but I had none at the time. The legs are 30 inches long; they took up one-third of the 8-foot 2 x 4. The rails and stretchers were cut to such a length that the top would hang over the base by 2 inches on all sides to allow plenty of room for clamping.

The stretcher sticks—cut from a 1 x 6 material ripped down the center—are positioned about 16 inches from the floor. I intended to use the stretcher assembly for storing spanner sticks and clamps, and I didn't want to bend to retrieve them any more than necessary.

Stock Preparation

Base

Other than cutting them to length, the only preparation for the base components was to straighten the upper edge of the skirt pieces. As I wanted this press as perfectly flat as possible, this was an important step. Now, you might think that a lumberyard 1 x 6 looks straight, but check it against the factory edge of a piece of MDF. If you find it perfectly straight, you are most blessed; otherwise, proceed to the jointer or use a hand plane.

Top

Being too heavy for me to muscle through the table saw, I rough-cut the sheets of MDF with a handheld circular saw and trued the edges of the first sheet with a router, using a straight 1/2-inch carbide cutter with the shank piloting the factory edge of a second sheet (6–2). (If you have a flush-trim bit that will cut the full inch, by all means use it.) After the first sheet was trued, it was placed on each of the others to true them, resulting in three sheets of exactly the same size.

After scuffing the surfaces that would receive glue with 80-grit sandpaper, I also pulled the teeth of an old handsaw over the surfaces, providing a little "toothing" (6–3). This is rather important, as the smooth surface of the MDF will cause the glue to bead up and puddle.

Spanner Sticks

After cutting the 2 x 4s to length, I passed each piece over the jointer to straighten the edge that would contact the press. I used these sticks the same day to

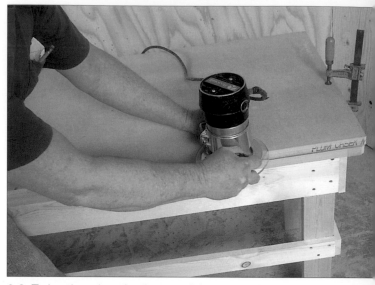

6–2. *Truing the edges for the top of the mechanical press.*

6–3. *Using a handsaw to "tooth" the top of the mechanical press.*

laminate the press top. Several days later, I found that the straightened edge had a slight bow. This I attribute to drying from the end of the 2 x 4s. I placed sticks between the 2 x 4s, allowing them to dry thoroughly. Periodically checking the weight of several of them, I found it took over a month before I could trust them to be stable.

After the spanners were thoroughly dry, I again straightened one edge and stuck three layers of scrap

6–4. Scrap veneer was applied to the center of each spanner for pressure.

6–5. Using a spirit level to ensure that the ends of the press top are level.

veneer in the center of each (6–4). When the sticks were put to use, the veneers would apply extra pressure at the center of the press—as much pressure as it takes to bend that piece of 2 x 4 about $1/16$ inch.

I had really intended to taper the edge of the sticks on the jointer, leaving a $1/16$-inch hump in the center. That particular day, one of the other guys was using my favorite jointer for edge-gluing a huge stack of boards. I wanted to use the press immediately; that's why the scraps of veneer were installed. Someday, I'll get around to tapering the sticks properly—honest.

Assembly

Base

I fastened all of the base's joints with $1^5/8$-inch drywall screws through a small pilot hole bored in the pine. A generous amount of yellow glue was used at each joint. The only caution is to see that the tops of the skirt components are perfectly flush and that the tops of the legs don't stand proud of (higher than) the skirt.

Top

Since I wanted the press top perfectly flat, the first step was to make sure that the base I was going to glue it onto was completely level. Using my trusty

spirit level, I made sure that each end was true, sliding a wedge under any leg that needed a little extra length to reach the irregular concrete floor (6–5).

Urea-formaldehyde, because of its no-creep properties, was chosen for laminating the three pieces that compose the tabletop. In operation, the spanner sticks will be slightly high in the center, tending to cup the top. If yellow or white glue were used for lamination, there is a good possibility that this cup would remain, as the PVA glues do permit some movement in the glue line.

The glue was mixed according to the manufacturer's directions. Then another five percent of water was added to make the excess glue a little easier to squeeze out. I spread the glue with a $1/16$-inch trowel tipped at about a 45-degree angle—which turned it into a $1/32$-inch trowel, the size recommended for urea-formaldehyde. After the whole surface was covered, I made several more passes with the trowel to ensure an even coating.

After all three pieces were in their correct positions, I laid out the straightened spanner sticks—the sticks I used the first day; not the ones I stuck the veneer scraps to later. The clamps were set in place with just enough pressure to prevent them from falling off. Starting with the center set, I began to tighten the clamps. Clamp pressure was firm and even. The object was to bring the surfaces into close contact, not to distort anything due to excess pressure (6–6).

The MDF itself provided some pressure, and in the right places. The moisture from the glue caused the outer pieces to cup. Because the center piece had glue on both sides, it remained flat. The cupping of the outer pieces applied increasing pressure in the center of the sheets, and the clamps provided pressure along the edges as the spanner sticks held the top sheet flat—a good example of letting nature do the work.

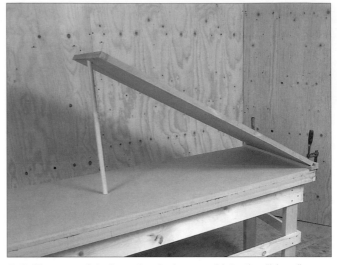

6–7. *The completed mechanical press. Note the "hinge" clamped to the end of the table.*

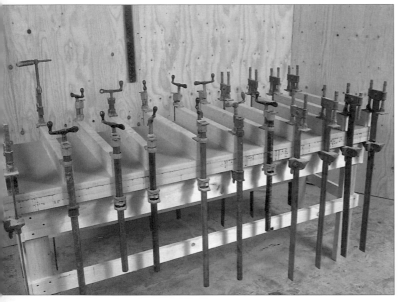

6–6. *Clamping the press base.*

I told the guys not to disturb the clamps until the next morning, so that the assembly would have at least 12 hours' drying. Most of the clamps stayed in position for several days, for, you see, I did not take them off myself. Knowing that the others would be needing clamps eventually, I let them remove them— a good example of letting someone else do your work.

Finishing Up

I began thinking of lifting that heavy cover sheet on and off the press, so I devised a "hinge." This was nothing more than a rabbeted stick clamped to the end to the table to prevent the cover from sliding off (6–7). I also drilled a 1-inch hole partially through one end of the cover sheet to receive a dowel that would hold the cover up for easy loading. It was a great idea at the time, but I found that what I had actually devised was a good deadfall trap. In the section Press Heater that follows, you'll see what I came up with next.

PRESS HEATER

Since I have spent over half my years as a professional woodworker and businessman, no one ever had to convince me that time is money. While there are always plenty of things to do while waiting for the glue to dry on a veneered panel, anything that can speed a project along is a worthwhile investment. It's why I added heating plates to my veneer press.

Solar Heater

Be it known that I am a fan of energy conservation. I drive an economy car. I have meticulously caulked all windows and doors in my home. And when my children were at home, I spent many hours turning off lights, TVs, and stereo equipment, to say nothing of firmly shutting off all dripping faucets. In addition, I'm a wee bit tight with a buck and see no reason to pay for heat when God, in His infinite generosity, sends it to me free. It is thus that my solar-powered veneer-press heater came into being.

The solar heater consists of no more than a piece of 2 x 4-foot x $^3/_{16}$-inch steel plate. The plate is placed on a couple of sawhorses in full sunlight. Within a short time—depending on the season—the plate gets hot enough that I can handle it only with gloved hands. Once the plate is set in position on the press, it takes over an hour to cool down—ample time for urea-formaldehyde to set with the heat.

Because the plate is brought into close contact with the veneer, and because the plate is steel, it does require a barrier sheet of plastic film between it and the veneer. This prevents squeeze-out from sticking to the plate, and we all know that water + wood + iron = blue stain. In addition, I usually cover the plate with a sheet of particleboard, providing insulation that slows the cooling of the plate.

My plate is slightly cupped—about $^1/_8$ inch. This I consider a blessing. I always put the convex side against the veneer and pull it flat with the spanner sticks. This applies pressure to the center of the panel first, forcing excess glue to the edges as clamp pressure is applied to the spanner sticks—how lucky can a guy get?

I keep telling myself that I'm going to have a smaller plate cut for smaller projects. As this will probably never happen, when pressing small panels I set out a few blocks the same thickness as the substrate being pressed to support the plate.

Steam-"Fired" Heater

My Maker does not always send sunlight to heat my veneer press. This could be a "reward" for my many digressions. Rather than try to explain my relationship with the Almighty to clients who are in a hurry for their project's completion, I built a backup press heater.

This heater consists of two separate lengths of $^3/_8$-inch copper tubing inset into a piece of 1-inch MDF (the tubing layout can be best seen in 6–13). I felt that the two separate "coils" would distribute the heat more evenly. Steam passing through the copper tubing is conducted to a plate of .090-inch aluminum that contacts the veneer, distributing the heat evenly. Of course, the heater does need a source of steam. No problem; see Steam Generator on pages 88 to 91 for more information.

Fitting the Copper Tubing

Cutting the Groove

To cut the groove for the tubing, I used a router with a $^3/_8$" straight bit, the shank of the bit being guided by a template of 1-inch-thick MDF (6–8). (A template bushing can also be used for such an operation, but I never did see the use in adding any more gadgets than absolutely necessary.) I made the cuts in two $^3/_{16}$-inch steps, and on the last cut I passed the router several times around the template—hopefully widening the cut slightly.

6–8. Cutting the groove for the tubing using a router.

While you have that router out, you will need to install a slotting cutter and cut some grooves to receive tabletop fasteners. See 6–14 for details.

Placing the Copper Tubing

Inserting the tubing in the straight cuts was easy; placing the loops was not. Here I eased the tubing around the groove, pushing it in with my thumb. Where thumb pressure wasn't quite sufficient, I encouraged it with a block of wood and a hammer (6–9).

6–9. Inserting the tubing and loop.

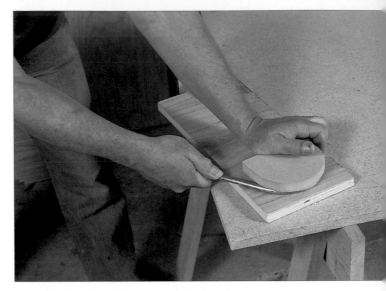

6–11. Pulling the tubing around the bender.

The first bend went so well that I got a little over-confident and kinked the second; I took a few minutes and built a tubing bender. This is simply a piece of pine glued to a scrap of MDF. The pine piece was planed to the same thickness as the tubing and cut to the radius of the bend (6–10). The pine piece and MDF were then glued to a scrap of plywood. After the glue was thoroughly dried and any squeeze-out cleaned away, it was a simple matter to firmly pull the tubing around the piece of pine sandwiched between the scraps (6–11).

I did have this project all planned out to use a 25-foot coil of copper tubing. When I got to my friendly neighborhood home improvement center, I found that it had only 20-foot coils. To make matters worse, it was out of 3/8-inch couplings. Undaunted, I slid the shank of a 5/16-inch drill bit into the end of a second coil of tubing and took it to the flat portion of my vise. Tapping firmly on the end of the tubing as I rotated it (6–12) caused it to expand enough to slip it over about 1/2 inch of the end of the untreated tube. It was then a matter of soldering the joint. Needless to say, the groove in the MDF had to be widened and deepened with a chisel at the point of the joint.

6–10. A tubing bender.

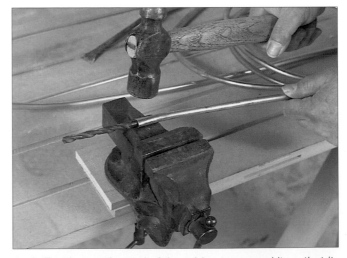

6–12. Tapping on the end of the tubing to expand it so that it can be slipped over the end of the untreated tube.

Finishing Up

Next, I removed the tubing and gave the surface of the MDF a thin coat of contact cement. After the contact cement dried, I placed strips of aluminum foil over the grooves—except those for the loops—and pressed the tubing back in, forcing the foil into the groove (6–13). This is a necessary step. Without the foil, the heat radiating from the small surface of the pipe is not very effective in heating the plate that is to be placed over it. The foil conducts heat from the bottom and sides of the tubing, and when the spanner sticks press the plate and foil together, the whole assembly works rather efficiently.

Don't expect the foil to stick to the contact cement just yet. It will stick the first time the press is heated, at which point there will be no chance of it moving about. Until then, handle the assembly carefully to prevent the foil from wrinkling and forming wads. On the ends, beyond the loops, I did put a piece of foil into some fresh contact cement. This had no heat-transfer properties; it served only as a spacer.

Fastening the Aluminum Plate

The first steam-fired heater I built had the aluminum plate fastened with flathead screws going through the plate-and it didn't work! The expansion coefficients of the plate and the MDF were so vastly different that either the plate buckled or the screws were torn from the MDF. It was thus that I resorted to the Z-shaped tabletop fasteners.

A groove is cut in the MDF to receive the end of the fastener. Holes are bored and tapped in the aluminum plate to accept a #8, 32 threads-per-inch screw (6–14); I used some spare cabinet hardware screws about an inch long from my junk drawer. Use extreme care in boring and tapping the plate. Aluminum isn't the strongest of metals. And don't overtighten the screws.

On the face side of the plate, I cut off the screws and filed them flush with the surface. This will allow pressing right to the edge of the plate with no fear of damage to the veneer.

6–13. Aluminum foil has been added to the grooves.

6–14. Holes have been bored and tapped into the aluminum plate.

6–15. Using a steam-fired press heater. Notice the bucket on the right, which collects condensation.

Operation

Steam is introduced into the tubes at the outer edge through a ³⁄8-inch rubber hose. The outer edge is where I felt the most heat would be needed. At the other end, condensation is collected in a bucket (6–15).

Normally, I put about a gallon of water in that bucket to keep escaping steam from dramatically raising the humidity of the shop—especially in the summer. Also, steam bubbling through the water will heat it; when it comes time to refill the boiler, I have a bucket of preheated water at hand.

Normally I leave the press closed until the aluminum plate becomes very hot. This also warms up the table. I did try putting the steel plate that I use as a solar heater on the table and heat it for pressing both sides of a panel at once, but I found that the heat from the MDF table was sufficient to cure even urea-formaldehyde.

When the panel to be veneered is set in place and the clamps are installed, the bubbling will stop for a time. That's because the heat is being transferred to the panel and the steam is condensing.

So how much time does the heat save? Urea-formaldehyde will cure rock-hard in about 15 minutes. Although white and yellow glues don't cure through chemical action alone, it takes about 15 minutes for the heat to drive enough moisture from the glue into the substrate so that the veneer is bonded firmly. Either liquid or hot hide glue takes about an hour.

As I mentioned in Mechanical Veneering Press, the stick that holds the cover open (6–15) made for a great deadfall trap. Once the press found a home, I came up with a little different method of holding it open (6–16). A piece of rope, strung through an old sash pulley nailed to a rafter and tied off to a screw on the press, did raise some noses, but it works.

Other Applications

The heated press has other applications: It can be used to flatten things. One of the panels that I pressed for the blanket chest described in Chapter 9 bowed slightly—about ³⁄16 inch. Because I wanted the lid of that chest to fit comfortably, even this a residential, exterior door. Considering what I charged my clients for these little feats of magic, if the various components returned to their twisted shape, I would have heard by now.

The heater press is also an excellent way to quickly flatten and dry veneer. For your viewing pleasure, I selected three wrinkled mahogany crotch slices (6–18). Two of these I sprayed with water and placed in the press. I put a cover sheet of plastic film under them to prevent the moisture from spoiling

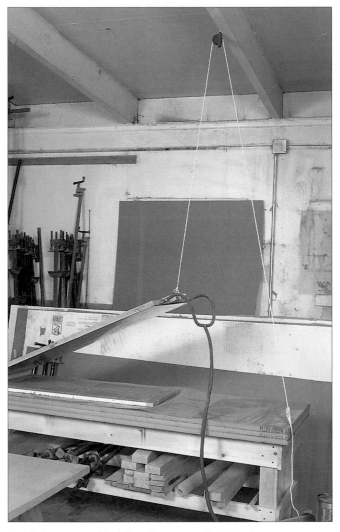

6–16. *A means of holding the steam-fired heater open.*

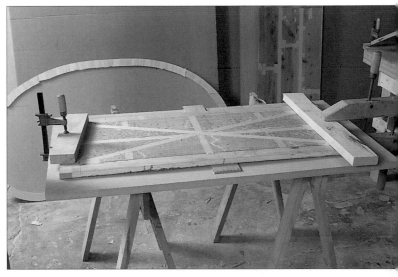

6–17. *Using the heated press to flatten a panel.*

6–18. *Flattening and drying crotch slices using the heater press.*

slight bow was intolerable. To correct the condition, I placed the panel in the press for about an hour, clamping the heater down lightly. Then I removed it from the press and clamped it to a piece of MDF with a stick in the center, forcing it to bow in the opposite direction (6–17). After being left to cool for a couple of hours, it was flat.

Does this heat treatment really work? Are the results long-lasting? Well, I got the idea from a piano mechanic who was using a little electric tool to straighten hammer arms and twisted keys. He assured me that heat worked. I've used the technique for years to straighten antique cabinet doors—even to twist drawers back into shape. I even used heat on the piece of particleboard they rested on (6–19). Initially I clamped the press lightly (6–20), tightening the clamps at intervals over a 15-minute period.

I then opened the press and placed a piece of Single-Side above and below the veneers (6–21) and closed the press once more. The clamps were replaced with light pressure.

Two hours later, I removed the two pieces of veneer. Compared to the third (6–22), they were very flat and as dry as a fresh potato chip.

6–21. *Corrugated cardboard has been placed above and below the veneers.*

6–19. *Plastic film has been placed under the slices sprayed with water.*

6–22. *The two pieces of veneer are much flatter and dryer than the piece not flattened.*

STEAM GENERATOR

I've described how steam can be used to flatten veneers and showed how to build a steam-"fired" press heater, so I had better present some ideas on how to generate steam for use in the shop.

For years, our shop was heated by a gas-fired boiler. I can't say that I was sad to see the old boiler go. I enjoyed the even warmth that steam heat provided during those cold winter months, but I didn't enjoy

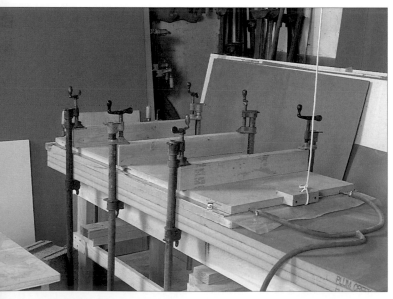

6–20. *The press is clamped lightly.*

feeding the vintage 1940 boiler. As I watched the contractor install the new, efficient forced-air system, I realized I was going to miss more than the high utility bills. I was going to miss the steam, for over the years I made good use of steam in my shop, not just for simple bending, but for other very important uses.

It wasn't two weeks after the boiler had been replaced that I had to flatten some veneers, and I had to do it quickly. I pulled out the steaming box, and then came to the sudden realization that I had no steam. I wandered into the kitchen—we have a small kitchen in our shop—and after scrounging around, found a teakettle and a hot plate. I carried these back into the shop; filled the teakettle; plugged in the hot plate, and in about 15 minutes I had steam . . . but how to get it to the box?

I wrapped a damp cloth around the steam hose and packed it in the mouth of the kettle. It worked, provided I propped up the hose to keep condensation from settling in it. I didn't have a tight enough seal with the damp cloth to build up enough pressure to force the condensation from the hose. A few days later, I improved this little rig by buying a rubber cork from a brewer's supply house, forcing a piece of 3/8-inch copper pipe into it and coupling that to the hose.

I always worried a little about the safety of such a rig, but in the times I used it I was never able to blow up the teakettle.

The system worked well even for generating steam for my larger wood-bending chambers. The only challenge was the constant refilling of the teakettle. It would only run for about 20 minutes before cooking dry. That was when I came up with the rig I will now describe.

My new steam generator is centered around a #20 (five-gallon) propane tank. The finished product is shown in 6–23, and the components in 6–24. (I have read articles that describe steam generators utilizing paint buckets and even fuel containers. I would not recommend lightweight containers because steam will rust them through quickly. I once built a heating chamber out of light, furnace duct pipe. It lasted only two years—and it was galvanized.)

Into a hole sawed near the bottom of the tank, I brazed a 1-inch pipe coupling to receive a 1,200-watt, 110-volt water-heater element (6–25). (I later built a boiler using a 2,500-watt, 220-volt heater, and, although the 2,500-watt element brought the pressure up quicker, I could detect little difference in operation.) In the threaded hole on top of the tank—where the valve was—I screwed a 4 1/2-inch nipple, which serves as a filler pipe. Into the nipple is brazed a piece of 3/8-inch o.d. copper pipe that is used as the steam outlet. The tin can on top of the nipple serves as safety pressure relief and as a conveniently removable filler pipe cap. The components of the can are shown in 6–26. The 4 x 1/4-inch bolt-along with the stack of washers-keeps the can centered and prevents it from falling off the filler pipe. A couple pieces of rubber—cut from an old inner tube— seal the top of the nipple.

6–23. Steam generator.

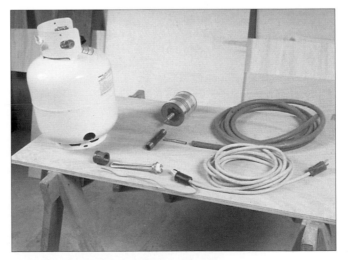

6–24. Components of a steam generator.

6–25. Sawing a hole near the bottom of the tank to receive a pipe coupling.

6–26. The components for the electric-fired boiler's tin cup, which serves for pressure relief.

Filling the can about three-quarters with lead wheel weights gives it enough mass to form a tight seal. If the pressure in the tank exceeds a safe level, it will gently lift the can and the excess will be released.

Rather than using the electric element, you may, of course, set the tank on a camp stove, propane burner, or even an electric range. Open flames in my shop scare me, and I don't even like things as hot as a range element. The choice is yours.

Construction Details and Instructions

If you have no experience in welding tanks, let me here do everything possible to convince you not to do it yourself. Your little handheld MAPP gas torch is not hot enough. If you have oxyacetylene equipment and must do it yourself, lay the tank on its side and fill it with water. Gases can accumulate in the empty container during the brazing process—even if it's a new tank—and they can cause a nasty "surprise." Perhaps explosion is a better word. Spend a buck; take it to a pro.

If you plan to build with a used tank, read the above paragraph several times, and be prepared for a terrible stench the first few times the boiler is used. If the water is changed every time the boiler is used, the stench leaves more quickly.

Rather than brazing the stub of the 3/8-inch copper pipe into the filler, appropriate pipe fittings may be used, but as long as you have a welder working for you let him do the work.

As you can see in 6–23, the 1-inch pipe coupling enters the tank at an angle, but parallel to the bottom. Pipe couplings do vary in size, but a 1³/8-inch hole saw worked for me. I did have to make a few passes through the hole with a rat-tail file, and it took one good blow with a hammer to set the coupling within brazing distance. Measure carefully and chose a hole saw smaller rather than larger than the hole required—brass will refuse to fill large gaps.

You may have some trouble threading the heating element into the coupling, because it has tapered threads and the element doesn't. Fear not; wrap a couple of layers of Teflon tape on the element's threads and screw it in snugly. Don't worry that it doesn't engage the rubber seal that was provided with the element.

That black thing on the end of the electrical cord in 6–23 is a plastic film can. It is slipped over the electrical connections and held with tape—this adds a safety dimension. Note also the green ground wire secured to the handle of the tank with a bolt. Don't omit it. Often, when heating elements "die," they short to ground or neutral. Should this happen and the ground wire is omitted, you could receive a nasty shock instead of the breaker being harmlessly tripped.

6–27 and 6–28. Close-ups showing the tank stored in the plastic container.

It is necessary that the boiler operate with some pressure. As water from condensation will form in the steam line during operation, there must be enough pressure to force the water out of the hose. Also, boiling water under pressure increases the temperature of the steam. Every few degrees can help.

A can filled with wheel weights used as a safety relief sounds a little "Rube Goldberg." However, it does the job, and it can be conveniently lifted off for filling purposes. But don't forget to save the can's lid. You can solder it back on after the bolt and wheel weights are in place.

Insulation around the tank is a must. It makes for fuel economy and in the summer the tank will remain cool. I chose fiberglass because . . . well, I had some, and I was concerned that any type of foam might melt in contact with the hot tank.

Placing the tank in the plastic container was one of my more brilliant decisions. In the past, I would have wrapped the tank in insulation, using bailing wire to hold it in place. Criticism would then flow from my children, my clients would wonder why I was storing trash, and my beloved would quietly mutter, "Slob." The plastic container is neat, clean, and, when the lid is on it, I don't have to explain to a visitor that I'm not running a still (6–27).

Operation and Safety Precautions

The electric heating element has one serious drawback: If the tank cooks dry, the element will self-destruct. Therefore, the element must be immersed in water. Before starting the boiler, I check the water level, inserting a small stick through the filler pipe. Starting with about three gallons, I've found that at an altitude 4,000 feet, the boiler (at 1,200 watts) takes about 40 minutes to build a head of steam and consumes about one gallon per hour. Keeping careful track of time is my only safety device.

I usually start the boiler with the filler-pipe cap removed. When steam flows freely from the filler pipe, I hold the hose in the air to drain any water trapped in it. I couple the hose to the appropriate fixture, and then I install the cap. This ensures that I don't handle a very hot hose.

Should I have occasion to remove the filler-pipe can to check the water level while the boiler is in operation, I drape an old bath towel over it, shown in 6–28. A significant amount of hot steam will be released, and it could cause some nasty burns. Also, a sudden release of pressure will cause the water in the tank to boil violently, often spewing out of the filler pipe. The towel insulates my bare hand and prevents steam from blowing into my face or any other interesting parts of my body.

MISCELLANEOUS VENEERING TECHNIQUES

Veneering Moldings

Often the cost of solid, exotic wood for moldings is prohibitive. Sometimes exotic species make very poor solid lumber—satinwood comes to mind. And then, there are those instances where you may want some decorative effect on a molding. In all of these cases, moldings may be veneered—provided, of course, that there is some attention paid to design.

It's a good idea to practice with a heavy piece of paper, planning the best way to attack the project. You will also note that the veneer hammer is going to be impractical. Practice will help you design the type of squeegee—or squeegees—that works best for the operation.

As long as you're going to the trouble of using moldings, do something different, something the eye doesn't expect. When I'm hammering a molding with hot hide glue, I spread the veneer and hammer one edge in a convenient character of the mold (6–29). After the edge has set for 15 minutes or so, I gently heat the unbonded portion of the veneer to remelt the glue, and then hammer it into the remaining portion of the character. I always work in some cross-grain veneer into the molds I veneer. Usually it's best to place these in a larger character or portion of the molding's design. Sometimes these pieces need to be pre-formed. This can be easily done by band-sawing a piece of scrap to fit the character (seen to the right in 6–29), placing the moistened pieces to be pre-formed between the molding and the band-sawn piece, clamping all of them, and letting them set overnight. I have to construct a "hammer" to match the curvature of the molding (6–30), but the effort is well worth it.

Veneering Turnings

Veneered turnings can also add a special element to any project. Small pieces of veneer laid over any flat spots on a turned component can make for an interesting design. A column veneered with olive ash or Carpathian elm burl can take on the appear-

6–29. Veneering molding with hot hide glue.

6–30. A shop-made hammer used for veneering molding.

ance of marble. A mahogany crotch can make a column appear as if it's on fire. The various decorative effects are endless. All are eye-catching, because the eye doesn't expect to encounter these effects on a round piece of wood.

To veneer the convex portion of a turning, you'll need a hammer that fits the diameter of the turning. Prepare a hammer that has a radius about 5 percent greater than the radius of the surface being veneered. Use only 15 degrees for the circumference. If the hammer has a greater circumference, you won't be exerting any pressure and the extra width will get in the way.

Veneering a simple cylinder requires little effort. Merely spread glue on the cylinder and wrap the veneer around it. Work out the excess glue with the specially prepared hammer, and double-cut the joint. If the glue is left a little thick, it will shrink as it dries, tending to tighten the joint. I have seen some rather impressive puddles of glue under veneer on curved, antique pieces of all sorts.

If the cylinder is not true, rather having a slight bulge—as with some columns—start at the bulge and try to stretch the veneer slightly around the greater surface. Wet the veneer in that area of the of the bulge and try to stretch the veneer slightly around the greater surface. If the veneer buck in the areas of lesser diameter, mash it as flat as possible.

If the diameter of the turning varies greatly, it will have to be veneered in pieces. These pieces need not be all of the same species. Some terrific effects are possible. The options are so great that space forbids considering even a few. I will recommend the use of patterns and experimentation. Discover the limitations of the species and turning being used and make necessary adjustments.

Spiral Veneering

Spiral-veneered columns are especially eye-catching. The process is simple and well worth the effort.

Once you have determined the width of veneer that will be worked, cut a piece of felt paper to the same width and wrap it around the column in order to determine the pitch of the spiral. Then make a mark to show where to set the veneer (6–31). In 6–32, I am using an iron to soften the veneer and prevent it from splitting. It will be bonded to the column with contact cement. The face of stubborn species should also be moistened. It's always best to work with extra-long veneer if possible and trim it after the glue has had a chance to set for a while (6–33).

6–32. Softening the veneer with an iron.

6–31. Using felt paper to locate where to set the veneer.

6–33. Extra-long veneer can be trimmed after the glue is set.

CHAPTER 7

Adding a Finish

Probably the reason you will choose veneer for a project is that you want to display the natural beauty of wood—a noble motive indeed. But just what is it that wood has that a piece of plastic laminate doesn't? Don't all raise your hands at once. Wood has iridescence . . . fire, depth.

When light strikes the surface of a piece of wood, it is reflected in many different directions by the cells and pores. When a clear finish is put over the wood, the pores and cells fill with this clear substance, turning it into tiny lenses and prisms that further diffract the light and even alter its color. With this in mind, all finishing processes should be geared to enhance this property.

In most cases, there is no simple one-step approach to finishing. A system that uses several steps of colors, fillers, glazes, and topcoats—all applied at the proper time in the process—will create a professional finish. Colors of different types and hues can be applied at various stages in the process to produce a wide range of effects (7–1). Fillers may be applied over bare wood, after sealing, or both. Topcoats may be full gloss or have a flattening agent mixed into them to obtain the desired sheen without the necessity for rubbing.

With regard to the finishing "system," I must add that if you live in a state that has outlawed the use of solvent-based chemical coatings, take your piece across the border, finish it, and then bring it home. While great strides have been made by the water-based coatings industry, as of this writing there is no system of stains, glazes, and topcoats that can compare with solvent-based products.

The subject of wood finishing can be volume length. That in mind, here I'll take a philosophical approach rather than treat any particular technique in depth. I'll point out some readily available products and their advantages and disadvantages in relation to maintaining the beauty of wood.

SANDING AND PATCHING

As you probably well know, the first step in any finishing operation is patching and sanding, and there is a lot of sanding involved. There is no beautifying finishing technique that hides scratches and other defects. More often, the finish magnifies these defects as it magnifies the beauty of the wood.

Often, there are spots such as a slightly open joint

7–1. Spraying on a finish.

or a hole in a burl that need a little patch. Even worms have to eat, and any evidence of their dining should be disguised. For most patching I use nitrocellulose putty. It's not only the most common product at the paint store, it also serves well in most instances. Usually I choose the lightest color available, preferring the stain to add color to the patch. If the stain doesn't color it sufficiently, I can add color after the piece is sealed. (It's always easier to make a patch darker than lighter.)

Where the species is likely to fade dramatically and this will become obvious, I "brew" a patch by adding dust produced from the piece I'm sanding to some thinned liquid hide glue. Because the particles in the patch are of the same species, they will fade at an equal rate and to the same color, and the transparency of the hide glue will let some iridescence still left in the particles shine through.

ALTERING THE COLOR OF VENEER

It may be that you have fallen in love with the grain pattern and texture of a particular veneer species, but are not crazy about the color. Don't fret; the color of wood can be altered, in many cases with only minor work. Altering the color of the veneer to a darker shade, or to a darker shade with a different hue, is probably the easiest. Altering the color to what appears to be a lighter shade can be done easily using dyes. Actually making the wood a lighter shade is more difficult and often compromises the iridescent properties of the wood because pigments or bleach will be required.

No one product or technique should be adopted exclusively. There are so many different species and techniques available that to limit your approach to a single method will mean not taking advantage of the versatility that is so important in wood finishing.

Pigmented Stains

Stains containing pigments are probably the most popular consumer product for altering the color of wood. They are easy to use, and blending the various colors of pigment to achieve a particular hue is also easy. Consumer pigmented stains are usually of the brush-on/wipe-off variety and may be solvent-, oil-, or water-based. With these stains, wood can easily be made darker and actually made lighter through the use of a light-colored pigment. And the pigments usually concentrate in the grain of the wood, enhancing the grain pattern.

Sounds good, doesn't it? Are you about to pledge yourself to the exclusive use of pigmented stains? Don't!

When pigments are spread over the surface of bare wood, they tend to fill the pores and open cells. While this characteristic does enhance the grain pattern, it can completely destroy the iridescent properties of the wood. Pigments are actually finely ground rocks. Their colors are lightfast (resistant to light), but they are not transparent and do not permit the passage of light. It's like looking at the surface through a film of mud.

Scratches and slightly open joints pick up pigments, so the full "beauty" of these defects is intensified.

Pigments tend to settle into end grain more than flat grain. Wavy species like maple will appear blotchy.

While pigmented stains are quick and easy to use, there are better ways to go. These methods are discussed below.

Dye Stains

Unlike pigmented stains, dye stains are fully transparent. They alter the color of the wood without affecting its iridescent properties. Unfortunately, they are not as lightfast as pigmented stains, and some fading can be expected through the years. But remember, if you are finishing new wood, it is not lightfast either.

Not as easy to find as pigmented stains, dye stains are supplied in powdered form or dissolved in a number of mediums: water, alcohol, oil, toluene, etc. Many liquid dyes are supplied in concentrated form and should be thinned to the desired shade. It's always best to thin the stain with the same medium as in the concentrate. If this is not possible, compatible thinners may be used. Water stains may be thinned with alcohol—to make them dry faster and minimize the grain-raising tendencies of the water. Alcohol stains may be thinned with lacquer thinner—if you don't have any alcohol on hand. In any event, if you have chosen a poor combination, particles will form on the bottom of the container. If you have thinned an oil dye with water, well . . .

Dye stains are not quite as easy to blend to produce a particular color as are pigmented stains. This is because the dyes are transparent, so the color of the wood comes more heavily into play. When the dye stain is wet, it will appear to be one color; when it dries, the color changes dramatically. Then, when the topcoats are applied, a third color results. This color is usually very similar to the color of the wet stain, but not always. If that isn't enough, because the dyes are fully transparent, the color will change as the surface is viewed from different angles. Suffice it to say that experiments should be carried out on scraps, and that the experimental pieces should be given topcoats and viewed under a number of light conditions to ensure a critical match.

Dye stains should be sprayed on. Trying to apply these with a brush or by wiping them on with a rag can be very tricky. Because they absorb and dry so quickly, lap marks will become evident—very evident. Spraying does give the advantage of being able to color the wood without being at the mercy of the absorption properties thereof. A specific amount is applied to certain areas of the wood, where it is absorbed. And while dye stains don't cover sanding scratches and slightly open joints, they don't accentuate them either.

For maximum effect, the dyes should be applied in heavy, penetrating coats—almost to the point where the dyes run. This happens quite often when I use dyes, so I keep a rag tucked in my back pocket that I use to blot them.

It is impossible to lighten a particular species with dyes, but it can be made to look lighter. When I want to quickly make new, deep-purple walnut look like old, faded walnut, I spray it with bright-orange dye. The bright orange makes the walnut appear lighter. The resultant color will not pass critical examination, but is a quick fix. There is beauty in the process in that if the piece is exposed to light, as the dye color fades, the natural color of the walnut develops. Bright-yellow dye, a dab of orange, and a dab of brown will work the same way in making new oak look like aged oak.

Are you about to select dye stains as the coloring technique of choice? Well . . . don't practice on your project, and be sure to read the section on glazing stains below, for wood colored with only dyes can be quite stark and will need to be toned down.

Combination Stains

Some consumer wood stains are a combination of dyes and pigments. If you put a stick in a fresh can of this type of stain, you'll find that the liquid alters the color of the wood. While stirring, you'll notice some solid matter (pigment) on the bottom of the can—the less the better.

These types of stain provide the best of both worlds. The liquid colors the wood while the pigment enhances the grain pattern. Because the pigment is held to a minimum, it does not completely hide the iridescence of the wood. Combination stains are about as close to a one-step coloring system as you will find.

Glazing Stains

If any one product were to be counted as the mark of the professional, it would be glazing stains. These pigmented stains are lightly brushed or sprayed on a thoroughly sealed surface, and then selectively wiped off, either with a rag or a dry brush.

A tiny bit of glaze left around the edges of a table or buffet top will subtly break up the single color of the surface. A light streak or two in the glaze can make grain appear where none really exists. And glaze left in the low areas of moldings, turnings, or carvings will make the features stand out.

If you have used a dye stain and are less than pleased with the rather stark appearance after the sealer dried, glaze can be used to soften this appearance. You may not be satisfied with the way that the dye did not enhance the pore pattern of the wood; in this case, glaze will settle into the pores and make them stand out.

A good glazing stain dries very slowly; some don't dry at all and have to be sprayed over with a coat of lacquer to set them. This gives ample time for experimentation and adjustments. If things don't work out right the first time, wipe all of the glaze off and start again. Try a different color. The effects of glazing stain don't become permanent until a topcoat is added.

Bleach

If your color selection is substantially lighter than the natural color of the wood, you will have to resort to bleach. One major manufacturer of cherry furniture routinely bleaches its pieces as a first step. This is to not necessarily make the piece lighter; it's to remove all color that will fade. The manufacturer then colors the cherry with a coloring system that is more lightfast and proceeds with the finish.

I'll not go into specific bleaching methods, because the safety issues would take several pages to deal with. I will recommend a three-part bleaching system specifically for wood that should be used only after you have completely read all the instructions and precautions on the label. Also, after bleaching wood, be sure to neutralize the bleach and wash any crystalline residue from the piece. That residue can dramatically interfere with any finishing system used.

Oils

If I had to recommend a simple "one-step" finish, it would be an oil finish. Oils produce a very durable finish when used in complete conformity with the instructions on the back of the can. Most are fully transparent; some have added transparent color that nicely accentuates the pattern of open-grain woods. The ones that do contain pigment contain very little.

Because oils penetrate deeply, they do have some drawbacks. I would not recommend using an oil finish on veneer that has been bonded with contact cement; the solvents in the oil can soften a contact-cement bond. Oils—especially colored oils—applied to close-grain woods can make them look blotchy. This is particularly true of woods with a curly figure-birch, maple, some alder, and some varieties of burl.

When choosing among the various types of oil, linseed oil would be a last resort. The various Danish oils are my first choice because of their durability and the fact that they come in an assortment of colors. (I've often used Danish oil as a stain, covering it with lacquer topcoats for extra sheen.) And while I rarely use tung oil, some blends are nontoxic and can be used on items that will contact food . . . or small children.

Fillers

If your veneered work is to have a highly polished finish, some type of filler is a must, especially on open-grained woods. Fillers may be tinted to match the background of the wood or to contrast dramatically with it, further enhancing the pore pattern. In order that the filler and the tinting colors don't hide the iridescence, it is best that they be applied after the surface is stained and completely sealed. Using fillers on bare wood, though more effective, requires a lot of sanding.

If you are spraying on lacquer sealer, spray several light coats rather than one heavy one. The light coats will not penetrate to the bottom of the pores. This will allow the solvent from the filler to be partially absorbed by the wood at the bottom of the pore, making it harden in the pores and dry much more quickly. As you wipe residue from the surface, less filler will be pulled from the pore.

After allowing the filler to dry overnight, sand any residue from the surface, and remember that fillers do not fill completely. If I ever invent one that does, I'll be a wealthy man. Several topcoats with sanding in between will be required before polishing.

TOPCOATS

Due to the persistent work of the advertising industry, the subject of topcoats is one I would rather avoid . . . but I won't. There are great claims made for various varnishes and lacquers. In the industrial spectrum of products, catalyzed lacquers have become very trendy. What to choose, and why?

Topcoats are evaluated by a number of criteria. Their hardness is evaluated by an "impact" test: A piece of wood is coated with the product. After thorough curing, a weight is dropped on the surface and the number of "impacts" it takes to cut through the finish are counted. Tests are also made to determine the coating's resistance to such things as alcohol, grease, and sunlight. The results of these tests can seem very dramatic, but should, taken with a grain of salt.

Several years ago, a sales representative tried to

convince me that I should use his polyurethane varnish in my furniture-finishing operation. His product would withstand 21 impacts. It was impervious to alcohol and grease. The UV inhibitor made it impervious to sunlight. Even spills of fingernail polish remover—if removed quickly—had minimum effect on the coating.

As I listened to his spiel, the immortal words of Archie Bunker came to mind: "Whoop-de-do, whoop-de-do." The impact test did not impress me; the lacquer I was using at the time was good for 18 impacts. The difference of three impacts was not enough to outweigh the slow-drying properties of his varnish, along with the dust challenges that would have to be met. While his product would "spray" well, successive coats wouldn't "bite." That is, the second coat would not dissolve the surface of the first coat and flow into it, as lacquer does. And the samples he showed me had a slightly milky appearance; I could just see this finish over a beautiful mahogany tabletop.

I was interested in all of the things his product was impervious to, but then I got to thinking. Being impervious to almost everything in the world, it would probably be impervious to paint remover—or at least make the remover work hard. As a fine piece of furniture is often refinished several times in its lifetime, a coating that is impossible or difficult to remove is not a blessing. And using a product that resists fingernail polish remover wasn't appealing; such spills have brought me a lot of refinishing work through the years.

What did I do with the two quarts of sample he left? I refinished the front door of the shop, that mahogany door that is exposed to the afternoon sun. In the years that followed, I found his product to be everything he said it was and more.

There is a place for everything.

Lacquer

If you have spray equipment, I highly recommend nitrocellulose lacquer. Do not use the water-resistant or catalyzed types. Both of these can be difficult to remove for refinishing, and before using some of the industrial catalyzed types, you have to don a space suit in order to avoid the added health hazards. Both

also require that all coats be applied within a specified period of time—usually 24 hours.

If all you have is a brush, a fine finish can still be applied. Choose a fast-drying brushing lacquer or a modified lacquer. Some of these products dry dust-free in as little as 20 minutes—which is very important—and dry to a point where another coat can be added in a matter of hours.

Shellac and Varnish

Both shellac and varnish have been around for centuries. I do use both, but mostly in French-polishing concoctions.

As far as I'm concerned, varnish can't hold a candle to lacquer. It is slightly more durable, but taking into consideration the slow drying and dust challenges, I can live without the extra durability and the yellowing that come with age.

Shellac, on the other hand, is a handy product to have around. I have used it as a sealer, for it's quite effective in sealing in pitch and other resins. Years ago, I used orange shellac to add depth and fire to my projects, but this has since been replaced with dye stains and dye toners.

Water-Based Topcoats

I use water-based topcoats very rarely, and due to the vast improvements that are being made in that industry, any information I could give here would be obsolete before this book is printed. Most seem to me to have a slightly milky appearance. I don't like spraying them, and some are difficult or impossible to remove. I have used water-based coatings over decoratively painted pieces and must admit that they are very durable.

Overall Considerations

No matter what topcoat is used, keep it thin. Let some of the texture of the wood show through. On a filled and highly polished tabletop this is, of course impossible, but for those vertical surfaces a little texture is most attractive. It has always been my opinion that the best-looking furniture finish is one that doesn't resemble a finish at all.

PART TWO

Projects

CHAPTER 8

Veneered Lamp

It's always nice to have a small project or two in mind to use up those leftover pieces that are far too precious to throw away. In the case of this project, I had not only leftover veneers, but also a few end cuts of poplar. And it also happened that the drawer full of electrical "stuff" had to be purged. Reviewing all of these things that could either be used or thrown away, I decided to build a lamp (8–1).

PATTERN

I had this vague mental picture of what I wanted to build. Using this visual concept and factoring in the dimensions of the assorted leftover pieces, I drew a pattern on a piece of roofing felt. I got lucky, and things looked good with the first attempt (8–2). That's probably because I had no idea what a veneered lamp should look like in that there are not many veneered lamps around.

SUBSTRATE (GROUND) PREPARATION

I sized two pieces of 8/4 and two pieces of 4/4 poplar. Down the center of the pieces of 4/4, I ran a $3/8$ x $3/16$-inch dado cut (8–3); this was to accommodate the electrical cord. Somewhere around the shop I do have a bit long enough to drill a hole that long, but I've always had trouble getting it to stay in the center.

   If you haven't seen this technique for lamp cords, keep it in mind. It can save a lot of frustration, and it can be fun. Many years ago, I turned a four-foot lamp shaft for a charming young couple who were going to build their very own wooden floor lamp. The young lady was very concerned about the hole down the center of the shaft and asked me several times if I was sure I could bore such a hole in something that long. I reassured her that I could.

8–1. Veneered lamp.

I prepared the turning blank out of two pieces with a dado cut in the center, but in order to mount it on the lathe, I put a 1-inch plug in both ends of the dado cut.

When the couple came to pick up the shaft, the young lady immediately noticed that I had forgotten the hole in the center. I apologized and told her that I would drill the hole. "Only take a second."

I picked up my drill and installed a $3/8$-inch speed bit. They both looked at me as if I were out of my mind. I drilled into one end of the shaft, and then drilled into the other. The couple looked at each other in complete disgust. I held the shaft to my lips and blew; shavings flew from the other end. Without a smile, I looked into four wide eyes and two open mouths and said, "That bit's a lot longer than it looks." All right. I admit it. I'm cruel.

CUTTING THE BLANK

After gluing the pieces together, I marked and, using a band saw, cut one pair of sides, being careful to mark the waste for the mating side (8–4). Then I

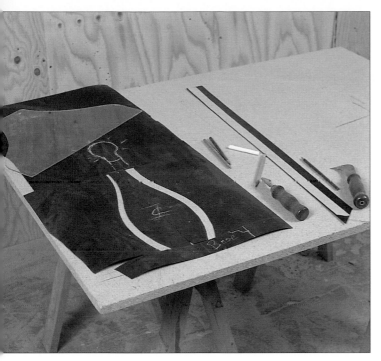

8–2. The pattern for the veneered lamp has been drawn on a piece of roofing felt.

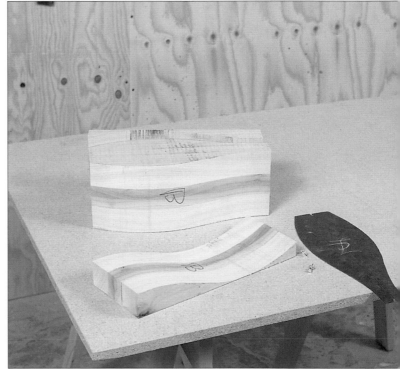

8–4. A cut pair of sides.

8–3. Preparing the substrate. A dado has been cut to accommodate an electric cord.

taped the waste back into position and marked the other sides (8–5). After the blank was cut, I used a rasp to smooth out the very slight irregularities left after my magnificent and almost perfect job (8–6).

PREPARING THE VENEER

I then set a piece of waste on the bench with the substrate on top of it and a magnificent piece of paper-backed olive ash burl between them. After marking this precious scrap (8–7), I cut wide of the line with scissors. The same procedure yielded all four pieces of veneer.

VENEERING THE FIRST TWO SURFACES

It was then a simple matter to spread the glue on the substrate (8–8), set the veneer in place, and clamp the sandwich together (8–9). Did I say simple? Not so. The sandwich tended to slip all over the place. To minimize the slipping, I forced the sandwich together with hand pressure. After readjusting all of the components, I installed the center clamp first. (The scrap of MDF shown under that center clamp in 8–9 is there to strengthen the thin section in that portion of the waste.) Drawing the center clamp down slowly, the slipping stopped. It was then a simple matter to install the end clamps and enjoy a cup of coffee as the glue dried.

After about 20 minutes, I removed the clamps and trimmed the veneer, leaving it ever so slightly long. I

8–5. Marking the other sides.

8–6. Smoothing out irregularities in the sides.

8–7. Marking the veneer.

8–8. Spreading glue on the veneer.

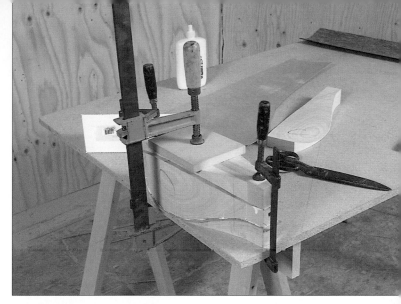

8–9. Clamping the assembly.

let the first two sides dry overnight and hoped that little extra length would not be eaten up by shrinkage.

The next morning, I sanded off that extra length with some stiff sandpaper (8–10) in preparation for veneering the other two sides.

OOPS

Above I mentioned that I did an almost perfect job of band-sawing the substrate. I lied. On the last side I cut, the blade came out of the block, leaving me a two-piece caul with no support in the center. Undaunted, I set the pieces in position and taped them together. That piece of paper shown in 8–11 is to prevent the masking tape from sticking to the substrate.

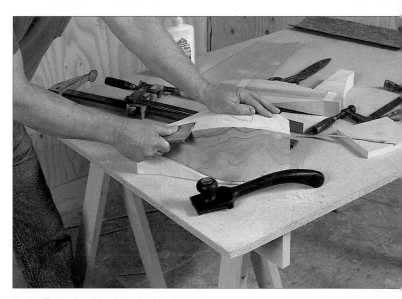

8–10. Trimming the bonded veneer.

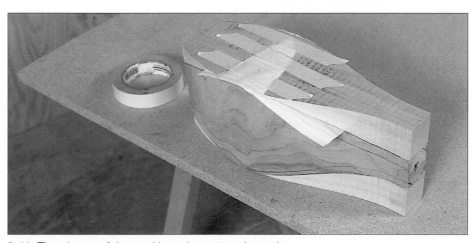

8–11. The pieces of the caul have been taped together.

The masking tape only met part of the challenge, because by the time I smoothed out the path of the wayward blade, the center of the taped caul did not fit quite well enough. This was corrected by placing a piece of outdoor carpet between the caul and the veneer to take up the slack (8–12).

FINAL PROCEDURES

After allowing the assembly to dry overnight again, I trimmed the last two pieces and sketched a line down one edge of the veneered block. That line tapered from the center of the bulge to one corner of an octagon I had laid out on the top. I then cut along this line with a spokeshave, smoothing the cut with a rasp (8–13). (You didn't think this was going to be a simple, four-sided lamp, did you? No way! Too easy. This lamp starts out square and becomes octagonal.)

Once I was satisfied with the cut, I used the side of a pencil to transfer its shape to a piece of paper (8–14). After cutting the paper, I used it as a pattern to mark the other sides (8–15). I installed the block in a fixture and shaped it with a spokeshave and rasp, turning the top end into an octagon. Then I spread glue on the bare surfaces, preparing them for veneer using the dry-glue process.

After bonding strips of contrasting veneer, I carefully trimmed the excess using my veneer saw—the

8–12. A piece of carpet between the caul and veneer ensures a good fit.

8–13. Smoothing the cut on the veneered block.

8–14. Transferring the shape to a sheet of paper.

8–15. *Marking the sides.*

8–16. *Trimming the excess.*

8–17. *Finishing the trimming using a curved stick with sand-paper.*

one sharpened like a knife (8–16). In any place where the veneer saw indicated it wanted to leave the veneer long, I let it do so and finished the job using a curved stick with sandpaper glued to it (8–17).

BASE

To accurately cut the veneer for the base—which will be bonded with dry glue—I first made a pattern for the pieces (8–18), referencing the bottom of the pattern to the bottom edge of the block.

Using the 45-degree lines on my paper cutter to check the accuracy of the pattern's marks, I cut the veneer (8–19), leaving the pencil line on the stock so that the stock would be slightly long.

8–18. *Referencing the bottom of the pattern with the bottom of the block, in preparation for making patterns for the base.*

8–19. *Cutting the veneer with a paper cutter.*

I bonded the veneer by setting it with the bottom edge and gently rolling it over the curve (8–20). Then I trimmed the slight excess on the curved edge flush with the sandpaper-covered stick (8–21). The opposing side was worked in the same manner.

To fill in the remaining sides, I cut pieces that had a little excess width at the bottom. I began bonding

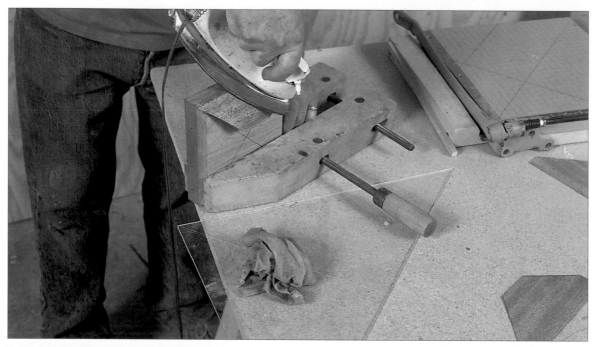

8–20. Bonding the veneer to the base.

8–21. Trimming the excess of the curved edge.

these pieces on the top of the block, making sure that the miter cuts fit perfectly (8–22). After trimming the bottom edge and a little sanding, I wet one corner with lacquer thinner and took a photo of it (8–23). Looks like it grew there, doesn't it?

Prior to a little sanding, I drilled a hole in the base for the cord and fastened it to the body with dry-wall screws. After the lamp's journey through the paint shop for clear coats, I installed the electrical fixtures. All that was left was shopping for a shade. This My Lady did, for there is no way I could ever do a proper job.

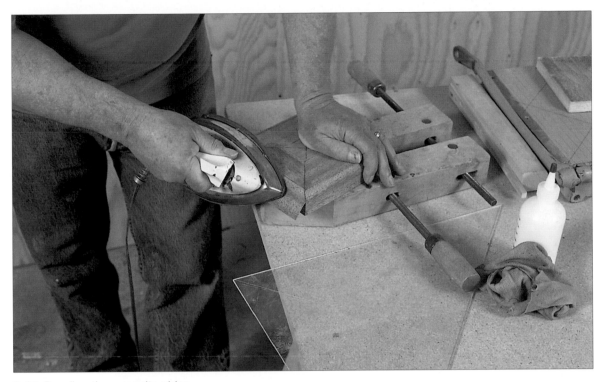

8–22. Bonding the opposite sides.

8–23. The finished base.

CHAPTER 9

Blanket Chest

Boxes of all sizes and shapes are fun things to veneer. Fun, that is, if the veneer itself is not difficult to work with. In the case of this blanket chest (9–1 and 9–2), my client selected lacewood from my box of veneer samples. I had made a mental note to remove and burn that particular sample after my last lacewood project, but the note got lost. Don't read me wrong; I think lacewood is beautiful, but it is very inconsistent in thickness. This commission was going to require the hot press in conjunction with urea-formaldehyde glue to make up for the inconsistencies.

There were a couple of things about the project that appealed to me. I did manage to persuade my client to select a blanket chest with dimensions that would conform to a pile of pecan plywood leftovers I had stored for some time. She indicated that she didn't want any metal lid supports inside the chest to snag blankets, and that no hinges should show. When she agreed to a simple removable cover, I began counting the profits.

Then when she mentioned a diamond match for the lacewood and rounded edges, the expense involved in making the chest grew to a point that I was sure I would loose the commission. I didn't. So, for your benefit, Gentle Reader, I'll describe the project.

9–1 and 9–2 (following page). Blanket chest.

9–2.

VENEER LAYOUT AND TAPING

As if having to veneer the outside of the chest with lacewood wasn't bad enough, the cedar I ordered for the lining came in short pieces. Had I used them vertically, there would have been too much waste. The alternative was to trim the ends and tape them into longer lengths (9–3). After taping several short pieces together, I cut the appropriate length for the inside of the chest, trimmed the edges, and taped them together to provide the needed width (9–4). As indicated in 9–5, a linoleum knife makes a handy straightedge for tearing tape. As also shown in 9–5, I had to employ lots of pins and any handy weights

to hold the cantankerous cedar flat. I sure wish I'd had a few more jointer planes.

After unpacking the lacewood, the first step was to make my squiggle chalk mark on one edge so that I would keep all cuts running in the proper direction (9–6). I did notice some iridescence variation from one side of the sheet to the other, but if a cut of this veneer is turned, the results are devastating.

After cutting a number of lengths about an inch longer than needed, to form a shorter diamond, I

9–4. Taping cedar pieces together to form the inside of the chest.

9–3. Taping the cedar pieces together for extra length.

9–5. Using a linoleum knife to cut tape.

9–6. Making a chalk mark on the edge of lacewood piece veneer.

9–7. Smoothing the veneer edges. The workbench contains layout lines, and will be used for the front and back of the chest.

9–8. Cutting the first diamond.

noted that the edges of the veneer were almost clean enough to make a good joint. A couple of passes with an abrasive shooting block made them perfect (9–7). As shown in 9–8 and some of the following photos, there are some layout lines on my "workbench." This workbench will be cut in half and used for the front and back of the chest; thus, the alder facing.

Once the pieces were taped together, using the layout lines on the bench I cut the first diamond (9–8). The waste pieces were then turned over and placed to form the second diamond. Note the X's on the waste pieces in 9–9. These are on the underside of the squiggle line. Theoretically, this should give both of these diamonds similar light-reflecting characteristics. In 9–11, it looks as if this is to be the case, but only after bonding and finishing will we know for sure.

The waste was then taped and trimmed to size . As shown in 9–10, a iron was used to firmly set the tape. After the longer diamonds were taped, they were slid under the shorter ones and marked for final trimming with the point of a linoleum knife (9–11). (No, I'm not cutting with that knife; I'm only making a very fine and accurate mark.) Once the diamonds were joined, the panel was complete for now. The periphery would be trimmed after bonding.

As I cut farther into the sheet of lacewood, it became necessary to trim quite a bit off one edge to maintain a good pattern match. But before trimming, I made another squiggle chalk line so that I wouldn't loose direction (9–12).

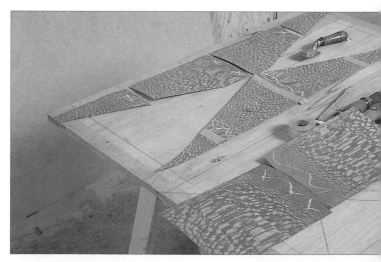

9–9. Forming the second diamond with the waste pieces from the first.

9–10. *Using a household iron to set the tape on the waste pieces.*

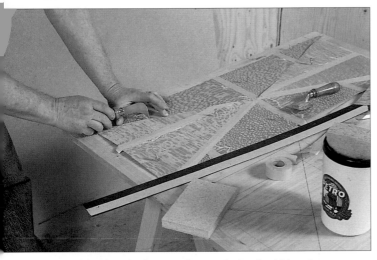

9–11. *Marking the longer diamonds for final trimming.*

9–12. *Another chalk line is made on the lacewood to ensure that the proper direction is followed.*

9–13. *Using perforated tape to join two pieces.*

Progressing even farther, I started putting more pieces of leftover scrap together. In some cases, I didn't know what side would be faceup, so I resorted to perforated tape for the joints (9–13). This tape is not as strong as the solid type, but it can be left in place even if it winds up in the glue line.

By the time I got to taping up the last small diamonds for the ends of the chest, I was picking up pieces from the floor. Most of these were devoid of chalk marks, but judging from the curl and holding them to the light, I was able to keep the reflections in order (9–14).

9–14. *Judging proper match from light reflections.*

PRESSING THE VENEER

After the cutting, fitting, and taping, I was relieved to arrive at the relatively fast-moving part of the operation. I chose urea-formaldehyde for this project because of the texture of the lacewood. This glue would fill the irregularities in the veneer and produce a much smoother surface than any other method I could think of. I mixed enough glue to bond the first panel (9–15). (I always save empty glue containers and other plastic containers for mixing glue. These I don't wash out, but let the glue dry in them. Usually some distorting of the container will free the dried glue, and the container can be used again.) For the lacewood, I wanted a slightly thicker glue, so I added glue to water in the proportions of one cup glue to one-third cup water. After mixing thoroughly, I added a dab more water—about one-sixth of a cup.

I then spread the glue with a notched trowel held at a 45-degree angle, being very careful to see that the glue was spread all the way to the edges (9–16). After making several final passes with the trowel, I set the taped cedar panel in place and secured it with masking tape on each corner to keep it in position (9–17).

Turning the panel over, I placed the diamond on it and reduced the thickness of the tape in the center

9–15. Mixing urea-formaldehyde to be used in bonding the veneer.

9–16. Spreading the glue.

9–17. Adding masking tape to the corners of the cedar panel.

9–18. Using a sanding block to reduce the thickness of the tape.

with a sanding block (9–18)—there were about five thicknesses of tape there. Then I prepared the face of the panel by running some paper and painter's tape around the area to which the lacewood would be bonded, placing the tape so glue couldn't reach more than ¼ inch beyond the area (9–19). This is to prevent glue squeeze-out from sticking to the substrate in the border area. The border will be applied with dry glue after the chest's assembly, and cleaning of the urea-formaldehyde squeeze-out could become a nightmare.

With the painter's tape in place, I set the veneers in position using the diagonal layout lines I had transferred to the painter's tape. Then I drew a few more lines and set marks around the veneers that were unlikely to be covered with glue.

After spreading the glue, I quickly replaced the veneers, securing them with masking tape as I did the cedar on the back side.

The press had been closed and the heater running for about an hour, so the table as well as the aluminum plate were quite hot. I set the panel into the press and, after installing the spanners and the clamps, I made several passes over all the clamps, pulling them down with equal torque.

As a final step, I placed a dab of fresh glue on the edge of the aluminum plate. This would tell me when the glue was cured.

That curing didn't take long. After ten minutes, I could no longer dent the dab of glue with my finger-nail. I waited another five minutes before opening the press, because the cedar on the underside of the panel was not exposed to as much heat as the lacewood directly beneath the aluminum plate.

When I opened the press, I noted that the squeeze-out from the cedar side was not rock-hard, so I flipped the panel over and closed the press again. This time, I only installed a few clamps, and these were not firmly pulled down. I wanted only to expose the cedar side to the higher temperature of the aluminum plate.

Five minutes after flipping the panel, I probed at the squeeze-out with a screwdriver. It was rock-hard.

The front, back, top, and ends were all pressed singly in the same manner. The bottom? Gentle Reader, I cheated. I only bonded the cedar, using no veneer on the other side. I wanted to see just how much the cedar would pull the panel. The glue had grabbed and the moisture had left the panel so quickly that the pull was slight. It only bowed the panel about ⅛ inch over its length. This slight bow could be easily removed when fastening the bottom in place. I made a mental note. (I also made a note on the wall; one that won't get lost unless we paint the shop—which is highly unlikely.)

After taking the warm panel from the press, I quickly removed the masking tape by pulling it back over itself (9–20). The press had done a good job of firmly seating the tape and I didn't want to take the chance of pulling off the surface of the veneer. Had I

9–19. Running tape around the face of the panel.

9–20. Removing the masking tape from the panel.

waited for the tape to cool, this would have been a likely situation—if I could remove the tape at all.

As the panels were removed from the press, I piled them on sawhorses with stickers between them, allowing the moisture to leave the panel. As I stacked the panels, I noted that the painter's tape did its job well. Squeeze-out from the veneer flowed over the surface of the tape rather than under it. And the tape did not hold firmly to the panel because of the heat.

After several days, I removed the painter's tape in preparation to trim the diamond edges. Removing the tape—and scraping squeeze-out from the edges—was a project that required safety glasses. The rock-hard blobs of glue shattered and flew from the paper as it was pulled from the panel, and pieces of the squeeze-out were propelled from the edge of the scraper with considerable velocity.

Using a router, 3/4-inch straight cutter, and a guide, I then trimmed the outer edge of the diamonds (9–21 and 9–22), setting the router to a depth that would just cut through the veneer. In any places where the router didn't cut quite deep enough—or cut too deeply—a scraper finished the job (9–23). This was a good test for the press, for the difference between "too deep" and "not quite deep enough" was only a couple of thousandths of an inch.

Before assembly, I removed all the tape and did some preliminary sanding on the lacewood.

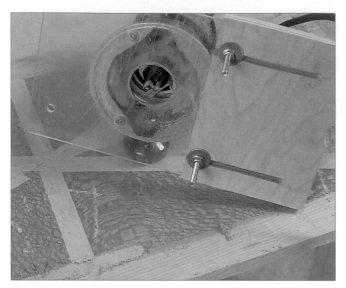

9–22. A close-up of the router and guides used.

9–23. Using a scraper to level the substrate in the trimmed area.

CHEST ASSEMBLY

After a trip to the table saw to cut the necessary rabbets, I assembled the chest with drywall screws and glue. Illus. 9–24 shows the 1/4-inch groove cut in the top edge of the pieces. A router and slotting cutter were also used to cut a matching groove in the edge of the pieces for the lid. After assembling the chest, I installed a spline in the groove and assembled the lid with nails (9–25). The spline would hold the lid in register and provide a seal.

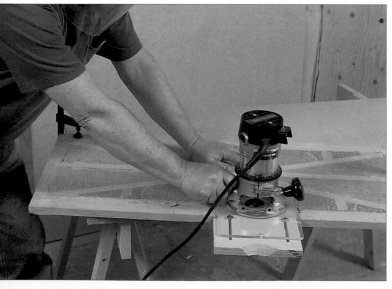

9–21. Trimming the outer edges of the diamonds.

9–24. *Assembling the chest with drywall screws and glue. A groove has been cut in the top edge of the pieces to accept the lid.*

9–26. *Spreading glue for the borders.*

9–25. *Using nails to assemble the lid.*

9–27. *Using a file to remove glue and dust particles from the edge of the veneer.*

I will confess that I had a difficult time prying the lid off, but then thinned the exposed portion of the spline with a scraper so that the lid could be lifted off easily. I was lucky; the lid could be replaced in either of its possible configurations—either with its front against the front or its back against the front.

I then rounded the edges with a router. I made a 1/2-inch radius around the top and a 3/8-inch radius down the sides. While spreading the glue for the borders, I was glad that I'd invested in a good brush

(9–26). Cutting that line along the already installed veneer would have been impossible with a cheap one.

After the glue was dry, I went around the edges of the lacewood with the edge of a file (9–27). This was to remove dust particles that might have settled near the joint and also to thin out any glue that might have collected in a puddle along the edges of the lacewood.

Next, I marked the location of the joints at the corner of the border, carrying the line onto the field

(9–28). These joints were not quite at a 45-degree angle. Rather, the line extended from the corner of the field to a point where the round in the edge started. I didn't want the tip of the top and bottom border pieces to wrap around the curve. You'll see how it works in the following photos.

On the face and back of the chest, I held a straight-edge against the field and marked its location with the tip of a linoleum knife (9–29); these lines were to be used for cutting the joint between the border and field.

After ironing a piece of border on the end of the

9–30. Cutting the miter joint.

9–28. Marking the miter joints on the border corner.

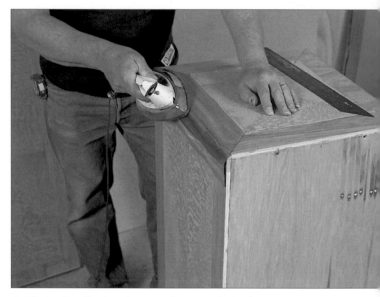

9–31. Ironing the border over the rounded edge.

9–29. Using a linoleum knife to mark the location of the field.

chest, I trimmed the corner joints using the lines that were carried onto the field as guides (9–30). Then I wet the piece and continued carefully ironing

it over the rounded edge, stopping about 1¹/₂ inches short of the joint on the other side (9–31).

After rolling the chest over, I clipped the ends of the cut so that I could see the marks made previously with the tip of the linoleum knife. Positioning the straightedge on the marks, I cut the joint using my modified veneer saw. Illus. 9–32 shows a piece of laminate backing sheet under the unbonded veneer to prevent the saw from damaging the edge of the lacewood.

I wouldn't want you to think that all of this work went without incident. That only happens in how-to videos and on Saturday-afternoon television.

9-32. A close-up of the cut joint. A piece of plastic laminate is being used under the unbonded veneer to prevent the veneer saw from damaging it.

9-33. Using a mallet to force a piece of border into place.

Ironing down one piece of border, I noticed that it overlapped the lacewood for about an inch at the end. To force it into place, I held a block of wood against the edge of the veneer and tapped the block gently with a mallet (9-33). Fortunately, the veneer was not completely bonded near the joint. The blow did crack the veneer, but once the errant edge was in place, the warm iron forced the crack back together.

I did try to cut the joints slightly long, but in one instance I left the piece so long that I had to slide a rod under the veneer to buckle it enough to get the

edges together (9-34). Illus. 9-35 gives an idea of how large a buckle can be forced down.

I also cut one joint a little short—about half the thickness of a utility-knife blade. After thoroughly chastising myself, I made a note to put a little patching putty in it. Putty is very difficult to detect when two contrasting woods meet.

After rounding those corner pieces, the straight pieces were easy. I merely pinned a rough-cut piece of border in place and marked the joints using the

9-34. Using a rod to buckle the veneer near a joint.

9-35. Using an iron to force down the buckle near a joint.

lines on the field as a guide (9–36). If the miter joints didn't fit perfectly, I adjusted them with a sanding block. And after the adjustments, if the whole cut came up a little short, I trimmed a little off the edge that met the lacewood.

As fate would have it, the pieces of veneer on hand were one inch short of making the long border cuts. So . . . I put a keystone in the center of the piece, to make up a design that would allow me to use the shorter pieces (9–37).

Even with the few minor challenges, the border work on the chest went well, and the pieces at the corners fit so well they looked as if they "grew" there (9–38).

The top posed a new set of challenges. To meet these, I resorted to pattern felt. After making a 45-degree cut in the end of a piece of felt, I held it against the intended joint with the lacewood and folded the 45-degree cut over the edge and around the corner. Then I made a mark at the center of the curved edge (9–39). Using that mark, I cut the felt at right angles with the edge that was held against the lacewood. Marking the veneer with the resultant pattern, I cut the first piece of border. After bonding this first piece next to the field, I wetted it and rolled it over the edge and around the corner, being careful

9–36. Cutting the final miter joints.

9–38. A close-up showing the fit of the chest border pieces.

9–37. Adding a "key stone" to permit the use of shorter veneers.

9–39. Marking a pattern to be used to cut the corner pieces.

that each tiny area was bonded before preceding. Loose spots in the rounded edge would be all but impossible to correct.

The first time I tried bending veneer lengthwise over a curved edge like this, I didn't wet it sufficiently. The face of the veneer fractured slightly, leaving tiny slivers standing. In the years that followed, I've used plenty of water and even let it soak in for a minute or two.

Next, I turned the pattern over and checked the fit. The fit was good except in the area marked with a chalked arrow in 9–40. The first piece was a bit long in this area because I had to force the veneer around that double-curved spot. After cutting the second

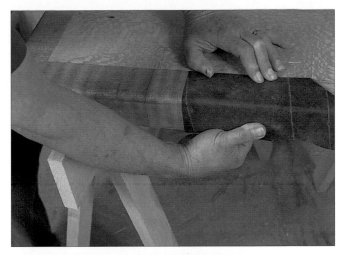

9–42. *Using a piece of felt to check the joints.*

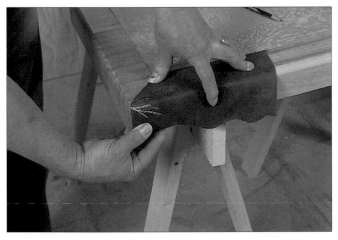

9–40. *Checking the fit of the pattern on the opposite edge.*

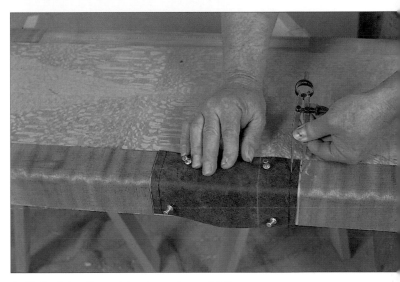

9–43. *Scribing the void onto a piece of felt.*

9–41. *A close-up of the fit of the corner.*

piece, I trimmed about 3/32 inch at the point of the arrow. Did the second cut fit? Take a look at 9–41.

Some of the pieces became slightly distorted as I bonded them. To check each to make sure a good joint would result, I used the straight edge of a piece of felt (9–42).

As I fit each of the corners first, I was left with four areas to fill in that were closed at both ends. To accurately cut the fill, I scribed the void onto felt (9–43). Then, using my straightedge held over the scribed line, I transferred the mark to the veneer (9–44).

No, all did not go perfectly. In instances where the fill was a bit long, I was able to compress it into place. In those other places, a sliver worked (9–45). I know I should be ashamed, but I'm not. The world is not going to stop turning because I fit a sliver into an open joint. The Old Timers often used far bigger slivers than I do.

ADDING A FINISH

After a good sanding, I gave the chest a very weak but penetrating coat of bright-orange dye stain. This developed the iridescence of the veneer. It developed to such an extent that the effects were quite harsh; the contrast between the diamonds made them look like completely different woods. After sealing and sanding the chest, I gave it a coat of burnt-umber glazing stain. The glaze was brushed on and almost completely wiped off. The tiny bit that remained on the surface softened the diamonds considerably, and the stain left in the pores developed the grain pattern most beautifully.

9–44. Transferring the mark to the veneer.

9–45. A sliver is used to fill an open joint.

CHAPTER 10

Kidney-Shaped Desk

Developments in man-made boards over the last few years have made the construction of curved cabinetry so easy that a great deal of the challenge is gone. Ten years ago, I would have built the case for this desk out of several layers of 1/8-inch-thick poplar plywood. Twenty years ago, I might have chosen a staved construction. The case described in the following pages is made of 3/8-inch luan "bender board."

If you have never worked with any curved cabinetry, consider this project (10–1 to 10–3) for your first time out. It is not as difficult as might first be thought. Although the case is curved, the drawers are square and fit into square openings. The only challenge comes in fitting the drawer fronts, and that is not so difficult.

My client chose nara as the field veneer for the case. This was bordered with movingue in the front

10–1 to 10–3 (next page). Three views of the kidney–shaped desk. Shown here is a front view.

10–2. A close-up of the top of the desk.

10–3. A rear view of the desk.

and zebrawood to the rear, around the drawers. Strips of mahogany were used to make the legs appear to flow into the case. Her eyes lit up when I showed her some olive ash burl I had in stock and suggested it for the top. That light faltered somewhat as she studied the wrinkled veneer and asked, "You will be able to get it flat, won't you?"

I smiled. "Gee, I hope so. If not, I'll throw in a big desk pad." Wish I had my camera to capture her expression.

Knowing that this desk would receive tender loving care, I chose to bond the case veneers with contact cement. The nara and movingue veneers were very flat, so I anticipated no challenges. Besides, the speed of working with contact cement would make up for some of the other challenges that I mention below.

PREPARING THE FORM FOR THE CURVED CASE

Layout

My client furnished general specifications. The desk could be no more than 54 inches wide. When she held out her hands to indicate the depth (" . . . about so deep"), I quickly drew my tape and measured the distance between her hands—28 inches. Also, "The desk must have two file drawers—for those hanging kind of files—two drawers for 'stuff,' and a pencil drawer in the center would be nice. Now, I don't want to be banging my legs on the sides of the desk, so give me plenty of knee room."

The next morning, after reviewing my specification notes, I gazed longingly at the ceiling and said, "Plenty of knee room, two file drawers, and only 54 inches wide. Lord, why is it that I always have to fit five pounds of stuff into a three-pound bag?"

Hearing no answer, I placed a sheet of particleboard on a pair of sawhorses and went to work. First, I laid out a centerline and the width and length extremities I had to work with, along with a 24-inch kneehole. Then I began making light pencil lines, locating the drawers—making sure there would be plenty of room for files. Working on the curved outline of the case, my lines increased in darkness as I arrived at the final shape (10–4).

When I found satisfaction with the outline, I drove some small finishing nails at 3-inch intervals along the darkest line and stretched a piece of 5/8-inch band steel along them. This would ensure that I had a smooth curve. I then marked the outline of the band steel with a red pencil to keep from confusing the final shape with all of the preliminary lines (10–5).

Using a tape measure, I plotted several points on the right side of the center so that I could draw a line to cut along that would leave me plenty of room for waste.

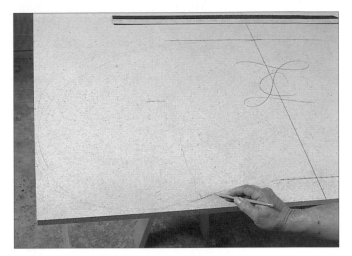

10–4. Drawing a pattern for the desk.

10–5. Marking an outline along the band steel.

Cutting the Form

With my trusty saber saw in hand, I cut out the left half of the desk to about 1 inch beyond the centerline as accurately as possible and freed the piece from the sheet by cutting along the plotted line on the right. I also cut in about 1/8 inch along the centerline. This would ensure that I never lost the centerline and could find it from both sides of the piece. Then I smoothed any irregularities in the cut with a horseshoe rasp (10–6). You know, I never could guide that saber saw through a sheet of anything with great precision, but I've become very proficient with that horseshoe rasp. At this point, I had a piece of particleboard, half of which could be used as a template.

10–6. Smoothing the cut with a rasp.

This piece I screwed to the opposite corner of the sheet of particleboard using four 1⅝-inch drywall screws. Then with a ½-inch straight cutter in my router, I followed the smoothed outline of the template, letting the bit's shank run on the template (10–7). As my bit had only about ⅜ inch of cutting flutes, I had to make several passes at increasing depths.

I could have rough-cut with a saber saw and used a router and flush trimmer—the bearing riding on the template—but I have an aversion for saber saws and resort to them when there is absolutely no other way.

With that cut made, I marked the centerline through the saw kerf I described above. After flipping the template over, I again screwed it to the sheet and cut the other side. Now, I was able to turn the assembly over and cut the rest of the first piece using the second as a template. Simple.

While the pieces were screwed together, I did some more layout work, marking the exact location of the drawers, letting the lines flow to the extremes of the piece and then continuing them vertically on the edges of both pieces (10–8).

10–7. Cutting, using a template and a router.

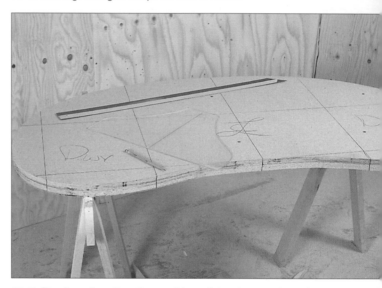

10–8. The lines locating the position of the drawers have been marked.

10–9. Assembling the form.

Assembly

After cutting eight pieces of 2 x 4 to length, I passed one edge of these pieces over the jointer several times to cut back beyond the eased edges. Placing a sharp corner of each 2 x 4 on several edge marks of the particleboard, I assembled the form, using drywall screws (10–9).

At the front of the form, I paced two 2 x 4s side by side. Here, unfortunately, there would be a joint in the bender board, and I wanted to have something solid behind it.

Preparing the Bender Board

An eight-foot length of bender board would span from drawer compartment to drawer compartment with a little length to spare–which was perfect. Unfortunately, my supplier was out of 8 x 4 sheets of bender board, so I had to splice two cuttings from a 4 x 8 sheet—one more step, but not a difficult one.

Clamping one piece of bender board along the factory edge of a piece of particleboard, I taped the second to it. The edge of the particleboard established a straight line, and I used paper veneer tape, of course. A couple of passes with a hand plane were required to make the joint fit true (10–10).

After the tape dried, I turned the pieces over and,

10–11. A stick has been placed under the bender board to help squeeze the joint together.

placing my hand under the joint, lifted it enough to run a bead of glue in the V-shaped opening. After retrieving my hand, I placed a stick under one piece of bender board, squeezing the joint together a little tighter (10–11). (Two strips, comprised of four pieces of bender board, were prepared in this manner.)

Now, you may think this is a poor way to join the edges of bender board. So did I the first time I tried it. But you will find the joint surprisingly strong, especially if there is time for overnight drying.

After scraping the squeeze-out from the joints, the next step was to spread the glue. Rather than use a brush, roller, or trowel, I used a glue bottle to dribble a $1/8$-inch bead of glue at 1-inch spacings both lengthwise and across the grain (10–12). As assembly time could be lengthy, this would ensure that

10–12. Spreading the glue on the bender board.

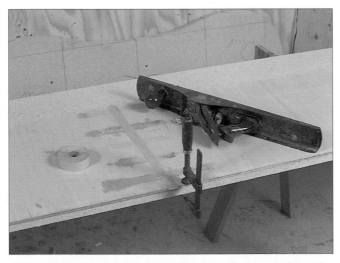

10–10. The two bender-board pieces have been taped together and the joint smoothed.

there would be fresh glue squeezed from the bead when the clamps were applied.

I then set the second strip atop the one that had been spread—offsetting the joints by 4 inches—and carefully carried them to the form. Positioning the strips so that the space between the joints was centered over the centerline, I drove one drywall screw through both into the form to hold the sheets in place. After bending the sheets around one side of the form, I recruited a clamp to hold them loosely against the 2 x 4 at the drawer opening; then I did the same with the other side. It was then a simple matter to install band clamps at top and bottom. Did I say simple? Folks, if you can draft some help for this operation, do it!

To ensure that the strips would be held firmly at the joint area, I screwed a couple of sticks over the spot, with 2½-inch screws passing through the sticks, bender board, and into the 2 x 4 (10–13). I also used a few screws at the drawer openings to ensure a good bond (10–14). As the screws didn't seen to distort the bender board, I decided to forgo the sticks that I used in the front.

The case was allowed to dry overnight.

10–14. Screws are also being used at the drawer openings to ensure that the strips remain firmly in place.

Bending the Moldings

While the case was still on the form, I decided to bend the moldings that would be needed. I selected lightweight mahogany for the moldings and cut the necessary pieces. After thoroughly wetting them, I let the moisture soak in for about a half-hour. Then, after screwing a couple of pieces of waste bender board in the kneehole area, I clamped the molding sticks in that area and began working them around the form (10–15).

I used an iron set on high to heat the pieces where they made the tight bend in the drawer area. You'll find it remarkable how pliable wood becomes with a little heat.

After the sticks cooled and dried for an hour, I removed them from the form. They did spring back considerably, but I had relieved enough tension from the wood that it would be easy to fasten the pieces to the case with glue and small brads.

Trimming the Case

Before removing the case from the form, I trimmed the waste at the drawer areas. This I did by screwing a couple of sticks to the form as supports for a platform over which I could guide a handheld circular saw (10–16). After the case was marked according

10–13. Two sticks are being used to ensure that the strips remain firmly in place.

10–15. Forming the moldings around the form.

10–16. Trimming the waste at the drawer areas.

to the drawing on the form, it became a simple matter to remove the waste in the right location and at the proper angle.

Drawer Fronts

After the case was removed from the form, pieces of a little more than sufficient width for the drawer fronts were spread with glue and held to the form with drywall screws (10–17).

Cutting the Legs

After squaring and sizing the stock, the first order of business was to cut the design in the upper portion of the leg. I cut the square or flat portion of the design on a table saw by making several passes over a dado head. Next, I clamped the four legs together and set up a guide for my router. The concave por-

10–17. The drawer fronts were added to the form.

tion was then cut with a router and 1-inch core-box cutter (10–18).

Normally, I taper legs on the jointer, but these being quite short, I thought it safer to cut the taper on the band saw. Besides, I wanted all of those wedges that would be the waste. It's always helpful to have a good supply of wedges on hand.

10–18. Cutting the concave portion of the legs with a router and core-box cutter.

I also used the band saw to cut the notch in the back of the leg that would fit around the case. The legs that fit next to the drawer compartments were a little tricky to cut. These were cut by eyeball and trial and error. A rasp was used to make the fit perfect, as shown in 10–22.

Drawer Compartments

Using the layout lines drawn on the form, I made a list of pieces needed for the drawer compartments (10–19). I also marked the location of the notches that would have to be cut for the legs.

Using a router, I then cut dadoes that would receive the drawer–compartment components (10–20).

After fastening the drawer-compartment components to the top of the bent case, I rubbed in a few glue blocks before installing the bottom (10–21).

The legs were then fastened using screws and a generous amount of glue (10–22).

10–19 (above left). Using the layout lines on the form to determine the pieces for the drawer compartments. 10–20 (above right). Cutting the dadoes for the drawer–compartment components.

Before I started to assemble the drawers and mount the hardware, I spread glue on and screwed two strips of bender board in the kneehole area to form

10–21. Glue blocks are rub-glued in place to reinforce the drawer compartment.

the pencil-drawer front. On the ends of the strips, I glued blocks on which to fasten the drawer sides. Illus. 10–23 shows the stick behind the clamp toward the center of the drawer. This is to hold the feathered edge of the block firmly against the bender board.

After the drawers were installed, pieces were

10–22. Fastening the legs to the case.

marked and band-sawn to support the drawer fronts. These can be seen installed on the small drawer, as shown in 10–24. Note that the false front of the drawer is installed square with the sides and that one drawer side (right) is slightly longer than the other, these dimensions having been taken from the layout drawing on the top.

10–24. A view showing the pieces used to support the drawer front.

Cutting the drawer fronts to size can be a little tricky because of the curve. I eliminated the curve by screwing the drawer-front stock to a flat piece of particleboard (10–25), allowing me to safely run the stock through the table saw.

10–23. Two strips of bender board have been screwed to the kneehole area to form the pencil-drawer front.

10–25. The drawer-front stock has been screwed to a piece of particleboard so it can be safely trimmed.

As the glue dried on the assembled pencil drawer, I patched and sanded the case (10–26). I used the disc grinder to do the heavy work on an ill-fitting drawer front, and then switched to a small belt sander.

I was now ready to veneer. I began the process by laying out the design. As it was difficult to draw lines square with the top of the tightly curved surfaces, I took measurements from the centerline using a story stick composed of a piece of 5/8-inch band steel covered with masking tape (10–27). When doing layout on curved surfaces, a good, flexible straightedge is a must (10–28).

Opening the package of nara veneer, I was delighted to find that there was a defect—pardon me, a natural wood characteristic—on one edge of several slices. This I planed for the center of the front panel (10–29).

With the veneers selected and the layout lines in place, it was time to spread the contact cement (10–30). I must say that spreading glue on the ben-

10–26. Patching and sanding the case.

10–28. Laying out the veneer design using a flexible straight-edge.

10–27. Laying out the veneer design on the curved case surface using a story stick.

10–29. The veneers laid out on the case.

10–30. Spreading the contact cement on the case.

der board felt like spreading a sponge. Two rather heavy coats were needed.

Normally, I spread glue on the entire veneer pieces before doing any cutting, because that coat of glue on the back of the veneer imparts considerable strength. Illus. 10–31 shows the veneer hanging over the bench-top slightly on one edge and one end. This way, I can spread glue to the edges without getting contact cement all over my worktable and the face of the veneer.

As the factory edge of the veneer looked good and straight, I did no more than run a shooting block over it to prepare it for the center joint (10–32). This

10–31. Spreading glue on the veneers.

10–33. Positioning the first cut of veneer.

not only smoothed out any irregularities, it also removed any contact cement that may have flowed over the edge.

I then carefully positioned the first cut. As shown in 10–33, a slip stick is placed under the body of the veneer and at the top and bottom. It isn't heavy brown paper, folks. It is plastic-laminate backing sheet. In this instance the plastic laminate is a must, because I intended to do a lot of cutting with the veneer and slip sticks in place. A knife wouldn't easily cut through the backing sheet, as would be the case with paper. At this point, retrieving pieces of slip stick would be impossible.

After withdrawing the center slip stick, I used a roller on the veneer, leaving the left slip stick in place a little less than 1 inch under the edge (10–34). I did avoid rolling the top, bottom, and the edge with the

10–32. Smoothing the veneer with a shooting block to prepare it for the joint.

slip stick under it. That way, I could trim the veneer for the next joint without the waste sticking (10–35). And while the slip stick was in place, I ran the shooting block over the joint edge (10–36).

With the first cut down, I set the second in position. Illus. 10–37 shows the steel rod placed about an inch from the joint. After rolling down the bulk of the second cut, I withdrew the rod and used a roller on the bulge it left. With my free hand, I made sure that the second cut didn't ride up over the first (10–38).

To make certain that both edges of the joint were firmly bonded and the surfaces even, I made a firm pass down the joint with the back of a linoleum knife (10–39).

The third and fourth veneer cuts presented a little challenge, as there was a small, severely wrinkled patch on both. Normally, I would have discarded those pieces, but have included them here for demonstration purposes. First, I moistened the area. Then I quickly warmed it with an iron set on one-quarter heat. Going to the edge of the wrinkled patch, I began to rock the iron back and forth lengthwise, slowly advancing it across the wrinkled patch (10–40).

With all the pieces of the field in place, I then trimmed the ends. Illus. 10–41 shows pushpins being used to prevent the straightedge from drifting. I had been using a veneer saw for cutting the joints, but noticed that I wasn't making much progress with it cutting across grain. To speed things, I switched to my "one-tooth" saw.

Removing the slip stick was a bit of a challenge, especially in the area that was ironed. But with a little lifting, twisting, and tugging and a few choice verbal encouragements, it did come out.

In the previous photos you've seen me using a roller to bond the veneer cuts. That isn't quite enough pressure to do the job completely. Were I to apply sufficient pressure to the roller, the roller would break apart. Often, I use my veneer hammer to complete the job, but on this occasion it was covered with hide glue from a previous project. Rather than clean it, I selected a soft pine scrap and proceeded to finish the job of bonding (10–42). How much pressure do you apply? Don't break the stick; just bend it a lot.

The thin strips of border went down quite easily. I

10–34. Using a roller on the veneer. The center stick has been removed, but the left one remains in place.

10–35. Trimming the veneer for the next joint.

10–36. Using a shooting block on the joint edge.

10–37. Setting the second veneer cut in position.

10–40. Smoothing out a wrinkled spot.

10–38. Flattening the bulge in the second veneer cut with a roller.

10–41. Trimming the ends of the veneer cuts.

10–39. Using the back of a linoleum knife to smooth the veneer joint.

10–42. Finishing the bonding process with a piece of scrap.

first mitered one end of the border with the paper cutter. Then, using plenty of slip sticks, I started at the mitered end and set the piece in place, forcing it against the field for a tight joint (10–43). Keeping a tight joint did cause some buckling of the strip, but as soon as the bonding pressure was applied, the buckles went down. Had they refused to go down, I would have again recruited the warm iron. It would relax the fibers of the veneer and make the contact cement more active.

10–44. *Using the back of a linoleum knife on the border veneer.*

10–43. *Setting a border piece in place.*

Again I used my linoleum knife to make sure the joint was well flattened. In this case, the veneers had such dramatic differences in thickness, I could only run the back of the knife on the border veneer (10–44). In a couple of spots, the joint was so tight that the back of the knife would not force that last little bit down. Here I used the top of the knife, rolling it over any high spots next to the joint (10–45).

With each piece of border, I cut the miter on only one end. After the piece was down, I cut the miter at the other end, using the lines I had extended onto the field as guides (10–46).

When all the borders were down, I did the necessary trimming with my trusty hook knife (10–47).

At this point, I had to leave the project overnight. The next morning, the contact cement was overly

10–45. *The top of the linoleum knife is being used to flatten the border veneer.*

10–46. *Making a miter cut on the end of a veneer border piece.*

10–47. Trimming the borders.

dry and some dust had settled on it. No problem. Rather than give all the pieces another coat of contact cement, I wiped the surfaces with a cloth dampened with lacquer thinner (10–48). This not only cleaned off the dust but reactivated the contact cement (10–48).

After setting the strip of mahogany above the leg and the movingue border piece next to it, I put down the next field in the same manner as the first (10–49). Well, not exactly; I did have to use a little masking tape to prevent the slip sticks and rod from falling off the case.

10–49. Setting down the next field.

After the case was complete, I started on the drawers. Here, the first step was the facing of the edges of each drawer front with zebrawood. Working with a full cut of zebrawood, I encouraged it to stick with a hammer rather then a roller (10–50). As the veneer would be exposed to considerable stress in trimming, I wanted it bonded as completely as possible.

Don't knock that dainty little hammer I'm shown

10–48. Wiping the border surfaces with lacquer thinner removes the dust and reactivates the glue.

10–50. Using a hammer to bond zebrawood veneer to the drawer-front face edges.

10–51. Removing overhang on the drawer-front face.

10–52. Trimming the zebrawood border on the drawer fronts.

using in 10–50. It has a large, smooth surface that won't put a ding in the veneer. Yes, I've tried a rubber hammer, but found that it can bend the veneer over the edge, causing it to fracture.

After the facing was bonded and trimmed, I used a shooting block to remove any slight overhang (10–51).

Next, placing the drawers in their compartments, I worked them as if they were a single piece, much the same as I did the case. After the field was in place and trimmed as a unit, the last thing to go on was the zebrawood border. It too was worked and trimmed as if the drawer fronts were one piece (10–52).

WORKING WITH THE TOP

After breathing a sigh of relief upon completing the case, I set it on top of a sheet of 3/4-inch MDF. Using a pair of dividers set for the amount of overhang I wanted, I marked the MDF (10–53).

I really wanted a 1-inch top for the desk, so I "beefed up" the 3/4-inch stock by adding pieces of 1/4-inch MDF around the edges. I let the pieces hang over slightly, and then trimmed them with a router and flush trimmer (10–54).

I next prepared the first two cuts of patched and flattened veneer by trimming away an area that was just too ugly to patch (10–55). This is one place

10–53. Marking the MDF top using a pair of dividers.

where a clear straightedge comes in very handy because it lets me see the whole veneer as I'm working. Aligning the pieces for a good pattern match, I marked the location of the joint on the second cut. As shown in 10–56, I also marked the face side boldly with chalk. Yes, I've accidentally spread glue on the face side . . . once over the chalk mark.

Now for the fun part: spreading the glue. Again, I let the veneer hang over the edge and brushed the glue toward that edge (10–57).

As I was spreading yellow glue for the dry-glue process, the moisture from the glue began to penetrate the veneer, and the veneer began to curl; this condition was eased by spraying the face side with water (10–58). As the glue dried, I kept an eye on the veneer, and if the curling continued, I simply

10–54. Trimming the pieces added to the top.

10–56. Marking the location of the joint for the veneer cuts.

10–55. Trimming away a section of the veneer too extensively damaged to patch.

10–57. Spreading the veneer with the glue.

10–58. Spraying the face side of the veneer with water to prevent it from curling.

10–59. Spreading glue on the field area of the border.

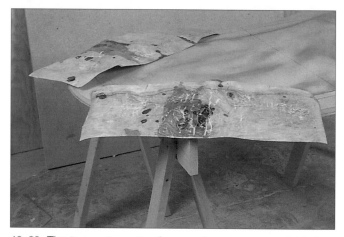

10–60. The two outer cuts of veneer became very wrinkled.

10–61. Using a hair drier to make the veneer cuts pliable.

sprayed a little more water. Spraying that face side must be done carefully; try to avoid the tape. If the tape gets too wet, it will turn loose. Patches will fall out, and the veneer can look very ugly. Use only enough water, and take heart; the second coat of glue will not cause nearly as much curling. And be sure to let the first coat dry before applying the second; remember that "dry" means no opaque areas.

Before spreading glue on the top, I marked the border and spread glue only on the field area (10–59). I like the glue to be less than eight hours old when bonding, and I wasn't sure that I would get to the border for several days.

After the second coat of glue dried, I put all of the veneers between pieces of coated 3/4-inch particleboard with a weight on top. The weight coupled with the residual moisture in the veneer helped flatten it substantially. In the case of the two outer cuts, I was afraid that their sever wrinkling would cause breakage if placed under the particleboard (10–60).

A little heat from my industrial–strength hair dryer made these two veneer cuts pliable enough for the flattening operation (10–61). Pieces with dried glue can also be placed in the hot-plate press described in Chapter 6. Should you try this, be sure to put the glued side down, against a sheet of plastic film. The glue will stick well enough to the aluminum plate that removal can damage the veneer.

Before beginning the bonding, I ran a sanding block

over the surface of the top (10–62). This was to cut the top off any particles that might have settled on the drying glue. If it were possible, I would have also passed the block over the veneer, but it was too wrinkled. To remove any dust produced by sanding, I wiped the surface with a damp cloth. That little bit of dampness also seemed to make the bonding go easier.

After positioning the first cut and securing it with a couple of spring clamps, I began ironing it down, working from the center outward (10–63).

I intentionally left this piece a little wrinkled just to show that a cut in this bad shape can be bonded successfully.

The bonding did take effort. After I did all I could

10–64. To compress the areas that were still standing, it was necessary to lean on the iron while heating the veneer.

10–62. Using a sanding block to remove imbedded dust from the top's surface in preparation for veneer bonding.

10–65. Putting down the bubbles remaining on the veneer.

with the dry veneer, I trimmed the joint and wetted a portion of it that was about three times the size of the iron's base. As the water soaked in, the veneer began to expand and a couple of bubbles immediately appeared. I could also hear some clicking, indicating that other areas were pulling loose. Heating the whole area, I began to lean on the iron (10–64). The moisture and heat made the veneer much more pliable, and the pressure of the iron caused compression of the areas that were standing. The heat also caused the veneer to dry quickly, aiding in its natural tendency to hold its shape. I continued ironing until all of the clicking stopped.

As I ironed over the wet veneer, I removed the tape and wetted the area under the tape. With a little water and heat, the tape peeled off easily.

After working the entire panel, I detected a few persistent bubbles. These I wetted. Then I heated the area and used extra pressure from the tip of the iron to put them down (10–65).

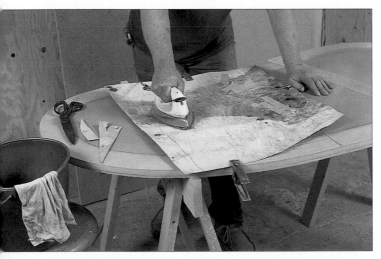

10–63. Bonding the veneer to the top using an iron.

I had pre-trimmed this cut for the outer-veneer joint, but after ironing out all those wrinkles, the joint was no longer straight. It was a simple matter to trim an additional 1/16 inch from the joint. As shown in 10–66, for this operation I used a linoleum knife and tilted the blade toward the straightedge for accuracy. I also pinned that slippery, plastic straightedge in place.

The waste from the joint came away, taking with it glue right down to the substrate. This I replaced by running a tiny bead of glue down the joint and smoothing it out with my finger (10–67).

I then proceeded with the outer veneer cut, bonding the area opposite the joint. Illus. 10–68 shows a steel rod under the veneer, about 1 1/2 inches from the joint. This was placed to make sure the veneer buckled and had a little extra length to make a compressed joint. I will admit that the rod was a bit redundant, because there were plenty of wrinkles in the cut to provide compression, but I'm a creature of habit.

Nonetheless, after the outer area was bonded, the rod was withdrawn and the joint was then completed (10–69). I then worked the veneer cuts on the

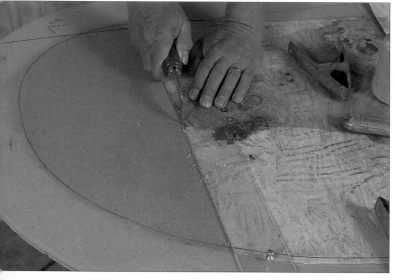

10–66. Trimming the veneer joint.

10–68. Bonding the outer veneer cut to the top.

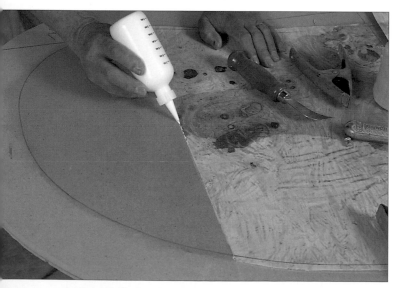

10–67. Replacing the joint's glue.

10–69. Completing the veneer joint.

10–70. *Bonding the opposite veneer cuts.*

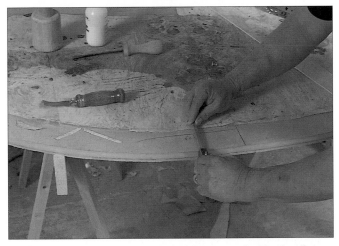

10–71. *Trimming the outer edges of the top, for the border.*

10–72. *Separating the outer edges of the veneer from the substrate using a chisel.*

opposite side of the joint in the same manner (10–70).

Once the field was down, I trimmed its outer edges for the border, using a needle scribe (10–71). For the most part, I was able to cut clear through the veneer with

the scribe. In places the needle didn't cut all the way through, I used a linoleum knife to complete the work.

I did try to avoid the outer edges of the field with the heat, but in some places the veneer was firmly bonded. These areas needed to be parted from the substrate with a sharp chisel (10–72), and in most cases the areas needed to be respread with glue. If the areas I had tried to avoid were bonded this well, I knew that the areas I had bonded were down tight. Just to make sure that all areas near the border were down, I wetted a strip about three inches wide adjacent to the border and passed the iron over it firmly until it was dry.

A couple of days later, I spread glue on the facing and border areas. While patches of glue were drying on the top, I installed the facing. Here I cut a number of strips of veneer with my paper cutter that were just slightly longer than the one-inch thickness of the top. In ironing these on, I let them stand just slightly proud of the top and trimmed them flush using a sanding block. After the trimming was done, I ran a tiny bead of glue over the top of the facing veneer and spread it out with my finger.

After scribing and fitting the first piece of border, I marked the joints by drawing an "eyeballed" line that was perpendicular to the tangent of the curve; this line I carried onto the field (10–73). These joints were cut and the first piece bonded.

The second piece was then scribed to the field. As shown in 10–74, the points of the dividers are par-

10–73. *Marking the border joint.*

allel with the grain lines of the veneer or parallel with the centerline of the veneer piece, which should be perpendicular to the tangent of the curve at its center. If you hold the points of the dividers perpendicular to the tangent of the curve while moving them along, you will cut the veneer short at the center.

The joint between the border cuts was marked using the line that was extended onto the field in a previous step, and the length of the cut was marked by drawing a pencil line on the underside, guided by the edge of the top (10–75).

In fitting these pieces, I used scissors to cut all the curved lines and a veneer saw to cut the joints between the cuts (the paper cutter tended to split the veneer excessively). The outer edge was cut to allow about a 1/8-inch overhang.

I will here again admit that I'm not perfect. Sometimes I let the scissors wander a bit in that hard zebrawood. Sometimes the scribe line wasn't where it should have been. I don't know what causes these things. What I do know is that minor errors can be corrected with a curved sanding block (10–76).

10–74. Scribing the second border to the field.

10–75. Marking the joint between the border cuts.

10–76. Using a sanding block to make minor corrections.

To perhaps simplify things a bit in this border–fitting operation, it should be noted that the border pieces should fit well to the field. Minor putty patching can be done because the putty will not be obvious where the character of the veneer changes as dramatically as it did in this project.

To make the border most attractive, the grain pattern at the joints should form an isosceles triangle (10–77). This was my goal, but in several instances I fell short. I didn't go back to attempt corrections because, in a top this "busy," only the most critical examiner will note this inadequacy.

My trimming with the needle scribe generally worked well, although in a couple of places the cut needed touchup. In one area, a knot deflected the scribe, leaving a small area that was slightly long. This was easy to correct using the edge of a flat file (10–78). I could have used the folded edge of stiff sanding cloth or the edge of sandpaper folded over a block, but I find the file easier to handle.

10–77. The chalk marks indicate the grain pattern of the borders.

10–78. Touching up the field with a file.

Throughout the border installation, I found the zebrawood to be substantially thinner than the burl field. To ensure that the border was bonded at the joint, I held the iron on edge and ran it along the joint (10–79); and, to provide for compressed joints in the border, I began ironing from the side opposite the joint. As the slight wrinkles in the veneer were ironed out, the joint was compressed slightly.

10–79. Using an iron to ensure that the borders are bonded at the joint.

After the top was complete, I checked for any loose spots by lightly passing the extended points of a pair of dividers lightly over every square inch of the top (10–80). A hollow sound under the dividers will quickly point out any loose spots. These I marked with chalk. Then I came back and wetted and ironed the areas.

ADDING A FINISH

After what seemed like days of sanding, I applied a thin coat of amber dye stain to the case and a thin coat of amber with a touch of brown to the top. The stain on the case brightened the movingue and accented the nara. Staining the top softened the contrast between the burl and zebrawood, which was quite stark.

After sealing and sanding, gloss lacquer was used to "build" the finish. The case was final-coated with a satin finish, and the top, after receiving many coats of gloss, was wet-sanded and then coated with a satin finish.

The desk pleased the client, and anything that pleases the client, pleases me . . . and my creditors.

10–80. Checking for loose spots on the top.

CHAPTER 11

Round Dining Table

Through the years, I've built many pedestal tables, but the design I'll describe here is one I rather enjoy. This is probably because I don't have to mount a 50-pound block of wood on the lathe to turn the pedestal. And I think that if I were offered a commission to build a solid-oak pedestal table, I'd turn it down. I've used so much oak in my lifetime that I now find it the most boring species I can think of—except when used for bending. For this table (11–1 to 11–3), I chose substrates of MDF, bender board, and poplar, and I used alder for the cove mold components; there was no particular reason for choosing the poplar and alder other than it's what I had on hand.

I chose zebrawood for the vertical surfaces and movingue for the base components. Benin was my

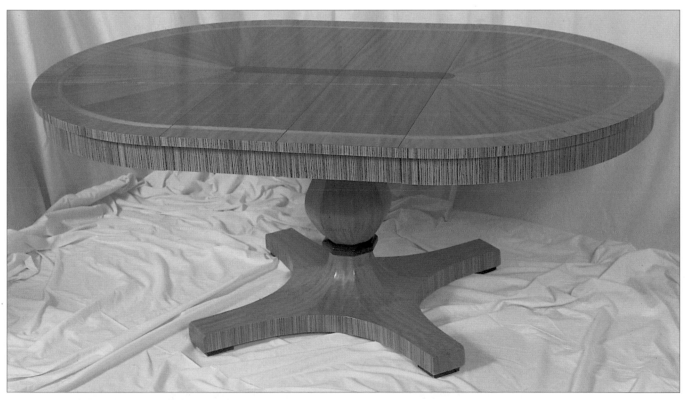

11–1 to 11–3 (following page). Three versions of the dining table.

11–2.

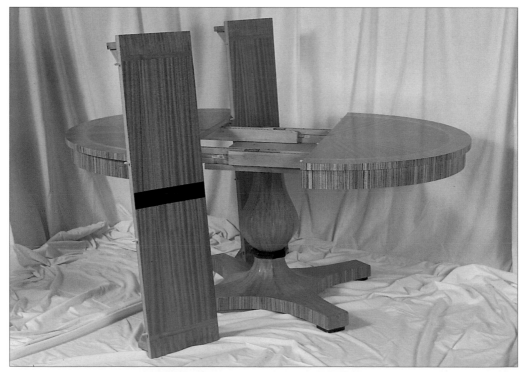

11–3.

choice for the sunburst. I have used mahogany crotch for several sunburst tabletops, but the crotches—like oak—are becoming boring. Movingue was used for the border. I used a bent piece of butternut to separate the movingue from the Benin sunburst.

PREPARING THE PEDESTAL AND BASE

I always start this type of project with a full-scale drawing. To the left in 11–4 I have drawn the pedestal, and to the right one–quarter of the base.

One critical component would be a piece of cove molding that I would cut on the table saw by passing the stock diagonally over the blade, lifting the blade in very small increments after each pass. I sketched this piece of cove using the saw blade I intended to use; this is also shown in 11–4. This assured me that the molding could be cut, and also gave me an idea of what angle at which to set the saw guide.

I cut out the pedestal pattern and used the remaining sketch to check the fit of end cuts taken from the cove mold components (11–5). It should be noted

11–4. Making a full-scale drawing for the dining table. A saw blade that will cut the cove molding is being used to check the curve.

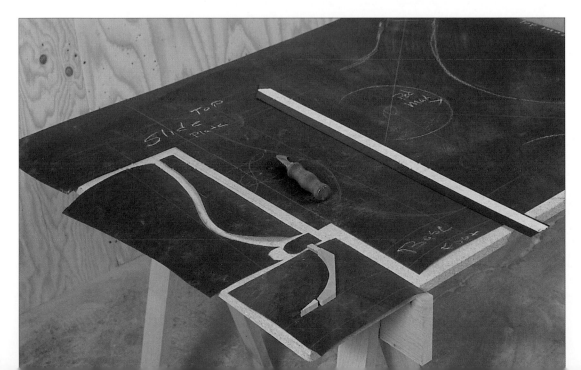

11–5. Shown on the left of the workbench is the cut pedestal pattern. On the right is the pattern for the base.

that I checked several lumberyards for a piece of stock cove that would work. And after the slow process of cutting that cove on the table saw, I made a mental note to take the time to grind knives for any molding machine, should I ever have to do it again.

Pedestal

The next step was to mark the components of the octagonal pedestal, using the inside of the blank as a reference (11–6). These were glued up from two pieces of 8/4 poplar; one piece cut to exact length and the other long enough to accommodate the shape.

11–7. Finishing the angle cut using a band saw.

11–6. Marking the components of the pedestal.

11–8. Gluing the dado cut to receive the spline.

After cutting the blank using a band saw, I cut the 22$1/2$-degree angle on a 10-inch table saw with the blade as high as it would go. The cut was then finished on a band saw (11–7). I do have a table saw that will take a 24-inch blade that would make these cuts, but it's a tilting table saw, and I don't care for tilting tables. Also, since that saw "bit" me several years ago, I tend to shy away from it except for very heavy work.

Any irregularities from the band saw were removed with a block plane. Then the components were returned to the table saw and a dado cut made to receive a $1/4$-inch spline. The spline does have some structural value and, as such, it should be glued into the dado (11–8). More than the structural value, the spline helps to locate all of the pieces

during assembly. I then spread a generous coat of glue on the side opposite the spline and on the spline groove, and assembled the pedestal (11–9).

Base

While the glue was drying on the pedestal, I cut out one-eighth of the base pattern. Then, scoring it at its center and folding it over, I used it as a pattern to complete the cutting of one-quarter of the pattern (11–10). I used this quarter section to lay out the complete base on a sheet of $3/4$-inch MDF (11–11).

After carefully cutting the base section with a saber saw, I trued and smoothed the cuts with my trusty horseshoe rasp (11–12).

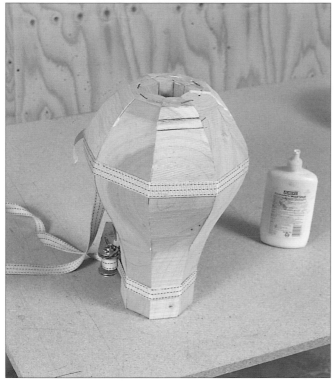

11–9. The assembled pedestal.

11–11. Laying out the entire base.

11–10. Cutting one-quarter of the base pattern.

11–12. Using a rasp to smooth the base.

11–13. Trimming the base pieces.

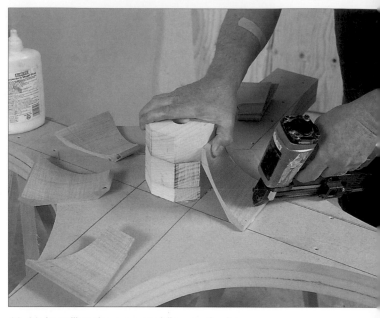

11–14. Installing the cove molding on the base.

I then began to build up the thickness of the base by gluing and screwing pieces to each side, trimming them to exact size with a router and flush trimmer (11–13). (The screws were removed as soon as the glue set.)

Next, I cut three octagons out of 8/4 poplar, drilled a 1-inch hole in the center of each, and rubbed-glued them together. While I was waiting for the glue to set, I drilled a 1-inch hole dead center on the base. (The base/pedestal assembly will be held together with a piece of 1/2-inch Allthread rod extending from the underside of the base to the top of the plate.) I also drew some lines from the extremities of the base assembly to guide the positioning of the octagons.

After cutting the octagon assembly to length on my band saw, I fastened it to the center of the base with glue and a couple of drywall screws through the bottom of the base.

Next, I installed the three-piece cove molding around the octagon (11–14). In the case of the lowest piece, a scrap and a clamp (a screw can be substituted) were used to hold down the feathered edge (11–15).

Even before the glue dried on the molding, I began patching the various screw holes and any gaps in the molding with auto-body putty. Yes, there were some places where the molding didn't fit perfectly. That's what body putty was invented for. Were I to chastise

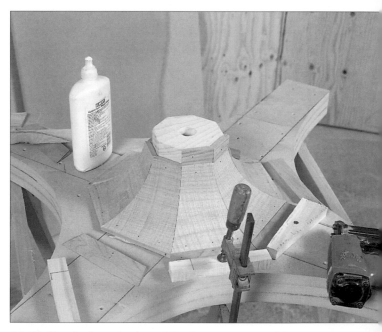

11–15. The feathered edge of the lowest cove molding component is held down with a clamp.

myself for such minor inadequacies, I would have spent a significant part of my life striking my breast and saying "Mea culpa, Mea culpa" in a low breath.

Once the body putty was dry, I began to prepare the base for the veneer. Here, a scraper and rasp came in very handy. I also used a 2 x 4 with the edge

11–16. Preparing the base for the veneer.

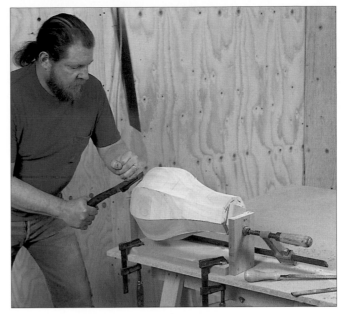

11–17. Smoothing the pedestal.

rounded off and a piece of sanding cloth glued to it with contact cement (11–16). Even my disc grinder came into play for a couple of the bad spots, but the photographer was reloading his camera and couldn't catch me using such an unorthodox tool.

The pedestal was next. There were some irregularities in the band-sawn pieces, and the coarse saw marks did have to be removed. Illus. 11–17 shows the jig I built for working the pedestal. After screwing a plug to the top and bottom of the pedestal, I measured the resultant length and cut the base of the jig to that length. I fastened the upright sticks with a couple of drywall screws through each. Another drywall screw in the top of each stick engaged the ends of the pedestal. The long, deep-throat clamp keeps

the pedestal from rotating—except when I want it to. Is it worth the trouble? You bet! It is well worth it to spend five minutes and use a few scraps to build a "vise" for that pedestal.

I next determined that there would be three distinct cuts needed to veneer the base and pedestal: one for the sides of the pedestal, one for the short section of the base, and another for the section that makes the foot. After making rough patterns of these, I laid the patterns out on the veneer for the most economical cutting. This allowed me to determine what length would accommodate all three so that I could cut the ten-foot lengths into something more manageable (11–18).

After rigging a fixture to hold the base in a work-

11–18. Laying out the patterns on the veneer.

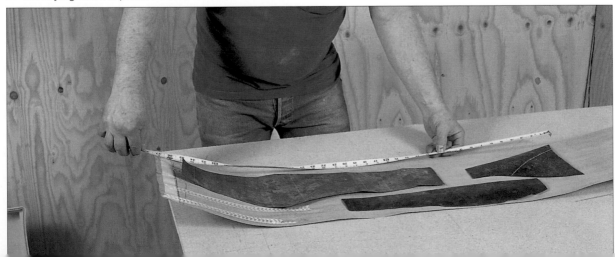

able position, I ironed on the zebrawood edge veneer using the dry-glue process (11–19). As very little of the iron's base contacted the veneer on that curved surface, I turned the iron on high and kept it moving through the curve.

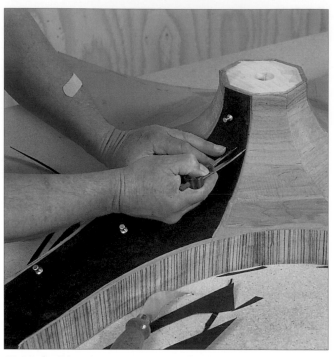

11–20. Scribing the veneer pattern for the base.

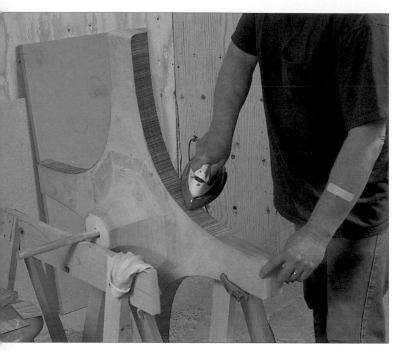

11–19. Ironing on the veneer to the edge of the base.

VENEERING THE BASE

Next came the fun part: fitting the eight pieces to the irregular base. To fit these pieces, I used a pattern. First, I cut a piece of #15 roofing felt that was smaller than the piece of veneer that would be needed. It is not important that this piece of felt actually be cut, only that it be smaller than the veneer all around. As shown in 11–20, I left it flush at the top, for convenience. With a pair of dividers set at about ½ inch, I scribed the pattern. This was done by letting one point ride on the base and marking the felt, and using the other point to follow the exact line the veneer should fall on. In all cases, the points of the dividers were kept perpendicular to the tangent of any curved surfaces.

In 11–20, I'm holding the dividers so that you can see them. The way I normally hold them—one that allows for far better control—is shown in 11–21.

11–21. Transferring the marking on the pattern to the veneer. The way I'm holding the dividers here—with my index and middle finger over the legs—allows for far greater control than the method shown in 11–20.

Holding the dividers in this way allows me to apply pressure with the appropriate finger, so I can let one point ride while the other marks or cuts.

Next, I pinned the pattern to the face of the veneer, and then transferred the marking on the pattern to the veneer (11–21).

Before transferring the pattern along the lines that would cover the edge of the facing, I opened the dividers about ⅛ inch. This would leave the veneer slightly long so that it could be trimmed later.

This whole process may sound a little difficult, but believe me, with a little practice you will find it simple and in many cases the only way to accurately fit complex pieces. The technique has been used for years by resilient floor-covering installers, especially for coved installations. I once installed kitchen floors in a subdevelopment using the pattern method. On the same project worked two other men who used the "cut, try to fit, and hack" method. I could install two kitchens to their one.

11–23. Putting the veneer cut down on the base.

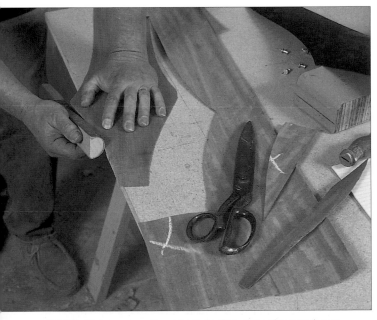

11–22. Using a sanding block to fine-tune the movingue veneer.

11–24. Rolling the veneer over the foot edge.

The movingue veneer was initially very brittle and hard to handle, but after the application of glue it became strong enough to cut with scissors. And of course, I used a curved sanding block to correct any of my "longcomings" (11–22).

I then pinned the cut in position and ironed it down. From this point on, the iron was set on high for the curved areas (11–23).

Before trying to roll this cut over the foot end, I wetted that section to make it more pliable. I then rolled the veneer over the edge, making sure that it was tightly bonded as I progressed (11–24).

11–25. Trimming a long spot in the veneer with a utility knife.

In one small area the veneer was slightly long, a condition quickly rectified with a utility knife (11–25). Had it been slightly short, I would have left it and rolled the next cut into the void.

In the same manner, I proceeded to cut and bond all four of the longer cuts for the base. These could have been installed without the pattern. Oversized pieces could have been bonded and then trimmed, using a bent straightedge. However, the pieces in between them necessitated the pattern. Scribing these

11–26. Scribing the shorter veneer pieces.

went far easier because there was the edge of the installed veneer for the divider point to ride along.

Illus. 11–26 shows the parallel lines near the center of the felt. These lines, made with the extended points of the dividers, are the first mark I make on any pattern. It tells me the setting of the dividers, should I suspect that they have drifted in handling or should I want to reset them for a longer or shorter cut.

VENEERING THE PEDESTAL

After veneering the base, the pedestal was easy. Here, I bonded oversized pieces to every other section, trimming them after bonding. Don't poke fun at the unusual trimming instrument shown in 11–27. That razor-sharp, French chef's knife held flat against the next section trimmed true and clean.

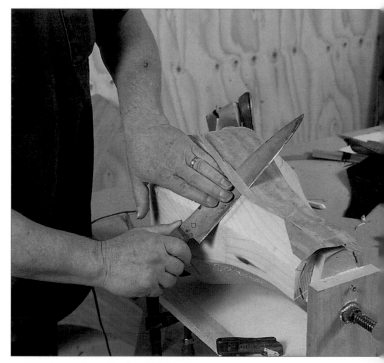

11–27. Trimming the oversized pieces for the pedestal.

After bonding, trimming, and sanding the edges of the first four sections flush, I spread a tiny bead of glue over the bare edges of the newly bonded veneer, smearing it out with my finger. I then bonded the remainder, letting them overlap the edges of the first, and then continued trimming, sanding, etc.

BUILDING THE RIM

Even though there was still some work to do on the base, it was time to get the glue drying on some of the other components, mainly the rim. After cutting out the halves of the top using a router (11–28), on the underside of one I mounted some reusable MDF fixtures, constructing a form for the bent rim. Around these I bent and clamped three layers of ³/₈-inch bender board, to form the table rim (11–29).

Had I an 8 x 4-foot piece of bender board on hand, I could have cut 6-foot lengths. Instead, I had to use a 4- and a 2-foot length, joining them with veneer tape and staggering the joints in the three pieces. As shown in 11–29, the clamping fixtures are spaced at about 6-inch intervals and there is a piece of scrap between the clamp and rim to distribute the pressure evenly. Rather than spread glue on the pieces with roller or brush, I dribbled four ¹/₈-inch beads along the length of the pieces—as in the bent-case pieces for

11–28. Cutting out the top halves.

11–29. Forming the table rim with bender board.

the kidney-shaped desk described in Chapter 10. I then taped them together loosely with masking tape, placed them on the form, and began clamping at the center. If you are putting a rim of this type on the form by yourself, you will think yourself deserving of a cup of coffee. After coffee—about 20 minutes—move each clamp to the space between the fixtures. You'll notice a little squeeze-out of glue, and you will be clamping the rim effectively at 3-inch intervals.

11–30. Bonding the rim to the veneer using an iron.

I intended to bond the rim to the veneer with contact cement and spread the glue on both the rim and veneer accordingly, but it wasn't until the next morning that I got to the bonding process. As the contact cement was quite dry, I used heat from an iron to aid in the bonding (11–30). This worked out well because there was no way to hold the rim so that heavy pressure could be applied to it to set the contact cement; the warm iron and moderate pressure were all that was needed.

I then "pinned" the top and leaves and assembled the top using a goodly supply of brace blocks—less than half of those that appear in 11–31. If you have never assembled a tabletop, here are some pointers: Use a doweling jig to bore for the pins and receiving holes, referencing the top. Work very carefully, as the pins will be responsible for holding the top and all the components in register—they will even slightly bend components that don't fit into register. Make sure that the slides are mounted perfectly square with the centerline break, and, if you are not inclined to use as many brace blocks as I, at least use them at every junction of the skirt with a dab of glue behind them. This will hold the skirt components plumb and in register.

11–31. Assembling the rim and top.

LAYING OUT THE TOP

After determining the criteria of the major components that I had to work with, I began the layout. The width of the veneer was important because I wanted no joints in the sections of the sunburst I had planned. Also important was the location of the border because I had bent some veneer for a divider in the border. (For that circular border, I bent a $7/8$ x $7/8$ inch stick of butternut and let it dry thoroughly. Then I cut off slices that were slightly less than $1/16$ inch thick. I didn't take photos showing the slices being cut on the table saw because I wanted no derogatory "fan mail" from some safety group.)

Perhaps the bent veneer was unnecessary, but I enjoy techniques like that. Those knowledgeable in veneering will look it at and say, " How the . . . did he do that?" Those not so knowledgeable will notice that there's something unique about this tabletop, although they won't be able to identify just what it is.

Once I determined that the bent veneer would fit the location I had planned for the border, it was a simple matter of walking a pair of dividers around a circle drawn with trammels to lay out evenly spaced sections of the sunburst (11–32).

After the layout was complete, I could then determine the length of cuts I would need and cut the sheet of veneer into more manageable pieces for spreading the glue (11–33).

11–32. Laying out the sunburst in even sections.

11–33. Cutting the veneer into more manageable pieces.

VENEERING THE PEDESTAL'S BEAD

As the glue was drying on the top and the sunburst veneers, I realized that I could no longer put off veneering the dividing bead for the pedestal. I made a pattern for the pieces I would need and used it to mark and cut pieces from the slice. Then I ironed every other section onto the substrate (11–34). After a little trimming with a sanding block, I went back and filled in the missing sections (11–35).

11–34. Ironing the pedestal bead pieces onto the substrate.

11–35. The voids in the bead pieces have been filled in.

VENEERING THE TOP

When I began veneering the top, I noticed that the grain pattern of the veneer I intended to use did not run parallel with the edges in all cases. To make sure I would have good-looking pie-shaped sections, I measured and marked the center of the butt end. Then, placing a straightedge on that center mark and, holding it parallel to the grain, I marked the other end. After positioning the marks on the centerline of the layout, I ironed down the first cut, doing the trimming after the cut was bonded (11–36). (To give you an idea as to how much the grain wandered through the cut, note the waste pieces shown in the lower right of 11–37.)

I continued installing the sections, using a steel rod to help make compressed joints (11–37) and doing the trimming after bonding. I only placed the rod about halfway through the length of the cut, because it would be useless at the narrow tip. That narrow piece I forced tight with hand pressure.

The iron I'm using in 11–37 may be considered an antique by some, but it's my favorite for work that is totally flat. The weight of that old iron will do the

11–36. Trimming the first veneer cut for the sunburst.

11–37. Installing the cuts on the sunburst.

11–38. Freeing the waste from a sunburst veneer after straightening the edge.

bonding almost by itself. That antique also helped me understand why ladies of that period were more respected than their counterparts today. After spending their days using a heavy tool like that, they must have had one devastating "right."

Things were going so well and the veneer was so heavenly flat that I began trimming the cuts before bonding. All went smoothly until I encountered one cut that did not have a straight enough edge for a good joint—even a compressed joint. After cutting about 3/64 inch from the erring edge, I used my veneer saw—sharpened like a knife—to free the waste (11–38).

After all of the cuts were down, I mounted a hobby knife in my tram-

11–39. Trimming the butt ends of the top using a hobby knife in a trammel.

11–40. The modified hobby knife used to trim the butt ends.

mels and trimmed the butt ends. Now, this is a little trickier than it looks in 11–39. Even though the knife blade was cut off, reground, and sharpened, as shown in 11–40, it still had some flex. And even if the blade didn't flex, the stick holding the trammels will bend slightly, destroying the accuracy of the cut if precautions are not taken.

What precautions? I start by making several careful passes, using little more pressure than the weight of the knife itself. After the path of the blade is well established, I increase pressure until the veneer is cut through. I counted seven passes in this particular operation.

After installing the bent border piece, I reset the trammels and used the knife to cut the curve of the other border pieces (11–41). You may have noted that there are no photos of me installing the bent border piece. Well . . . the moisture of the glue caused the bent piece to open considerably, and it took a little persuasion to force it into shape once more. During that critical period, I didn't need flash strobes going off in my face. I'm also glad my grandchildren weren't present, as they may have acquired some unwanted additions to their vocabulary.

(When I was finished with the bent border piece, my son Nick came over to my corner of the shop and said, "Gee, Dad, that's real neat, but I don't think anybody will appreciate all the trouble you had to go to." I replied, "Son, does this mean I've prostituted my time and talents on the altar of frivolity?" Nick's eyebrows wrinkled; his mouth opened, and he said, "Huh?")

After making the first curved cut in a border piece, I determined the length needed to provide for a little overhang and made a pencil line on my workbench—which, as 11–42 shows, is a table leaf that has not yet been spread with glue. This allowed me to keep sliding the stock forward and cutting with no further measurements. Illus. 11–42 also shows parallel pencil lines; these aided me in clamping the stock in the proper register.

11–41. *Cutting the curves of the border pieces.*

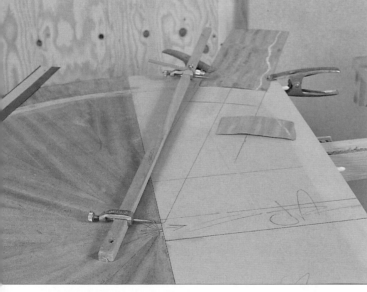

11–42. *Marking to determine the length of curve in the first border piece.*

11–43. *Marking the joints between the border pieces.*

The movingue border veneer was so hard that I barely was able to cut through it. Rather, I scored it deeply. Then I lifted the piece from the table, breaking it off—sort of like scoring and breaking a piece of plastic laminate.

With a straightedge set on the centerline, joints between the individual pieces of border were accurately marked for cutting with a paper cutter or scissors (11–43).

With the border installed, the next step was to fit

11–44. Cutting the center character.

the center character. I cut the outline of the half-circle using a pair of dividers with a very sharp point (11–44)—thinking of that sharp point as one tooth of a veneer saw. I used the same dividers to cut the inlay from a piece of veneer I had taped to prevent from splitting under the stress of the dividers.

I have done several of these sunbursts without the center character. I vowed to never do this again. Trying to contend with all of those tiny slivers is more trouble than it's worth.

From here on it was a matter of straight cuts and simple bonding to complete the leaves. A router with a flush trimmer handled the overhang, and as shown in 11–45, I still used the project as a workbench, but have protected the fresh veneer with a piece of plywood.

ASSEMBLING THE BASE

I'd been putting it off, but it was now time to finish the sanding on the base and assemble it. Movingue is one of those veneers that look blotchy where it is being sanded; there appear to be dark patches that could be dirt spots or—gasp—scorch marks from the iron. After doing all I thought was necessary with the sandpaper, I wetted the surface with lacquer thinner to see if the spots would disappear (11–46). They did.

To assemble the base, I screwed the bead character

11–45. Completing the leaves.

11–46. Using lacquer thinner on the base surface to eliminate the dirt spots.

to the pedestal and drilled two $^3/_8$-inch holes through the bead into the pedestal. I then removed the bead from the pedestal and screwed it to the base. Using the $^3/_8$-inch holes as a guide, I drilled into the base and installed dowels (11–47).

I used no glue on the dowels because they were

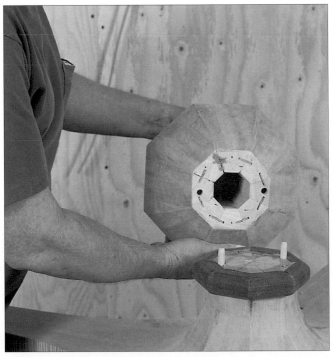

11–47. The completed base with drilled dowels on the pedestal. Also shown is the bead character.

there only to hold the pieces in register. What held the entire thing together was a piece of $^1/_2$-inch Allthread rod; after screwing the plate to the top of the pedestal, I installed the Allthread. No, I did not cut the Allthread with the hacksaw shown in 11–48. I put the assembly on a cart, wheeled it to the opposite side of the shop, and challenged one of the other guys to cut it without nicking the nut. I stood behind him quietly snickering, and, of course, acknowledged his great skill and thanked him.

ADDING A FINISH

This table received a very simple finish. I used a weak coat of amber dye-stain to accentuate the yellow of the movingue and to bring out the "fire" of the Benin. From there on it was sealer and clear coats of glossy lacquer. The final coats were of satin lacquer.

11–48. Installing the Allthread, a rod used to hold the assembly together.

CHAPTER 12

Bombé Chest

This project (12–1 and 12–2) was inspired by a fortunate lumber purchase. I was able to pick up a quantity of partially air-dried 3 x 6s at a price one-fifth that of any other lumber. Normally, I wouldn't think of building furniture with lumber that is not thoroughly cured, but I wanted to try an antique "forgery" and wanted to see if I could contend with the challenges faced by woodworkers of old.

12–1. A front view of the bombé chest.

12–2. A close-up of the top of the chest.

I inquired as to the species of my purchase and the old fellow I had been dealing with gave me a toothless smile, rolled his chew a bit, spat, and said, "What 'ya got there, sonny, is American softwood." I felt so elated about being called "sonny" that I didn't want to consider the rest of the answer. I felt so good in fact that I bought twenty-five 1 x 8 x 8-foot pieces, knowing that I would need some 1-inch material for drawer bottoms, backing, etc.

The old boy helped me load the material, and I noticed that the 3 x 6s felt rather dry. The 1 x 8s, on the other hand, felt wet. I asked, "How long have these 1 x 8s been air-drying?"

Another shift, another spit: "About two days." I made a mental note not to use the 1 x 8s until they lost substantial weight.

So it was on to the "forgery," which incidentally could not stand close examination by even the least observant. Further, the chest bore my trademark, and beneath that trademark I drilled a shallow hole and inserted a shinny penny bearing the date 1999.

DRAWINGS AND PATTERNS

After a couple of lines and rough dimensions on a piece of paper, I proceeded to make a full-scale drawing. Because I only like to draw once, I made the drawing on a piece of 15-pound roofing felt from which I could remove patterns for cutting the individual pieces of the chest. You may be partial to drawing on large pieces of wrapping paper or cardboard, but give the felt a try. It is economical and far more substantial than paper for patterns. It does have the disadvantage of not being erasable, but that can be overcome with the use of different-colored pencils and scribing devices—as you will see.

After flattening the felt by pulling it over the sharp edge of the bench (12–3), I trimmed the left edge square with the bottom. I then drew in the chest top—30 inches from the bottom. Then, placing a piece of the actual stock I would be using on the felt, I outlined it in red (12–4). (This piece of stock was cut from one of the more twisted 3 x 6's, faced on the jointer, and planed, giving me an idea of the maximum dimensions I would have to work with.) Normally, I would outline the stock with a

12–3. Flattening the felt.

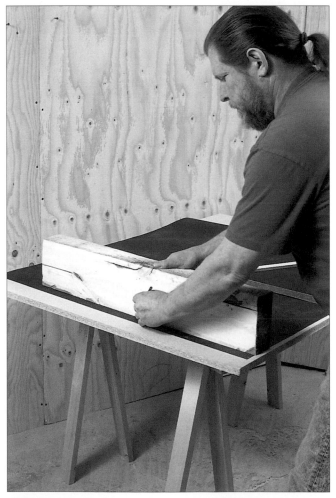

12–4. Drawing an outline of the stock on the felt.

scribing knife for a more accurate line, but I used the red pencil for benefit of the photos.

Next, within the confines of the marks of the stock, I drew a bold curved line that pleased me, and then marked out the approximate position of three graduated drawers and the skirt (12–5). This would leave a leg approximately eight inches long that would flow into the skirt. It was then I noticed that there would be too little "meat" where the skirt joined the sides. Not being able to erase my original line for the side curve, I modified it using a different-colored pencil (12–6).

12–5. Marking out the position of the drawers and skirt.

If you are making a drawing like this, at any point you can stop, pin it to the wall, and stand back to get a truer perspective.

To make sure the curve was smooth, I drove a number of #3 finishing nails along it and bent a

12–6. Modifying the line where the skirt meets the sides.

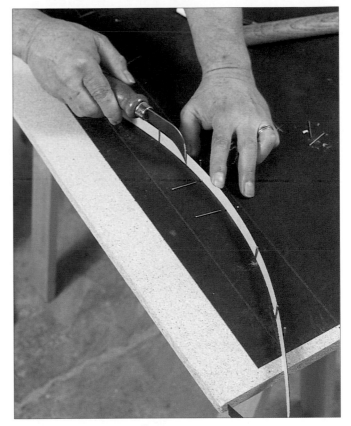

12–7. Marking the felt along the band steel with a linoleum knife.

piece of ⅝-inch band steel along the nails. (You may notice in the photos that the band steel has been covered with a piece of masking tape. This was done to make the steel show against the black felt and also because in the following photos the steel will be used as a measuring device. Pencil marks will be made on the masking tape.) Two of the nails did not fall in line with the steel. These were replaced by two that did. After all nails were in contact with the steel, I lightly marked the felt along the band steel with the point of a linoleum knife (12–7)—although a scribing knife or needle would work as well.

It was then a simple matter to pull the nails and cut the line. As the knife cut partially through the felt in the marking operation, it followed the partial cut accurately and effortlessly on the second pass.

Straight cuts were then made on the red lines marked on the stock, releasing a piece of felt that could be used as a pattern for the side and front of the leg . . .

almost. I fastened the waste felt I'd cut from the left side of the pattern to the right of the pattern, using masking tape on its underside. This, incidentally, is what is going to happen with the wood. The waste will be glued back to the stock to complete the leg.

After positioning the leg pattern back onto the drawing, I used a pair of dividers to scribe a line parallel to the side of the leg. (Although the leg will be tapered, it's easier to draw that taper with the parallel line as a reference.) Again using a colored pencil, I finished drawing the inside of the leg flowing into the skirt (12–8).

After I finished cutting the patterns (12–9), I had a good idea of the rough sizes of the material that would be needed. I left the patterns/drawings and went to the lumber pile, where I cut the rough lengths and placed sticks between them to let the pieces acclimatize somewhat (12–10). The thickness of the 1 x 3 would remain wet longer than the width.

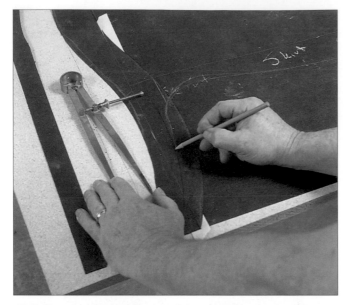

12–8. Drawing the inside part of the chest leg on the felt.

12–10. The rough-cut chest components set on stickers to acclimatize.

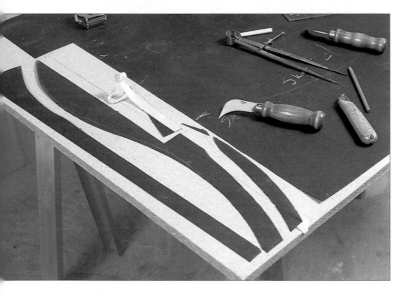

12–9. The cut patterns.

PREPARING THE COMPONENTS

Side Pieces

Once the stock was faced and planed to provide clean, parallel surfaces with square corners, the first step was to mark out the face of the side's core pieces. I used a square to draw a square line for the top edge and the upper part of the leg pattern on the face of the stock (12–11). After the piece was cut, the resulting waste was glued to the back side of the blank, producing a piece of stock from which I could cut two side core pieces.

Illus. 12–16 shows the side pieces assembled with clamps.

Once out of the clamps, this blank was marked. (If you are a little careless and the pieces do not fit perfectly, it's a good idea to run the blank over the jointer to true the edge. Otherwise, the blank will teeter on the saw table and the cut won't be perpendicular with the edge.) There are two ways to do this. The first way consists of using a pair of dividers, one leg riding the face and the other making the mark (12–12). It is necessary that the dividers be kept perpendicular to the straight line of the joint, because keeping them perpendicular to the tangent of the curve will produce a curve different from the pattern.

Another way is to mark the center of the blank at several places and again use the upper part of the leg pattern to mark the rest of the blank (12–13).

In any event, make sure that the top of the pattern is placed accurately on the blank, as this top line will become the reference for all of the side components.

Once all of the blanks were cut on the band saw, they were glued to form the core of the side (12–14).

Legs

I pinned the pattern to a piece of leg stock with the straight part of the pattern aligned with the back of the stock, and then marked only the face (12–15). After the cut was made, the lower piece of waste was glued back to the blank (12–16), providing "meat" for the lower inside of the leg .

12–11. Drawing a leg pattern on the stock face.

12–13. Another way of marking the blank is to mark its middle and use the leg pattern to mark the rest of it.

12–12. Marking the leg blank using a pair of dividers.

This was done very carefully, as I made sure that the top and face lined up as well as possible. Inconsistencies in thickness of the pieces I let show on the inside—I'd take care of that later.

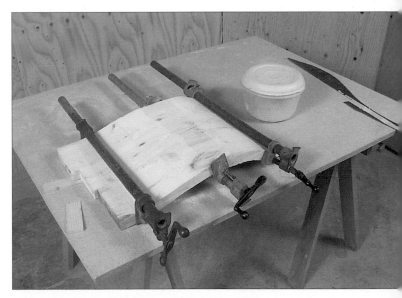

12–14. The assembled pieces for the side core.

Note the stick spanning the featheredge of the waste pieces. If you look carefully, you will also see some small nails driven partway through the waste. These are there to prevent the pieces from slipping in the glue as the clamps are applied. Another technique to keep the components from slipping is to rub the glued surfaces together, pull them apart, and let the glue "tack up" for a minute or so. In any event, apply the clamp pressure slowly, letting the excess squeeze out.

While the glue was drying on the legs, I took a few minutes to clean up the inside of the side core pieces. My inshave served well for the task (12–17), for the object was not to provide a perfectly smooth surface. Rather, I wanted to disguise the joints somewhat and remove any evidence of the yellow glue.

Once the glue was dry, I returned the pattern to the blank and marked out the full leg (12–18).

Now I chose to cut only two 5¹/₂-inch-wide blanks. Ripping off the width required for a front leg left enough material for a back. This I did on the table saw—not the safest of operations. If you feel the least hesitant, either cut the legs individually or set up a rip fence on your band saw to accomplish the feat.

12–16. Spreading the glue for adding the waste.

12–15. Marking the pattern on the face of the leg stock.

12–17. Cleaning up the inside of the side core pieces with an inshave.

12–18. *Marking out the entire leg.*

Finalizing the Case Sides

With the legs cut, I measured their combined width and cut the core blank to the proper width. All pieces prepared, I glued the components of the case side together (12–19). Care should be taken that they all are flush along the top. Otherwise, there will be work with a hand plane to true the top edge. You could, of course, pass the top of the side over the jointer, but I don't recommend it unless you are skilled and comfortable with such operations.

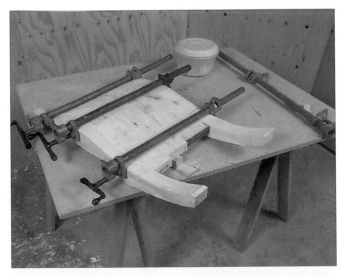

12–19. *The side components glued and clamped together.*

Caution: Be sure that you glue the sides up so that there is a pair consisting of one from each side rather than two of the same side. Yes, I've done it . . . more than once.

12–20. *Drawing the pattern for the front.*

Once the glue was dry, I marked out the cut needed at the front. Because the pattern was too short to conform to the curved surface that existed, I started the marking by setting the pattern flush with the bottom of the leg—straight portion against the joint between the leg and the core. After drawing the line about a third of the way up, I shifted the pattern so that the bulge lined up with the bulge of the case, continuing the line to the bulge (12–20). The final marking was done with the pattern flush with the top of the case.

Gluing Back the Waste

Once the front was cut, the waste had to be glued back to give enough stock to finish cutting the shape of the front leg—the front leg also needs a little extra strength at this point. This is a little tricky in that the

12–21. *Marking the notch for the waste piece.*

waste piece will need to be notched out to fit around the core. To mark the notch, I placed the waste above the position into which it must fall, set a pair of dividers to the amount of offset, and then scribed a line on the waste (12–21).

Cutting the Side Scallop

With the waste glued back, I sketched the scallop I wanted, marking my final decision with a red pencil (12–22). Saving the waste piece from the cut on the left side, I used it to mark the right (12–23).

After the scallop was cut, I got excited and spent a couple of minutes cleaning up the joints in the core and the legs with a hand plane (12–24). I only worked until I detected perspiration. It was that perspiration, Gentle Reader, that convinced me that I should cheat and use a power tool—read on.

12–23. Marking the opposite side with a waste piece.

12–22. Sketching the scallop.

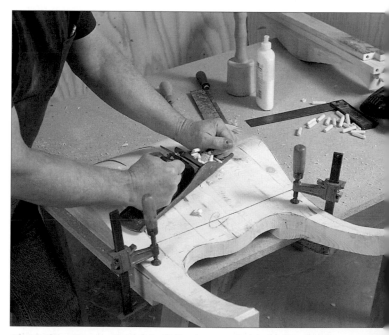

12–24. Cleaning up the joints in the legs and side pieces using a hand plane.

Preparing the Lower Scalloped Rail

I returned to the felt and drew a pattern for the lower rail—which was also to be used for the upper rail. Knowing that I wanted a minimum drawer front thickness of 1 inch and that I had 2¹/₂-inch material to work with, I drew a curve that started 1¹/₂ inches back from the face, flowing to a bulge in the center (12–25). With the pattern I marked a full piece of stock (12–26), later ripping off a piece to be used as the back, lower rail. After cutting the face on a band saw, I sketched in the scallop and used the waste from one side to mark the other.

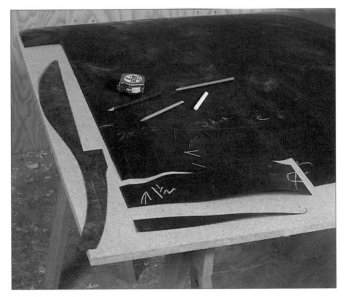

12–25. Drawing a curve for the lower scalloped rail.

Next, I drilled holes for dowels in the end of the rail and, using dowel points, marked the side of the case for boring (12–27). To properly locate the piece, I held it parallel with the joint between the front leg and the core.

Preparing the Upper Rails

After drawing the location and angles of the drawer fronts and rails on the left leg, I assembled the pieces I had—without glue—to get an accurate measurement for the balance of the rails (12–28). The front rails were also doweled into the case, but I also left a tab on the end of each that would be glued to the back of the leg (12–29).

12–26. Marking a full piece of stock.

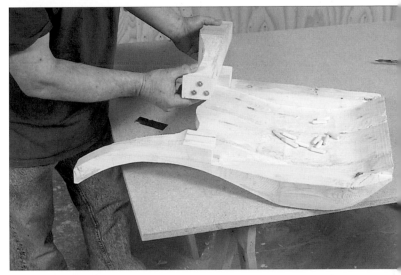

12–27. Dowels have been marked in the end of the rail, and the side of the case has been marked with dowel points for boring.

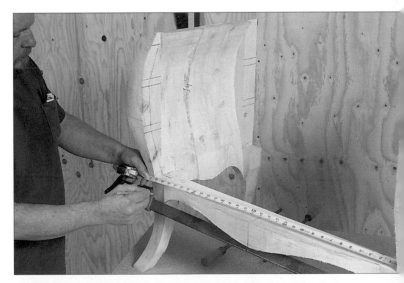

12–28. The components have been assembled so that the rails can be measured.

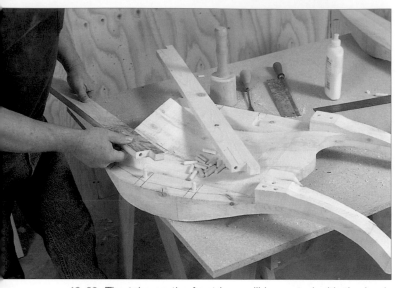

12-29. The tabs on the front legs will be mated with the back of each leg.

ASSEMBLY

With glue and plenty of clamps, I assembled the case, making sure that the drawer openings were square (12–30). Illus. 12–31 shows how the upper rails are glued to the core. Also note that the rear rails float in mortises cut in the back legs. This will permit expansion and contraction of the sides without disturbing rails and drawer guides, which, at this time, are just set in place.

12-30. The assembled case.

12-31. This view of the assembly shows how the rear rail floats in a mortise in the back legs.

DRAWERS

With the case assembled, the next step was to fit the drawer fronts, using the red lines drawn in 12–28 to determine their size and angles (12–32). I was then able to cut the remainder of the drawer components with all required dadoes.

After cutting the dado in the drawer bottom, I decided to dress it up with a few marks from a hand plane (12–33), and then set about beveling the edge using a drawknife (12–34).

I assembled the drawers with nails that I set with an old screwdriver ground to resemble the head of a square hand-cut nail. When the nail holes are patched, they do appear to contain an old nail.

12–32. Rough drawer fronts fit to the case.

12–34. Beveling the drawer edge.

12–33. Using a hand plane to dress up the drawer bottom.

SHAPING THE DRAWER FRONTS

With the drawers in place, the next step was to shape the drawer fronts. This can be done with a mallet and gouge—if you're a purist and need the exercise. If you're proficient with a chain saw, have at it. Those small chain-saw discs that fit in an angle grinder will also work. I prefer an air chisel with a gouge. Illus. 12–35 shows the wedges standing in the margins at the ends of the drawer fronts. These are in place to prevent the drawer from shifting in the opening and knocking the drawer guide out of alignment.

A few paragraphs back when cleaning up the core and sides, I mentioned that I intended to cheat and use a power tool instead of a hand plane. Well, if the air chisel wasn't enough to shape the drawer fronts, consider the angle grinder (12–36). With a disc of 16-grit "rockpaper," all of those tool marks disappear—to say nothing of the joints on the sides and the band-saw marks on the legs. With paper that coarse, there is also little dust floating around the shop.

Rather than switch to a finer disc that would produce dust, I finished the shaping with scrapers and every other tool I could think of (12–37).

As shown in 12–37, there is a rather wide margin

12-35. Shaping the drawer fronts using an air chisel and gouge.

12-36. Shaping the drawer fronts using an angle grinder.

12-37. Finishing the shaping of the drawer front.

at the top of the center drawer. Gremlins, right? Well, it could also be shrinkage, but I'll take the blame. I also fixed it by gluing a thin strip to the top of the drawer front (12–38).

With all surfaces prepared for veneering, I removed the drawers and turned the case upside down on the first layer for the top, letting it hang

12-38. A thin strip is added to the space at the top of the center drawer.

over the back edge ½ inch to allow for shrinkage. This margin was trimmed off the back edge before assembly. Then I determined the amount of overhang needed to accommodate the shape and marked it with a pair of dividers (12–39). After the shape was cut, I used the same technique to mark the finished top, using the first layer to guide the dividers.

12–39. Marking the overhang.

After preparing the top for veneer, I set all pieces aside for about two months to dry. After that time, I found a few new checks and discovered that the drawer fronts needed a little scraping to get them to fit perfectly, but the components cut from the 3 x 6 had not shrunk as dramatically as I'd anticipated. The knots were standing slightly proud of the surrounding wood, as I'd hoped; so as far as I was concerned, the project was a success . . . to this point.

VENEERING THE DRAWER FRONTS

In keeping with my policy of doing the hardest part of the job first, I started with the veneering of the drawer fronts. Now, if you're trying this for the first time, it may be helpful to place a heavy piece of paper over the front of one of the drawers and try to get it to conform to the shape. You'll find that it's impossible without wrinkling or tearing the paper.

You may then decide that the veneer being thicker and more tenacious would pose an even more impossible task. That was my thought the first time I tried a bombé front, but as there was no one to tell me that I couldn't do it, I blundered on.

I have seen veneered antique bombé chests, and I'm sure they were veneered using hot hide glue. Had I chosen walnut or mahogany veneers for this chest, I would have used hide glue just for demonstration purposes. But the rosewood veneer I did choose was far too cantankerous for hide glue unless I were to use all kinds of clamps, sandbags, few well-placed nails, and some words that I would prefer not be printed beneath my name. Not wanting to look like a complete fool, I took the easy way and veneered with dry glue—at least for the case.

I find it best to start in the center of the drawer. I had selected three consecutive slices of veneer of ample width, each containing a pin knot and attractive grain pattern in the center. After placing a push-pin through that pin knot, I secured the veneer with a couple of spring clamps and proceeded to iron down one-fourth of the veneer at the center (12–40).

12–40. Ironing down the veneer on the drawer front.

12–41. Continue along the center of the drawer front.

Then I began inching my way along the center of the drawer front's width (12–41), wetting the veneer slightly to make it more pliable. From there, it was only a matter of working the veneer down to the edges.

Sounds simple, doesn't it? Well, it is to a point,

12–42. A close-up of the drawer front shows a piece of veneer has been folded over.

12–43. A close-up of the drawer front showing the folded area after sanding.

but there were some things that had to be dealt with. On the first side of the drawer, I was just zipping along, a little overconfident, and I allowed the veneer to fold over in a small area (shown just beyond the chalked area in 12–42). I folded this crease over and flattened it as much as possible. After a little sanding, the crease disappeared (12–43). There was slight evidence of it that may have required some attention in the finishing process, but I doubted it.

12–44. A close-up of the drawer front showing bubbles (the dry, or lighter, areas).

I was more cautious with the other side of the drawer, spreading out potential creases and bubbles and making sure they were small enough to deal with. I allowed the tops of a couple of these bubbles to dry for demonstration purposes (12–44). Once these spots—which stood almost $3/16$ inch high—were bonded, there was evidence of the compression, but only you and I know where to look, and I won't tell if you don't.

Once the veneer was completely bonded, I carefully trimmed off the ends with a veneer saw (12–45), marking each piece because I was not through with this cut of veneer. I installed the drawers and bonded each trimming to the case front adjacent to the drawer whence it came (12–46). That straight line at the juncture of the drawer ends and the case can be rather unattractive in this type of construction, but continuing the veneer pattern of the drawer fronts to the border distracts the eye from the straight line.

Once all of the pieces were in place, I cut the ends with a scribe to fit the border (12–47). I did bond the pieces in several areas too strongly and had to use a chisel to free the areas that didn't separate easily (12–48).

12–45. Trimming off the ends of the veneer on the drawer fronts.

12–47. Cutting the ends of the drawer front so they will fit the borders.

12–46. Bonding the end veneer to the case.

12–48. Freeing the ends with a chisel so they can be trimmed.

As a precaution, I ran a veneer saw—one with set teeth—down the juncture of the drawer fronts and case, trimming off any overhang of the pieces just bonded (12–49). Had I removed the drawers and chipped the newly bonded veneer, I would have become rather unpleasant.

Moving right along, I attacked the sides. After straightening the edges of the three pieces of veneer I intended to use, I bonded the center cut. I next bonded the second cut for about an inch along the joint, pulling the joint tight as I went (12–50). After the

area along the joint was completely bonded, I went back and bonded the rest of the cut, forcing any wrinkles toward the joint. As there was no way to use a metal rod under the veneer to buckle it for a compressed joint, this technique was my second choice.

To trim the field for the border, I used the little scribe/cutter described in Chapter 2. It's a fine little tool, but it can be a bit challenging when used on tight curves. There is no way that it can cut too deeply, but it's possible it can start to follow the

12–49. Trimming off the veneer overhanging where the drawer fronts and case meet.

12–50. Veneering the sides.

12–51. A close-up showing an errant scribing mark made when trimming the field for the border.

grain or, if not held at quite the right angle, not cut deeply enough (12–51).

In one area I was in such poor form that I had to smooth out the cut using a wood-carving tool (12–52).

Using a pair of dividers, I began scribing and fitting the pieces of border. As shown in 12–53, many narrow pieces are used on the tight curves. This is necessary to make the border look like it follows the curve. When finished, it will look even better from a distance than in the close-up photo.

Pressing the veneer into the tight curve on the inside of the legs posed another challenge because the iron could not heat enough of the surface quickly enough to make the veneer sufficiently pliable to conform to the sharp curve at the top. Here I did some pre-forming by heating the veneer on a flat surface, and then quickly bending it and clamping it into position (12–54). After it cooled, it fit the tight curve very nicely.

12–52. Using a wood-carving tool to smooth a curve.

12–53. Fitting a piece of border to veneer.

12–54. Pre-forming the veneer so that it will fit on the curve on the inside of the leg.

VENEERING THE TOP

It was finally time to veneer the top and get my hands covered with hide glue. Early in the morning, I set up a small table with the things I would need. Among the tools and items shown in 12–55 is a glue pot in the process of melting a fresh charge of rehydrated glue. Beside it, I put a couple of plastic cups of glue flakes. The cup to the left contains dry flakes, a few of which I scattered on the bench in front of it. The cup on the right contains flakes that soaked in water overnight. Both cups contained the same volume of flakes, so you can get an idea of the increased volume the soaking process produces.

Also shown is my trusty iron, bathing in about ¼ inch of water contained in an old electric skillet. The skillet is not heated; it just happens to be the only container I have that is big enough for the iron. The water bath will dissolve any hide glue that may accumulate and dry on the iron.

I also broke out a new bristle brush. The one I had been using was . . . well . . . embarrassing. That brush is not disposable. At the end of the session, I may wash it in warm water, or I may squeeze out all excess glue and let it dry. It will, of course, dry hard and appear to be ruined, but a couple of hour's soaking in cold water and gentle heating in hot glue will completely restore it.

Next to my shop-built veneer hammer is an automobile window scraper and squeegee. Just in case the veneer is very fragile, I'll use the scraper instead of the hammer.

Most important of all are the bucket filled with warm water and the towel. Should I get glue on my hands, I'll seek the refuge of the warm water to remove it—lest I'll not be able to let go of anything I may touch.

Before I started assembling the equipment, I gave the face side of the top a good coat of water to begin the pre-cupping. As I waited for the glue to melt, I kept wetting the top. After about an hour, the center was standing about ½ inch above the rest of the board; it was time to begin veneering.

Before beginning, I "toothed" the surface; that is, I cut some grooves to hold the glue. I've never had a toothing plane, but I find that dragging the teeth of a saw across the surface works very well (12–56). On another occa-

12–55. *The tools and items needed to veneer the top.*

12–56. *Dragging the teeth of a saw across the surface to "tooth" it.*

sion I may have, at this point, heated the top, but on this day the shop was a heavenly 85 degrees.

This particular top was somewhat challenging because I glued it up from boards that weren't completely dry. The knots were standing slightly proud, and two of the boards had cupped slightly—just what I had hoped for.

Next, I sprayed the face side of the veneer and quickly spread glue on the top (12–57). If the face side is not wet, as the hot glue comes in contact with the back the veneer will curl, making it impossible to get down.

After the veneer was set in the hot glue, I passed my hands over it to push out any large air bubbles and slide the cut into exact position (12–58). Then, starting at the center, I went to work with the hammer, squeezing excess glue to the edges of the cut and forcing the veneer down (12–59). I pulled the ham-

12–57. Spreading glue on the top.

12–59. Forcing out excess glue using a veneer hammer.

mer both with the grain and across it, taking care to squeeze any thick spots of glue from around knots or in the bottoms of the cups. I picked up puddles of glue around the edges with a putty knife and return them to the pot.

At this point, I poured a cup of coffee and let the piece set for about 15 minutes. Then I trimmed the joint at the centerline (12–60). I had let that first cut hang about 1/4 inch over the centerline, and when I had first placed the cut, the edge was reasonably straight. After the 15 minutes of expansion, it was at least 3/32 inch out of alignment.

Before trimming the joint, I had sprayed the face of the second cut and set it aside to expand a bit. After about five minutes, I trimmed it straight, spread glue on the substrate, and set the veneer in place. On the second cut, I began by working the area next to the joint, pulling with the hammer to make sure that the joint fit tightly (12–61). This is

12–60. Trimming the veneer joint.

12–58. Smoothing out the veneer with the hands.

12–61. Using a hammer to ensure that the veneer joint fits properly.

a little tricky in that the glue can only exit at the joint and can cause the veneers to overlap, but with a little care I've found it the best way to ensure a good, tight joint. After working the cut down, there was one tiny spot that refused to stick. For this, I enlisted the aid of a small block of wood and a clamp. Illus. 12–62 shows the piece of paper beneath the block to prevent it from sticking to the veneer.

It is fair to use a clamp or two in a hammer operation. Sandbags can also be used, and I have a couple of heavy babbitt (a soft metal used for pouring bearings) ingots that I often press into service. I once fantasized that "when my ship came in" I would use silver or gold ingots for this purpose. Well, my ship did come in; it turned out to be a rowboat, and, believe me, there was no silver or gold aboard.

You may have noticed in the photographs that the substrate is not yet trimmed to size. The excess provides a place for the glue to go, rather than dripping onto the floor or, more importantly, my shoes. Hide glue sticks well to leather, and people tend to look down their noses at those with blobs of amber-colored stuff stuck to their shoes.

Nonetheless, I did have to cut the front edge to final shape so that I could use my cutter/scribe to prepare the field for the border As shown in 12–63, I have put a piece of veneer tape down the joint. I never rush to tape joints, because I want to make sure that they aren't going to curl up before placing the tape. And just to make sure that the tape doesn't pull moisture from the joint, causing it to curl, I dip the tape in water rather than just moistening it. This also expands the tape, and—hopefully—as it shrinks, it will pull the joint even tighter.

I cut the straight pieces of border with a paper cutter, but scribed the curved front pieces and cut them with scissors (12–64).

I put the border down working from the corners (12-65). This was to give each piece a chance to settle before placing one next to it. By the time I got to the border, there were quite a few little bumps of glue in the border area that were dry. That's why the scraper was close at hand.

You'll also see in the photographs that I've moved the glue pot closer to hand, insulating it from the field with a block of wood. I always keep a stirring

12–62. *Using a clamp and a block of wood to press down one spot on the veneer.*

12–63. *Trimming the field for the border.*

12–64. *Scribing a piece of veneer to the field.*

12–65. *Hammering down a piece of border.*

12–66. *Trimming with a utility knife.*

stick in the pot to stir in any scum that may form on the glue. But its most important duty is to prevent the brush from sliding to the bottom of the pot.

After securing clamps and blocks over a couple of joints that were starting to buckle, I trimmed the front edge using a utility knife (12–66). I prefer to use a downward slicing action rather than pulling the knife along the veneer. The warm, wet veneer slices easily, but will buckle if sideways pressure is applied to it.

As I was taping the border joints, I noticed a couple of loose spots in the field. Gently warming one with the iron, I held it down with my fingertips as I warmed the other (12–67). By this time, the glue under the veneer was drying so it was very viscous and sticky. With just that little amount of heat, it reactivated, and after a minute's worth of finger pressure, the veneer stayed down.

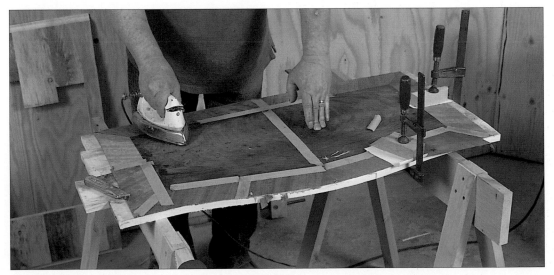

12–67. *Warming a loose spot in the field to put it down.*

MAKING THE BACKING AND DUST PROTECTOR

As the top stood in the corner drying, I fit some ⅜-inch tongue-and-groove boards into the bottom to form a dust protector and secured them with blocks dipped in hot hide glue (12–68).

After fastening the false top with a few small nails, I turned the case over and secured it with glue blocks, much the same as the dust protector. Then I installed the backing, which was also composed of ⅜-inch tongue-and-groove boards (12–69). I fastened these with a pneumatic nailer, but then went back and set the nails with a screwdriver ground to look like the head of a square-cut nail.

Just before leaving the shop for the evening, I clamped the top between some 2 x 4s (12–70). Just in case my calculations were wrong, I didn't want to return in the morning and find the top looking like a cinnamon stick. I also put a piece of paper under the 2 x 4s to prevent them from sticking to any glue that might still be active.

After the top dried for several days, it would be only a matter of trimming it to size, running a router around it to cut a bead, and then fastening it to the false top with several slot-head screws. I must add that after I removed the 2 x 4s the top did cup slightly, but the screws easily pulled it down.

ADDING A FINISH

Next came the sanding, and, believe me, there was a lot of sanding. Not wanting to destroy the effect of the slightly high-standing knots—or cut through at those points—all sanding was by hand with a piece of soft sandpaper. I can't say I enjoyed it, but I'm sure the workout did me good.

For a little accent and to soften the contrast, I gave the chest a wet coat of weak, light golden oak dye stain, followed by several coats of sanding sealer. All of the interior and drawers were generously sealed. For the purpose of Illus. 12–1 and 12–2, I finished up with a coat of satin lacquer. (The light reflections off a high-gloss finish are just too much to contend with.) Eventually, I'll French-polish the piece. That will add authenticity, and I guess I could use another workout.

12–68. The boards fit into the bottom of the case serve as a dust protector.

12–69. The backing is being installed.

12–70. Two x fours have been clamped to the top to prevent it from distorting.

INDEX

METRIC EQUIVALENTS CHART

INCHES TO MILLIMETERS AND CENTIMETERS
MM— Millimeters   CM—Centimeters

Inches	MM	CM	Inches	CM	Inches	CM
⅛	3	0.3	9	22.9	30	76.2
¼	6	0.6	10	25.4	31	78.7
⅜	10	1.0	11	27.9	32	81.3
½	13	1.3	12	30.5	33	83.8
⅝	16	1.6	13	33.0	34	86.4
¾	19	1.9	14	35.6	35	88.9
⅞	22	2.2	15	38.1	36	91.4
1	25	2.5	16	40.6	37	94.0
1¼	32	3.2	17	43.2	38	96.5
1½	38	3.8	18	45.7	39	99.1
1¾	44	4.4	19	48.3	48	101.6
2	51	5.1	20	50.8	41	104.1
2½	64	6.4	21	53.3	42	106.7
3	76	7.6	22	55.9	43	109.2
3½	89	8.9	23	58.4	44	111.8
4	102	10.2	24	61.0	45	114.3
4½	114	11.4	25	63.5	46	116.8
5	127	12.7	25	66.0	47	119.4
6	152	15.2	27	68.6	48	121.9
7	178	17.8	28	71.1	49	124.5
8	203	20.3	29	73.7	50	127.0